I0605223

I Am a Georgia Girl

I Am a Georgia Girl is the story Ann Hite has yearned to tell since she was nine years old. That's when her grandmother shared with her the horrific experience of seeing Leo Frank's body hanging from a tree limb, the victim of a lynch mob avenging the murder of Mary Phagan. Hite delves into this sad chapter of Georgia history by focusing on Frank's wife, Lucille. It's a remarkable portrait of a quiet but strong young woman courageously defending her beloved husband against insurmountable forces that ultimately ripped him from her forever. The roles of Lucille Frank and other women swept up in the Leo Frank saga have often been underreported. Thanks to Ann Hite for so vividly bringing their stories to life against the backdrop of one of Georgia's most infamous episodes.

—John Pruitt, retired WSB-TV news anchor
and author of *Tell It True: A Novel*

In this new biography, *I Am a Georgia Girl*, Ann Hite reexamines the horrific lynching of Leo Frank which occurred in Georgia on August 17, 1915. He was accused of murdering the thirteen-year-old factory worker, Mary Phagan. With extensive research and meticulous writing, Hite looks at the hatred, antisemitism, and mob violence of vigilantism which was rampant at the time. But Hite concentrates on the life of the young wife of Leo Frank, Lucille, who spent the rest of her life trying to prove his innocence. Her life was shattered, too. This is an important book for which Hite should be commended.

—Carolyn Newton Curry, award-winning
author of *Trudy's Awakening*

I Am a Georgia Girl, Ann Hite's nonfiction feat, gleams with precision, humanity, and expert storytelling. This tautly rendered, compelling account of the courageous life of Lucille Selig Frank and events surrounding the 1915 lynching of her husband, Leo Max Frank, weaves the timely and momentous story of gross injustice, antisemitism, and the suppression of women's voices. Lucille Selig Frank would be proud.

—Robert Gwaltney, award-winning
author of *The Cicada Tree*

Many of us know the story of Leo Frank and Mary Phagan—the murder, tabloid trial, "guilty" verdict, and lynching, which led to a rise in antisemitism, a rebirth of the Klan, and the birth of the Anti-Defamation League. But the story we don't know is that of Leo's wife, Lucille. Now, for the first time, Ann Hite's *I Am a Georgia Girl* gives Lucille a voice, and it's a poignant one rendering a heart-breaking story. No longer bound by society and forced to bear silent witness to the events that surrounded her husband, Lucille (and Ann) gives an indictment on race, class, religion, gender, and history that must not be ignored. History cannot be allowed to repeat itself.

—Jeff Clemmons, author of *Rich's: A Southern Institution*

The late University of Georgia law professor Donald Eugene Wilkes, Jr., introduced generations of his students to the horrifying story of injustice that Ann Hite so well recounts here, with excellent research and narrative, in her book *I Am a Georgia Girl: The Life of Lucille Selig Frank, 1888–1957*. I was shocked to be reminded how relatively recently this happened, Mrs. Frank being the age of my grandparents. I have friends who are descendants from families on both sides of this horror story, and a statue of one of the most culpable in causing this horrific injustice still stands on the Georgia State Capitol grounds. We must keep this story, raw and painful to read today, ever-present in our minds, as Professor Wilkes was intending. The words of George Santayana, who said "Those who cannot remember the past are condemned to repeat it," underline the importance of reading this book.

—McCracken Poston, Jr., author of *Zenith Man: Death, Love, and Redemption in a Georgia Courtroom*

I Am a Georgia Girl

The Life of Lucille Selig Frank, 1888–1957

Ann Hite

MERCER UNIVERSITY PRESS
Macon, Georgia

MUP/ H1057

Published by Mercer University Press
1501 Mercer University Drive
Macon, Georgia 31207

Books published by Mercer University Press are printed on acid-free paper that meets the requirements of the American National Standard for Information Sciences—Permanence of Paper for Printed Library Materials.

Printed and bound in CANADA.
This book is set in Adobe Garamond.
Cover/jacket design by Burt&Burt.
Illustrated map courtesy Jerry C. Hite

ISBN 978-0-88146-998-1 (print)
ISBN 978-0-88146-997-1 (eBook)
Cataloging-in-Publication Data is available from the Library of Congress

To

Inas Hawkins Lord (Granny)
Thank you for sharing how you were taken to see Leo Frank hanging from the tree in Marietta when you were six. I hope I have told the story you intended.

Glover Allen Swafford (Dad)
Thank you for teaching me through example that there are rights and wrongs in this world, and we must stay on our toes, remembering history repeats itself.

Lucille Selig Frank
I only hope I did your story justice.

MERCER UNIVERSITY PRESS

Endowed by

TOM WATSON BROWN
and
THE WATSON-BROWN FOUNDATION, INC.

Contents

I Am a Georgia Girl

Alpharetta.
Marietta.
The Temple
Atlanta Ga.
National Pencil Co.
NATIONAL Pencil Co.
S.S.S.
OAKLAND
ANN Hite

Cumming
Georgia Back Roads
Eatonton
Litte River Ferry Crossing
State
Prison
Milledgeville
Jerry C. Hite
Feb. 12, 2025

Introduction

Lucille Selig Frank

This book began as a little germ of a thought: *Why not write a historical novel about the life of this woman?* After all, fiction is my comfortable place. At that point, I had published four historical novels and one novella. The new book would be about Lucille's marriage and what led to the lynching of her husband. So, I began the tireless research I do for my novels. What a complex story! But this wasn't my first introduction to this heartbreaking event.

I became acquainted with Lucille in 1966 when I was nine and had returned to Marietta, Georgia, after living for five years in Germany. My maternal grandmother, known to me as Granny, told me stories from her childhood to engage me and get my mind off my parents' upcoming divorce. She told me the story of seeing Leo M. Frank hanging from a tree in Frey's Grove in Marietta in 1915. She had been one of the many children brought to view Frank in the carnival-like atmosphere. The spectators wore their Sunday best and crowded around the dead man hanging from a smallish oak tree. Many in the crowd had brought picnics, and the crowd's mood was quite jovial because, after all, justice had finally been served.

As a spunky nine-year-old on her way to becoming a writer, I wondered how Granny ended up as one of a thousand-plus people visiting Frey's Grove that fateful day. When I was told the part of the story where Leo gave his wedding ring to someone in the mob to be returned to Lucille, I knew, even at nine, I would find out more about this woman, that the thought of her receiving her dead husband's wedding ring would never leave me. I guess it could be said this book began with that first telling fifty odd years ago.

While scouting public and private archives for letters, documents, books, photos, and court documents, the story built itself into a nonfiction narrative. Books written about the Phagan case—centered around the murder, trial, and lynching—hadn't yet given the women woven into this case a voice. Was I up for telling Lucille's story? What did Lucille have to say when her husband was accused of murder? How did she handle being a target of people like Tom Watson, a politician, journalist, and editor of the *Jeffersonian*? Did Lucille really wait two weeks to visit Leo in jail because she was conflicted about his innocence, as Hugh Dorsey accused? Who was Mary Phagan? Who were her mother and sister? The more I researched, the more I saw the injustice in these women's narratives being marginalized. Their convictions and ideas were, if told at all, buried on the back pages of the newspapers.

Lucille was twenty-five and had been married three years when Mary Phagan was murdered. I have four daughters and often found myself thinking *What would I have done?* So, I set out to write this biography of voices. As far as I know, I'm the first woman who isn't a member of the Phagan family to take a long, unbiased look at the women who make up this story. Josephine, Lucille's mother, and Regina, Lucille's grandmother—who took her two daughters and fled on the last train out of Atlanta before the city burned in the Civil War—played a supporting role to Lucille and Leo. Mary's strong paternal great-grandmother learned early that women are often judged with a special set of rules. Fannie, Mary's mother, set out to warn the girls in the city with her story of heartbreak. Mary's sister Ollie had a deep love for her youngest sibling. These are just a few of the women whose voices have yet to be heard.

An old sepia photo became my North Star. Taken on 17 August 1915, in the woods outside Marietta, it showed several generations of a large family dressed in their Sunday best. The photo put faces to the devastating stories, and in doing so, deepened my empathy and compassion for the victims of these horrific events of 1913–1915. Within these two years, White mobs lynched 162 Black Americans and eighteen Whites, for a total of 176. Only one victim, Leo M. Frank, was Jewish. Lynching, or mob-violence vigilantism, was common in these years.

There are always several sides to a story of murder. I have done my best to represent those sides. The family photo is one photo in a set of three. The other two show long tables covered with slices of watermelon and bottles of soda. A party. A celebration. Behind the group is the site where Leo was lynched by a mob, which wanted justice for Mary after Georgia's governor John Slaton commuted Leo's death sentence to life in prison. Governor Slaton believed Leo to be innocent, but he knew that a complete pardon would be signing Frank's death sentence. When I looked into the background of the photo, I saw a fuzzy image of other spectators with children in tow. The lynching was quite the event that early morning in Marietta, where people celebrated what they felt was a true justice.

What makes this group of well-dressed people different from the others who showed up after the lynching?[1] This is the maternal side of Mary Phagan's family. This haunting image reminded me there is always more than one point of view in a tragedy. Mary—a teen only two months from her fourteenth birthday—was last seen alive when she went to pick up her pay envelope from the National Pencil Company in Atlanta, where she worked twelve- to fourteen-hour shifts. Leo Frank, the pencil factory's superintendent, was the last known person to see her alive. This photo told me a story from multiple angles: a young girl's brutal death—and the family left behind that loved her and still do now, generations later.

What kind of people have their photo taken where a man was lynched by a mob of the most powerful men in Georgia's justice system? Did this family see Frank's murder as redemption for the wrongs done to Mary? Is there a swagger to the men in this family portrait? A boastful pride in how they hold themselves? Are the women thinking of Mary and how hard she worked for her family? What about Mary's mother, Fannie? Did she feel guilt that her daughter had to work in a factory at such a young age? Did the family discuss the use of cheap child labor? Mary's great-nephew described the family as poor and living a hardscrabble life.

Newspaper accounts from the time agree with him. Child labor was normal for the time and expected for a family in this economic state. Families had to put a roof over their heads and food on the tables. I came to know most of the faces in this photo during research. I learned their names, where they lived, and their relationship to Mary. Like most authors, I researched far beyond what this book required because I was caught up in the story, devouring the details of people involved. For every fact that went into the book, there are five that didn't make it. The old rule for authors is to write what you know. My belief is we never know enough. We have to continue to seek the stories that show our humanity—or lack thereof.

While other authors have recorded the story of Mary's murder and Leo Frank's trial in great detail, I listened for the women's voices, so often silenced through history. Until Steve Oney's book *And the Dead Shall Rise*, Lucille had been barely mentioned. Very little is publicly known about her, but what exists is compelling. Her story tangles in many ways with those of the other women and girls connected to this event.

This is the story of Lucille Selig Frank, the youngest of Emil and Josephine Selig's three daughters. This is the story of twenty-five-year-old Lucille, who paid a heavy price for fighting this injustice because she believed it was a wife's duty. Her father would die before Leo was sentenced to death but not before he testified on his son-in-law's behalf. The story of Lucille Selig Frank and the women involved in this case is just as timely today as it was in the early 1900s.

In early 2021, Steve Oney wrote an opinion piece for the *Washington Post* questioning just how far the state of Georgia has come since the sixties when Lucille's nephews, fearful that their aunt's grave would be desecrated, put her ashes in the trunk of a car and secreted them to Oakland Cemetery in Downtown Atlanta to be buried between her parents. On 6 January 2021, as the insurrection in Washington, DC, unfolded, Jon Ossoff, the first Jewish man to hold such an office since

1974, was declared the winner in Georgia's Senate race. Oney pointed out Ossoff's opponent, Republican senator David Perdue, had used a caricature of Ossoff as a "big-nosed elitist." Oney said that in today's world, the lynching of Leo Frank would be seen as domestic terrorism. In the present day environment, is it too hard to conceive antisemitic incidents similar to those in Leo Frank's time?[2]

In April 2019, the first of Georgia's Conviction Integrity Units was established in Fulton County. These units (now in Chatham and Gwinnett counties as well) review claims of innocence in old cases. Former governor Roy Barnes, a consultant to the Fulton County District Attorney's Conviction Integrity Unit, played a pivotal role in advocating for Frank's case to be reopened. His wife's grandfather drove a getaway car for the mob, and Barnes is convinced that Leo Frank is innocent of Mary Phagan's murder. But just as many, if not more, people believe Leo Frank killed Mary, including the Phagan family.

This story has many diverse characters, and I would argue that its setting is one of the most influential characters in this story. Granny was only six when she saw Leo Frank hanging from a tree, yet she seemed ashamed that her father took her to this event. At the age of seventy-seven in 1986, she said, "That old man needs to be quiet." She was addressing Alonzo Mann, Leo Frank's former office boy, who, in 1982, at the age of eighty-three, said he had encountered Jim Conley holding Mary's dead body those many years before. My grandmother believed Mann should have left well enough alone—that any new truths should stay buried. She wanted to walk away and pretend nothing but the accepted story ever happened. She was not alone in these beliefs.

With all the complexity, I hope telling this story will help others see that the history of anti-Semitism, the silencing of women's voices, and mob vigilantism should not be allowed to recur. Recent headlines reflect that we have elected officials who are comfortable encouraging mob mentality.

I am honored to tell Lucille's story and the intersecting stories of other women. This research and writing taught me that we hold the power to make a change. What is the price of using this power? My great-grandfather believed in the mob's right to take the law into their own hands. How many were complicit in Leo's journey? How many today choose to stay silent instead of speaking the truth? Don't we owe future generations more?

This book leaves the decision to the reader.

Chapter 1

Ribbons and Nylons

"I am a Georgia girl, born and reared in this state, and educated in her schools. I am a Jewess"[3]

Those that say you care are flawed. Your passion is not about Mary,
a child working hard to help her family survive.
You turn your head so as not to see young hands toiling
before the sun comes up, stopping only
when the sun dips down, earning what breakfast costs for a day.

Mary, a child, a girl, who plays with friends when free time allows.
Mary, who shied from men because she was innocent.
Mary, running a machine in a dark factory,
Mary, thoughts of playing outside, sun shining, friends laughing.
Mary, dreaming of a life with flowers, new clothes, happy times.

Mary, found in the dead of the night
at the bottom of the pencil factory,
coal dust, pencil shavings, and soot.
Nightwatchman, making his rounds,
running to the office to call the boss
ring, ring, ring.

"They perhaps are not entirely to blame, fed as they were on lies unspeakable. Their passion aroused by designing persons."

Designing persons, you lined up young girls, children,

one after another, paraded them to the witness stand.
Each walked the aisle in their Sunday best,
pointing a finger.

Designing persons, you opened the windows to the heat outside.
Crowds straining to catch a glance,
hanging on every word.
Mary's family, friends, co-workers filling seats.

Those who could see their own daughters
in the picture you painted.
Crowds outside the window packed in a frenzy,
a deep need for judgement,
a need for erasure so murder couldn't happen again.
Where was God on those hot, hot days?

Kill the Jew
sang on the rooftops.
Buildings the Jews fought to build, a city
where hate wouldn't exist
but now echoes through the air.
A price to pay, Death.

Mary, a child with dreams,
dashed in the basement of the pencil factory.
Beautiful lavender dress stained with blood, her blood.
Gray heels smudged, broken.
Bows ripped from auburn hair.
Matching umbrella ground into coal dust.

"I am also Georgian, and American, and I do not apologize for
that, either."

Where were the designing people who now seek revenge?

Where were they on the day of Mary's death?
Did not they protect her? Did they know her?
All marching in a parade,
a celebration of bondage,
of cruelty and death,
speeches and flags,
ribbons and nylons.

"Guilty," repeated twelve times
with each chime of the clock tower.
Outside the windows,
cheers and hats in the air.
His sharp, delicate face, small-boned,
wire-rimmed glasses perched
on his slender nose.
Her hand touching the wooden bench,
not unlike a church pew in an unholy place,
Fingers wanting to caress his vulnerable neck.

Christians believe Christ can heal with a mere touch
of a hand to the hem of his robe.
Roll up your mat and walk.
Belief in the courtroom that justice was done.
Hearts believe what they are taught,
whether right or wrong,
weak or strong.

"Some of them, I am sure did not realize the horror of their act.
But those who inspired these men to do this unlawful act, what of them?"

Someone must pay for the death.
And what becomes of the blood on your hands, designing persons?
An eye for an eye,

a rope around the neck,
a tomb with no bed.

"Will not their consciences make for the hell on Earth, and will not their associates, in their hearts despise them?"

Chapter 2

A Feather of a Soul

A tree that takes a life must be big,
a trunk, arms can't encircle,
sprawling limbs twisting into the sky.

If a tree can take a life,
the weight must be massive,
the bark thick with age.

The site of the crime was not planned,
like the deed, a kidnapping
in the middle of the night.
Phone lines severed. Isolation.
A parade of *Bravo! Congratulations!*

Taken in the dead of the dark morning,
taken in only a nightshirt. Gentleman,
or so they say, suits and ties,
shiny shoes and bowler hats,
Winchesters and cigars.

Men of substance,
of breadth and proper language,
of money and privilege.
Gentleman seeking revenge
through the back door,
thieves in the dark,
hearts with holes.

Parade stretching from one
distant point to another.
ruckus and cheers,
waking folks deep in their sleep.
Tired men who push plows and plant,
shaking their heads in agreement
just for peace.

The dusty gray on the horizon,
time when spirits walk and
cry out for help for those about to die.
Rhythmic engines keeping time with each other,
keeping time with each other,
forming a train of death, dark hearts,
bad intentions.

Starry night escapes into bondage,
to the woods, to the gin,
an apple table pushed close to the tree,
hardly a tree, twisted and knotted,
a Y in the limbs spread like a claw of prey.

Only a white nightshirt,
men, fine men, gentlemen gather
around, stomping, crushing.
Neighbors close their windows in the hot
August morning, a Tuesday morning,
a workday.

A length of strong rope,
braided with toughness, strength, dependability.
Rapid-fire words: *Did you? Say you did.*
Only one sentence is uttered,

as white nightshirt is forced onto the apple table,
his weight slight, almost a feather of a soul.

"I think more of my wife and mother
than I do my own life."

His hands bound together in front,
a coat tied around his waist,
a pure white blindfold,
as if seeing the faces of those who commit this
crime is cruel and inhumane.
Blood running from an old throat wound,
torn open by sheer force.

Spectators come from far and near,
lining up to view the slight tree,
slight like its victim.

Neighbors wearing their
Sunday best, children in tow,
to learn the lesson of indifference, revenge,
defiance, justice taken into the bloody hands
of upstanding gentleman.

Twisting, turning anger, hatred
for what is not known or understood.
Burning hell-fire justice.

A wedding ring, a gift,
a legacy, a will of testament.

"I think more of my wife and mother
than I do my own life."[4]

Chapter 3

The Death Sentence

A letter from Rachel "Ray" Frank, Leo Frank's mother, dated the day before everything she hoped for died, before life as Lucille Selig Frank knew it was altered irrevocably.

August 16, 1915[5]
My Dear Leo,

Just got your postal card, happy as always to know you are well. We are enjoying good health, and dear mamma seems to be gaining energy. God will heal her someday.

Charlie and Ron just left for the train, and I will go to Sara's later. Alex has not come back yet. Charlie's N. Y. address will be Hotel Cosgrove 72nd.

It is very hot to-day. We have had some rain and it looks as if we will have more.

Best love and many kisses to both.
Your Loving Mother

Lucille woke that Monday morning to temperatures hugging ninety degrees in the Central Georgia city of Milledgeville—the capital of Georgia during the Civil War, but by 1915, best known for the Georgia State Penitentiary and Central State Hospital. At twenty-seven, Lucille was a fashionable woman. Her dark hair and eyes, along with a milk-and-honey complexion, provided her with a beauty few could match. Lucille had faced more than most women twice her age. For the first time in two years, life was taking a turn for the better: Leo had narrowly survived a grievous wound to his throat in an attack by a fellow inmate, and Governor Slaton had commuted Leo's death sentence to life in prison. Somewhere in his mere existence was a touch of hope. Did Lucille dare let down her guard long enough to relax and embrace the newfound reason to go forward? Could she do that?

The morning air was thick as Lucille wrote the daily letters to keep family and lawyers informed. All good news flowed through her fountain pen. Leo's improving health and spirits made the task easy, almost enjoyable.

☙

Meanwhile, in Marietta, more than 120 miles north of Milledgeville, some of the most notable men in Georgia's justice system—who couldn't risk being recognized, men in high places with too much to lose—had hand-picked a mob of twenty-five men, largely viewed as upstanding and moral, with a variety of careers that lent to their mission.[6] Designated leaders "Black Newt" Morris, Gordon Gann, and George Daniell were ready to leave. They were prepared to enact their organizers' plan for justice, which was to gift a murder to the people of Cobb County, especially the family failed by the so-called state justice system. Seven automobiles left different locations of the city at staggered times so as not to garner too much notice. They would meet in a secret place along the route to form their convoy for the remaining distance.

☙

The sun, low on the horizon, was still bright in the hazy sky when Lucille visited Leo at the prison. Surrounding the brick building were fields of cotton where prisoners in striped uniforms worked in the unbearable sun. The next morning, Leo would reenter the inmate population. Because of his math and engineering skills, he had escaped hard labor and instead worked in administration. The couple's visits wouldn't be so free and frequent since Leo had healed. Before the attack, actor and filmmaker Hal Reid produced a documentary, *Leo M. Frank (showing Life in Jail) and Gov. Slaton*, which depicted Leo in the warden's office as well as conversations Reid filmed with Lucille, Ray Frank (Frank's mother), and Sally Francis Grant (Governor Slaton's wife). Surely, the massive exposure would help Leo prove his innocence. He was obsessed with the film. *Variety* pointed out the following after a preview of the documentary: "So much publicity has been given to the case this film should create a general interest...."[7] The documentary played to full houses in New York. Even Leo's mother, Ray, had seen the movie in Brooklyn.

The cicadas hummed so loudly it was hard to hear anything else, like every evening Lucille said her goodbyes to Leo, their plan for another campaign to gain a full pardon, an exoneration, a return to happiness, agreed on. A group of lawyers and well-meaning friends stood fervently ready to help. Lucille wouldn't find peace until she succeeded.

When Lucille left the penitentiary, Leo's high spirits infected her own. Soon, she would once again take up the task of proving Leo's innocence, the goal she had sought from the day in April 1913 when he became a suspect in the murder of thirteen-year-old Mary Phagan, an employee at the National Pencil Company where Leo was superintendent. The event had divided their lives into stark halves—before the murder and after. This was understood, but what stretched in front of her was a life that once again could be lovely, laced with promise. At least Leo and her had a chance to return to happiness thanks to Governor Slaton. Leo was her heart.

The next morning, Lucille planned to visit her aunt Emma at her home in Athens, a retreat where she could rest and heal. Atlanta still crawled with reporters, who, wanting more of Leo's story, would exploit anything that Lucille said and make up stories when she didn't speak. Her family understood her best. Her Uncle "Bud," M. G. (Moses Gershon) Michael, who founded a successful department store in Athens with his older brother Simon, made her laugh and kept her busy.[8] This trip's fun, private events would prove a welcome distraction and bolster her spirits. Hope. Finally, there was a future.

ଔ

Each man in the Marietta mob had been assigned a rifle and pistol. One of the cars in the convoy carried a box of explosives and a thick rope expertly knotted into a hangman's noose. Around dusk on 16 August 1915, the convoy came just outside of the penitentiary in Milledgeville. Yellow Jacket Brown, an electrician, spent the previous days on his motorcycle, tracing the phone lines in the small city. When he spotted the cloud of dust moving his way, he cut the phone lines, robbing most of Milledgeville of communication with each other and the outside world.

Vigilante: "a member of a volunteer committee organized to suppress and punish crime summarily (as when the processes of law are viewed as inadequate)."[9] The vigilantes were heard traveling the road to the prison—a prison with an armed tower guard watching the gate—before they arrived at the barbed wire–wrapped gate. F. J. Turner, a prison trustee, tried to convince the night watchman, Mr. Hester, to send Leo out the back with a guard, but Hester didn't take the situation seriously. The gate was opened to the vigilantes. The tower guard didn't attempt to stop them.

The Marietta group broke into three small groups—one going to Warden Smith's home, the next heading to Superintendent Burke's home, and the last to disable all vehicles on the grounds.

When Burke answered a knock at his door, he stood looking at two men who held shotguns and two men armed with pistols. Handcuffs were snapped on his wrists, and the four men marched Burke to the penitentiary building. The second group proceeded to Warden Smith's residence. Handcuffs were placed on the warden while his wife screamed and pleaded with the men to allow the warden to remain with her. The vigilantes agreed and left behind Lawrence Haney, one of the group.[10] Only two of the mob bothered to wear masks, and none of the group seemed to fear paying any sort of price for their deeds.

When the vigilantes came in search of Leo, the trustee extinguished the oil lamp. One of the mob demanded he relight the lamp.

The trustee denied having any matches. The vigilante insisted the trustee find a match fast and pointed his pistol in the trustee's face.

As this took place, Leo was in the next room, wide awake, listening. Horror and resignation must have frozen him. There was no place to run, no way to protect himself.

The mob found Leo, wearing only a white nightshirt, monogrammed with *LMF*.

"May I get dressed?"

"Where you are going, you won't need clothes," one of the men responded.

They led Leo to the stairs out front where two men took him by the arms, and two men took a leg each, and a man grabbed his hair. The men bumped Leo down the stone steps and threw him into the back of one of the cars.[11] Leo moaned, his throat wound not yet healed. One of the mob held up the hangman's noose in front of Leo's face.

The mission of "justice" was completed in a matter of minutes and without resistance. A man who fit the description of Black Newt Morris yelled, "All right boys; make for the swamps."[12] As the men jumped back into the cars, Superintendent Burke asked if he could be released from the handcuffs, but the men responded that he would have to go with them. "Damned if I go anywhere with you," he retorted.[13] The seven automobiles, lights bright, sped off. The only mishap came when Haney—who guarded Warden Smith—was left behind.[14] As the automobiles turned onto the highway, two circled back to pick up their partner.

The cut telephone lines meant Warden Smith and Superintendent Burke had no way to call for help. The prison's bookkeeper was awakened when Superintendent Burke sent for him, and he found a vehicle the mob hadn't disabled. He left for Milledgeville to spread the news. In town, he found no one had a working phone apart from one long-distance line to Augusta that was still intact. Word of Leo's abduction was sent to Augusta to let anyone along the route know to watch for the mob. Smith and Burke assumed that the vigilantes were headed to Mary Phagan's grave by the shortest route.

ᘓ

Prison officials called Lucille at the Alfords' home in Milledgeville, where she lived with friends of Leo's uncle Moses Frank while Leo recovered from the nearly lethal prison attack. Lucille was summoned to the phone. Before the prison official could finish telling Lucille that Leo was in danger, she dropped to the floor and began to have what were then called "convulsions." Prison doctors were called to aid Lucille and revived her with great difficulty. The *Atlanta Georgian* later reported that Lucille had been near death.[15] Because newspapers of that time frequently exaggerated women's emotions and conditions, her condition can't be confirmed.

Prison officials sent a courier to the home of Sheriff Terry of Baldwin County to inform him of Leo's kidnapping, and they contacted Representative Ennis, captain of the Baldwin Bugs, a militia company. Word, at long last, began to spread.

Lucille, waiting for more news, remained with the Alfords. What she feared more than anything during the past two years was coming to pass.

ᘓ

Ten miles north of Milledgeville, at Little River, the vigilantes lost time searching for the man who ran the ferry. The mob used the delay wisely by cutting phone lines around them. The route north they chose took much longer than the route they used to come south. Gordon Gann's car had a tire problem and was abandoned by the road. Meanwhile, Leo sat silent in the second car between Luther and Emmett Burton. During the trip, the brothers attempted to engage Leo in conversation.

"Is there anything you would like to say before your execution?"

"No," Leo answered.

The journey continued, silent except for the drone of the engines and hum of the cicadas.[16]

The vigilantes used a route to the northeast and circled small communities as if they were coming out of the North Georgia Mountains rather than Central Georgia. This route took time. Around daybreak on 17 August, the mob reached Alpharetta, then the Milton County seat.[17] Here the story grows strange. Judge Newt Morris was in Alpharetta for the Blue Ridge Circuit Court, which would convene that morning.[18] John Wood, an attorney from Canton, had accompanied his good friend Judge Morris and happened to be out for an early morning walk, where he met a line of automobiles.[19] In the back of one, Wood noticed a figure he felt sure was Leo Frank. He went to get Judge Morris. This means both John Wood and Judge Morris were early risers that August morning—or was there a chance that the two men were waiting for the convoy that wasted no time moving through Roswell, taking the road to Marietta? The mob was just a short distance from their destination, Frey's Gin.

"Is there nothing you wish to say?" Luther and Emmett Burton again asked Leo.

"No," he answered again.[20]

Frey's Gin—owned by William Frey, former sheriff of Cobb County and the man that tied the hangman's noose—was two miles from Mary's grave and faced the Benton place, Mary's home before she was nine.[21] Most important about Frey's Gin was its setting—trees surrounded a clearing and shielded the view from the road—and an apple table, a sturdy piece of furniture on which good apples were sorted from bad. It would ensure the execution would not fail.

Nearby families denied seeing or hearing anything from the convoy that Tuesday morning. Automobiles were not ubiquitous in 1915, so six cars traveling up a road first thing in the morning had to be noticeable.

Only members of the lynching party were present in the woods that hot morning. Leo remained visibly calm, showing nothing but dignity.[22] When removed from the car, Leo asked if he could write

Lucille a note. Permission was granted. He wrote in what was believed to be German, but it was more likely Yiddish. Nervous about what it might say, someone in the mob destroyed the note.

Leo had worn his wedding ring throughout his entire two-year ordeal, but now he removed it from his finger to be given to his wife.[23]

The hangman's noose was thrown over a branch—photos of the tree reveal it was small, with much larger trees nearby. The men likely chose it because they could throw the rope over a low branch. They blindfolded Leo and forced him onto the apple table. Was he blindfolded because the mob didn't want to look into his eyes as they put him to death? The likely leader of this so-called justice, Judge Newt Morris, pronounced the verdict. "Mr. Frank, we are now going to do what the law said do—hang you by the neck until you are dead. Do you want to make a statement before we do it?"

"No," Leo answered.

"We want to know whether you are guilty or innocent of killing little Mary Phagan."

For a moment, all was quiet. This was a time when some of those responsible for Leo being at Frey's Gin questioned their decision.

Then Leo spoke. "I think more of my wife and mother than I do of my own life." And that was all Leo Frank had to say.[24]

The leader, likely Judge Morris, kicked the table out from under Leo's feet. The jerk of the noose tore open his throat wound, and blood spilled down his white nightshirt.

Leo M. Frank died by hanging.

ꝏ

On Tuesday morning in Milledgeville, Lucille learned that Leo had been lynched in Marietta. Those present said Lucille did not show surprise. How could she? This outcome had been one of her greatest fears since the nightmare began in 1913. Lucille went into Milledgeville that morning, taking care of errands that an unexpected death brought to task.[25] Condolence telegrams poured in, and she answered some. She settled her bills with local stores and went to the prison to collect Leo's belongings, then returned to the Alfords' home to say her goodbyes. Uncle Bud drove from Athens to take her home to Atlanta. Friends were planning a funeral service, but Lucille put a stop to this: She would not bury her husband in Georgia. She was of the mind, like many others, that Leo died for being a Jew. Many had his blood on their hands, both in Marietta and Atlanta, the place where she had been born and raised. No, she would take his body home to New York, to his parents, away from the place that killed him. This was the last gift she gave him.

Chapter 4

A Jewish Community Grows a City

To tell Lucille's story, we must go back to the foundation of Atlanta, where generations of her family carved a history from the land, the setting of what would become a great progressive city.

Atlanta came into existence on what many described as the first piece of flat land after leaving the Appalachian Mountains. This expanse of territory, called Canebrake, belonged to the Cherokee and Creek Nations, who had lived there long before the European settlers arrived.

In 1820, Andrew Jackson—the country's future president—stood at Shallow Ford on the Chattahoochee River and posted a warning sign demanding White families on Cherokee land to vacate. If they ignored this order, their homes and crops would be destroyed before they could gather them. This same man would be the one who brutally removed the Cherokee and Creek Nations from their land. By 1835, the Cherokee and Creek were gone, forced West, and the federal government built a post office in the area and called it Whitehall.

With the post office came transportation that could move people and goods. Stephen Harriman Long, army civil engineer, explorer, and inventor set out to bring the Western and Atlantic Railroad to this flat piece of land. His efforts gave the area its temporary name, Terminus, in September 1837. This name was never intended to be the small town's permanent name. Between 1837 and 1842, the town was called Deanville for Lemuel Dean, native of Palmetto, Georgia, and then Thrasherville, after John J. Thrasher, founder of Norcross. In 1842, an official name, Marthasville, was chosen to honor the daughter of then-governor Wilson Lumpkin. Later J. Edgar Thomason, the chief engineer of Georgia Railroad, changed the town's name to Atlanta after

Martha's middle name, Atalanta, meaning a fleet-footed goddess.[26] After Reconstruction and into the early twentieth century, Atlanta became known as the "Gate City" because it was at the intersection of four rail lines, so most overland traffic that passed between the North and South to points west moved through Atlanta.[27]

ଓ

Immigrant families coming to the United States faced many changes and adjustments. Most wanted their new country to accept them, not see them as strangers with strange customs. Some sought to reinvent themselves in their new home. Some changed their surnames to sound less "foreign," but others retained their birth names with pride. Jewish immigrants in the South, many from Germany, Poland, or Russia, often found acceptance difficult. Jewish families choosing Atlanta as home would have to conform if Georgians were to accept them. These fine citizens were slow to trust non-Christians or anyone born outside the South, or both.

One of the first Jews to live in Atlanta was believed to be Jacob Haas, who emigrated from Germany with his family in 1842. Atlanta officially became a city on 29 December 1847, and Haas's daughter Caroline, born 13 November 1848, was the first Jewish person born in the city.[28] Jacob opened a dry goods store with Henry Levi in 1846. By 1850, the Gate City was home to twenty-six Jewish people—1 percent of the population. These families were part of Atlanta's backbone and helped turn it into one of the most innovative cities in the country.[29] Still today, one can drive through Downtown Atlanta and see the influence of these early Jewish immigrants in the street names.

Most of the Jews who helped build Atlanta began their lives in America's larger cities, such as New York. These men began as peddlers or partnered with extended family in businesses before they set out for the South, where they provided a variety of much needed business and industry. Morris Rich is one example. Rich, who changed his name from Reich to Rich upon entering the country, and his brothers moved

South from Cleveland, Ohio, to build a mercantile business that would become Rich's department store, an Atlanta institution.

During the Civil War, media portrayed Jews as caricatures making money off the war while watching from the sidelines. This perception couldn't be further from the truth. Three thousand Jewish men—a number greater than their proportion of the population—served on the side of the Confederacy. Many were officers, and more than five hundred died.[30]

In 1860, less than twenty years after Atlanta's founding, the Hebrew Benevolent Society was established "to obtain a burial ground and provide relief for the Jewish poor."[31] When Rabbi Isaac Leeser of Philadelphia came to Atlanta in early 1867 to conduct Atlanta's first Jewish wedding, he suggested Atlanta Jews create their own congregation. On 1 April 1867, the Hebrew Benevolent Congregation, an outgrowth of the Hebrew Benevolent Society, received its charter. The congregation bought and established a burial ground in Oakland Cemetery. These graves were walled off from non-Jewish graves as was Jewish tradition.

The Jewish population continued to flourish. Jonas Cohen, Lucille's maternal grandfather, was a co-founder of the new temple. On 31 August 1877, the Hebrew Benevolent Congregation dedicated the first synagogue built in Atlanta on the corner of Forsyth and Garnett streets. By 1902, a new synagogue was built on the corner of Pryor and Richardson streets. This would have been the synagogue Lucille and her sisters attended.

Atlanta's population in 1880 was 37,409, of which six hundred were Jewish. Many of these Jews were savvy businessmen who helped grow Atlanta's industry. In 1889, Jacob Elsas recognized a need for cloth and paper containers for shipping cotton to the North and incorporated the Fulton Bag and Cotton Mill. By 1900, Elsas's mill was Atlanta's largest employer. A mill town called Cabbagetown grew up around the factory; some say the name evolved because the streets were filled with the sharp aroma of boiled cabbage the women cooked for dinner.

H. Mendel & Company was founded by a one-time peddler, Hyman Mendel, who arrived in the country in the 1880s. This company grew into the largest dry goods wholesaler in Atlanta and elsewhere.

With the growth of the Jewish population in Atlanta came a need for more burial plots. The Temple established the Ahavath Achim section of Oakland Cemetery in 1892.

Atlanta gained new prominence by hosting the Cotton States and International Exposition in 1895. It was held in what is now Piedmont Park in Atlanta, and around eight hundred thousand people visited that year—one of them, seven-year-old Lucille, bought a silver souvenir spoon to mark the occasion. The exposition, chaired by Emanuel Rich (one of the Rich brothers), comprised thirteen main buildings and six thousand exhibits on Southern industries, such as mining, manufacturing, and railroads.

The same year, the National Council of Jewish Women was founded. The Atlanta section was committed to community service and issues related to women, children, and education. This group of women went on to found the Free Kindergarten Association, the Jewish Educational Alliance, and the Children's Dental Clinic. These projects are evidence that these women had a social and moral conscience that left a lasting mark on Atlanta.

In 1896, Atlanta's Jewish community marked a significant milestone. Dr. David Marx became the Temple's first American-born rabbi; he would hold this position for fifty years. Rabbi Marx was a native of New Orleans and was a Classical Reformed Jew. He changed the way Atlanta Jews were seen in the community. By 1900, Marx had done away with the bar mitzvah ceremony and allowed head covering and prayer shawls to become things of the past. He established Sunday services, which helped the community fit in with the Christian churches. He firmly believed the Jews were a religious community instead of a nation.

Both the Seligs and Cohens, Lucille's extended family, were among the innovative Jewish men and women who helped form Atlanta into the city it would become.

Chapter 5

A Legacy of Strong Women

The name "Lucille" (like Lucilla and Lucia) comes from French and Latin words for "light."

Emil and Josephine Selig chose the name *Lucille* at their third daughter's birth. It represented shimmery light and predicted a quality of hope that would carry the child into adulthood. Photos of Lucille tell a story of a happy child. When she was three or four, she was taken to a photographer's studio in Rome, Georgia. Her beautiful dark hair is pulled back from her face with a ribbon. She wears a light-colored tulle and sits in front of a studio backdrop of clouds with a slender vine of English ivy across her lap. Her expression is intent. She has bright, curious eyes and chubby cheeks to complete the almost too-adorable package. On her feet are black patent button-up boots with a half-inch heel. Stylish. Her sense of style began at a young age.

The next photo is an oval portrait of her as a teenager, probably in her last year of school. She's wearing a wide-brim hat, a high collar, and a bow of dark satin ribbon around her slim neck. There is a sophistication to her but an innocent half-smile.

Another photo shows an older Lucille as she sits on the beach with cousins. With sea grass on both sides of the trio and a sand dune behind them, the setting looks much like one of the Georgia barrier islands. Lucille relaxes on the sand, left of a teenage boy, who appears to be tolerating the older girls. Lucille leans in and has her hand on his opposite shoulder. He wears a light-colored button-up shirt with sleeves rolled up to his elbows and a sport jacket folded on his lap. His tie is perfect, not loosened. Lucille wears a light-colored dress with elbow-length sleeves and a matching hat perched on her hair that is swept into a style that was popular in the early 1900s before the short cuts of the Roaring Twenties. Lucille's smile lights up her face.

The girl on the right side of the boy holds a woman's wide-brim straw hat on his head. It's a joke that isn't making him laugh. This girl looks to be slightly younger than Lucille. There is a good chance the unnamed boy and girl are Aunt Emma and Uncle Bud's children. If so, the girl would be Helen Michael, who will sing at Lucille's wedding in the near future.

In Lucille's engagement photo, she is twenty-two and looks to be the same age as in the beach photo. The two photos reflect an innocent, hopeful young woman, still starry-eyed with confidence. At this point, there had been no need to dip into the courage, strength, and loyalty passed on to her by the role models in her family. Life is happy and promising.

ᘛ

Jonas Loeb Cohen immigrated to Vermont from Hesse, Germany, when he was twenty-eight (ca. 1858). This area was liberal and accepting, but the Jewish community was nonexistent. The land was fertile and he had come from a farming town, so the fit had seemed good. Soon after arriving, he left for New York City, where he found the companionship of other German Jews and a choice of a different kind of life. Not too long after his arrival in New York City, he met up with Regina Abraham, whom he knew from back home. Regina was twenty and had traveled to America with her brother, Augustus, on the SS *William Frothingham*. Regina and Jonas married in 1859, and a year later, Augustus in tow, they moved to Dalton in the North Georgia Mountains. Jonas opened a mercantile, a much-needed business for the area. Not long after, the couple made their way to Atlanta, where they bought a home at Whitehall and Harris streets. Augustus followed and started a family. At home in Atlanta, Regina kept a cow in the backyard. The city was still small, but a cow in the backyard must have been a sight.

The Civil War began in 1861, but Jonas and Regina's lives were not immediately affected. Like many in the city, they went about their business of making a life. The news of war was distant, unreal, a story about a far-off land. Many people believed the fighting would never reach as far south as Atlanta. Regina and Jonas's first child, Josephine, was born in 1862. The city's population had grown to ten thousand; two thousand were enslaved. As the war went on, more men joined the Confederate Army, and men from Atlanta made up a large segment of Georgia's soldiers. For whatever reason, Jonas was not one of them.

Then, the Confederate Army lost Middle Tennessee to the Union troops. This news made many citizens uncomfortable, especially when Atlanta became the medical base for the wounded. Regina and Jonas watched as Atlanta Medical College (later to become Emory), hotels, and city government buildings became hospitals filled with wounded soldiers. Refugees flooded the city, and the population in 1863 climbed to twenty thousand. Atlanta became a key supply center for the Confederate Army. The factories made nails or railroad tracks and iron plating for gunboats. Now, Jonas, Regina, and baby Josephine saw how close the war was to them. The Union troops surely would be stopped before they made it to Atlanta.

In 1864, the war had inched much closer to Atlanta, and the worst of the battles were taking place. Regina gave birth to Sarah, the couple's second daughter in the basement of their home. In late spring, Jonas left on a train for Nashville to take care of some business that must have been important since parts of Tennessee had fallen to the Union. Regina remained with the children in Atlanta, still a much safer place.

Word came that Union troops were advancing closer to the city. Confederate soldiers built earthworks on the banks of the nearby Chattahoochee River to keep Sherman from crossing into the city. Confederate troops were positioned in North Georgia to meet General Sherman. Atlantans were becoming alarmed, but the city newspapers urged calm. By 25 May 1864, Regina heard the distant booms of cannon fire. General Joesph E. Johnston held Sherman's army at bay for the time. The Confederate leadership moved the weapons arsenal to Macon and

Augusta. When the Battle of Kennesaw Mountain was lost on 27 June 1864, the wounded were moved to Milledgeville and Eatonton, and Atlantans packed their belongings and left. On 5 July, General Johnston ordered all military hospitals to get out. When Union troops crossed the Chattahoochee River near Roswell, Georgia, a few miles from Atlanta, General Johnston withdrew his army from the river on the nights of 9 and 10 July. This news heightened the panic in Atlanta, and citizens fought with medical officers for space on trains.

While these events took place, Regina sold her family's home for three thousand dollars in Confederate money, gathered her girls, now two years and five months, and took the last train out of Atlanta to join Jonas in Nashville.

On 9 August, three to five thousand shells exploded in downtown Atlanta, damaging or destroying most of the buildings. Some people still refused to leave and sought shelter in basements. All the stores were shuttered, and the remaining people, about three thousand citizens, had to make do with produce from gardens and the rations occasionally distributed by the Confederate troops. The army began leaving Atlanta on 1 September. Days later, Sherman ordered all remaining citizens out of Atlanta. Atlanta was in shambles. On 15 November 1864, Sherman burned nearly all of the captured city. Atlanta would have to rise again.

Sometime after the war ended in April 1865, Jonas and Regina returned to Atlanta. Jonas and Sigmond Selig opened a clothing store called Cohen & Selig on the corner of Whitehall—later Peachtree Street—and Alabama streets. With grit and determination, Regina created a good life for her children. She and Jonas would go on to have a total of five daughters.

ଊ

Rudolph Emil Selig was born on 10 June 1849 in Bavaria, Germany, to Simon and Sarah Selig. Emil had nine siblings, but by the time he was ten, five had died. Sarah gave birth to triplet boys who lived only twelve days. She had two more children who lived only two years. Still,

Sarah raised her remaining children to be strong, successful adults who would leave their motherland to make a new life in America. Emil Selig arrived in his new country in 1867 at the age of eighteen. All his siblings made the journey, leaving behind their parents. Simon Selig would die in 1872, five years after Emil left Germany.

In 1880, Josephine Cohen was seventeen and lived at 111 Garnet Street with her parents and four sisters, Sarah, Henrietta, Carrie, and Emma. Thirteen years had passed since Emil Selig had come to his new country. At thirty-one, he lived in Atlanta with his older brother Sigmond; Sigmond's wife, Sophie; and their son, Simon, at 133 Forsyth Street. Also living in the Selig household were Emil's younger siblings, Jonas, Jacob, and Alice. Emil and Sigmond were both clothiers; Jonas and Jacob were bonnet-makers.

The Jewish community in Atlanta remained small. Emil and Josephine both attended services at the Temple and became acquainted. Josephine's father, Jonas Cohen, was a co-founder of the Temple. When it opened in 1877, Josephine, fifteen, and Sarah, thirteen, were part of the celebration ceremony. The Selig family would have attended this celebration. The families must have interacted with each other outside of work and The Temple services. The family spent much of their time focused on services and activities there. On 8 March 1882, Josephine, who was nineteen, married thirty-three-year-old Emil in Atlanta's Fourth Ward. The young couple settled within walking distance of their families. On 25 November 1883, two years after Josephine and Emil's wedding, Josephine gave birth to Sarah. The following year brought another daughter, Rosalind.

When Jonas Cohen died on 13 January 1885 at the age of sixty-one, Sarah, Henrietta, and Emma helped Regina with all aspects of running the household, and twenty-three-year-old Josephine lived close enough to help as well. Levi was buried in the Cohen family plot in Oakland Cemetery.

In December 1887, Josephine's sister, Sarah (age twenty-three), married Harry Silverman from Pennsylvania. Emil and Josephine, who was seven months pregnant with her third daughter, Lucille, attended the wedding. A leap-year baby, Lucille was born on Sunday, 19 February 1888, in the midst of progressive changes happening across the city and country. Did Josephine sense what would befall this beautiful daughter when she held her for the first time? Likely not. Life has a nasty habit of dropping shocking news out of nowhere.

A few months later, Sarah Cohen Silverman gave birth to her first child, Helen, on 23 September 1888. Lucille and Helen were first cousins and would become playmates. Regina Silverman, Sarah's second child, was born 27 October 1891. The future looked bright for these new families.

At some point after the birth of her second daughter, Sarah became ill with consumption and was sent to a hospital in Alto, Georgia, some eighty miles northeast of Atlanta. She wrote to her daughters as often as she could. On 10 February 1894, days away from Lucille's sixth birthday, her aunt Sarah, just months from her thirtieth birthday, died, leaving behind her two daughters, Helen and Regina, and her husband, Harry. Grief-stricken, Harry had a large marble statue of a beautiful woman erected in Oakland Cemetery as Sarah's headstone. Helen and Regina stayed close by, living with extended family, while Harry lived in a boarding house in the general area. Though he never remarried, he remained in Atlanta, earning renown as a pioneer in Atlanta's restaurant industry. He became a member of the governor's staff and served eighteen years under several executives. In May 1925, Harry was found in his son-in-law's garage with a fatal gunshot wound to the head. Family and friends insisted the shooting was accidental, that Harry had shot himself while firing at cats that had been after his chickens and pet birds. Thirty-one years after his wife's death, Harry was buried next to Sarah.

ൽ

By 1900, the Selig clan was scattered. Josephine and her daughters rented a house at 16 Brotherton Street. Sarah and Rosalind were now seventeen and sixteen, with Lucille trailing at twelve. There is no mention of Emil on that year's census. Josephine is listed as the head of the household but marked as married. Emil's younger brother Jonas lived in a boarding house at 249 Whitehall Street with his wife and their two children. Forty-six-year-old Jacob lived with his wife and son in New York City. Emil became a naturalized citizen in 1902.

Lucille, like her sisters, attended Girls High School located at the corner of Mitchell and Washington Streets in the donated John Nepal/William Lyon home, a drafty old mansion previously used as General Sherman's headquarters during the occupation of Atlanta. City Hall stands on the site today.[32]

The Girls High School, founded in 1872, was the only school exclusively for girls, and it had an excellent academic reputation. Eventually, an annex—a warmer, multilevel brick building—was built so more girls could attend. Lucille was one of these girls. GHS, later renamed Roosevelt High School, is one of the seven schools that became part of the original Atlanta Public School System.

By 1896, Sigmond Selig opened the Selig Chemical Company. The business did well, with all the brothers working for their oldest sibling. Emil worked the rest of his life as a salesman for West Disinfection (a division of the Selig Chemical Company), which claimed to be the largest manufacturer of disinfectants in the world. Emil provided a good income for his family. With the exception of Sarah Silverman's death, Lucille had a childhood untouched by tragedy.

☙

Lucille graduated from the Girls High School in 1906 with secretarial skills and became one of Atlanta's working women employed by offices in Atlanta's booming industry. At the age of eighteen, Lucille became a stenographer for the Atlanta Paper Mills Company. By 1910, she was working as a stenographer for the Practice Company.

Affluence surrounded Lucille's home on East Georgia Avenue, but Emil and Josephine were upper-middle class at best. Still, the family did not want for anything. Emil made a good living, which allowed Josephine to hire help with the housework and cooking. Emil rented a spacious two-story house that he shared with Josephine; Rosalind;

Lucille; his oldest daughter, Sarah; her husband, Alex Marcus; and their five-year-old son. In the 1910 census, Alex Marcus was listed as head of the house.

Sigmond Selig now lived in a house on Washington Street, around the corner from Emil, so Lucille's maternal and paternal families were together in one neighborhood.

Levi Cohen brought clout to Lucille's family and provided them honor within the German-Jewish community. Emma, Josephine's youngest sister, had married M. G. Michael, who, with his brother Simon, had founded Athens's earliest department store, Michael Brothers Wholesale and retail Dry Goods Store. The brothers built matching Greek Revival homes on Prince Avenue, a wealthy neighborhood near the University of Georgia. These connections helped Lucille's parents, Emil and Josephine, have a place at the table with the wealthy Jewish elite of Atlanta even if they were not one of them. Lucille was comfortable and happy. She was practical, sewing many of her own clothes, but also bright, fun, almost carefree, with a romantic side. Lucille could throw caution to the sky and splurge on Gibson blouses, all the rage, and new dresses with matching accessories. Lucille possessed a natural beauty and a sunny personality that attracted attention. Her love of the arts and her fun-loving approach to most situations made her quite the catch. Then, she met her one and only true love.

Chapter 6

Love Blooms

While Lucille grew into a fine young woman in Atlanta, a man only two years her senior, Leo M. Frank, worked on his college education in the North. Neither had an inkling about the other. Both lived lives they saw as happy and productive.

☙

Leo Max Frank was born on 17 April 1884 to Rudolph and Rachel "Ray" Frank in Cuero, Texas, known as the stopping point on the Chisholm Trail cattle route to Kansas. Rudolph served as the local postmaster. Three months after their son's birth, the small family moved back to Brooklyn, New York. Rudolph initially settled in Brooklyn in 1869, when he left his career as a physician in Germany and came to America. Brooklyn would be Leo's home until his career pulled him away.

On 18 October 1886, Leo's little sister, Marian, was born in Brooklyn. The siblings, two years apart, were close and would remain that way throughout their lives.

Leo attended public schools and graduated from the Pratt Institute in 1902. He excelled on the school's debate team.[33] His stellar grades earned him admission to Cornell University, which he attended from 1902 through 1906. He majored in mechanical engineering. His extracurricular activities were photography, chess, basketball, and tennis, and he played on all the school's teams. Leo was a member of the Henry Morse Stephens debate team throughout his stay at Cornell.[34] Many photos of Leo during his college years exist and show a popular, well-adjusted young man. One photo shows Leo with a large group of friends crowded together and acting goofy. Leo stands in the middle, looking slightly shocked to be in the center of such a gathering but enjoying it all the same. This awkwardness would come to haunt him in later years as a professional.

After Leo graduated from Cornell, he worked as a draftsman for B. F. Sturtevant Company in Hyde Park, Massachusetts. In fall 1907, he took a job as an engineer and draftsman for the National Meter Company in Brooklyn, which was founded in 1879 and employed Lewis H. Nash, the engineer who invented the Crown water meter.[35] Leo was working in this position when his uncle Moses Frank, who lived in Atlanta, invited him to take a job in his factory.

Moses Frank, Rudolph's brother, was well-traveled and known in business. He came to Atlanta in 1856 from Dudelsheim in Hesse-Darmstadt, Germany. When the Civil War began, he joined the Confederacy. By 1865, he became a citizen and made his fortune speculating in cotton and cotton oil. Moses Frank and manufacturing magnate Sigmund Montag co-owned the National Pencil Company, located in Atlanta.

Leo agreed to join his uncle in this endeavor and was quickly offered a management position. Leo traveled in November 1907 to Germany, where he began a nine-month apprenticeship to study pencil manufacturing at the Ever and Faber Pencil Factory. This company had been manufacturing pencils in the United States since 1861 and had had a factory in Brooklyn since 1874. At the end of his apprenticeship, Leo returned home and visited his parents for a few days before he boarded a train on 4 August 1908 for Atlanta. He arrived in the Gate City on 6 August, where he checked into one of Atlanta's finest hotels, Kimball House, on Peachtree and Decatur streets. He was fulfilling his dream of success in business by becoming the superintendent at the National Pencil Company. Most of Leo's friends described him as considerate and responsible but somewhat rigid. These traits helped him to establish his career at the age of twenty-four. Of course, having an uncle who was part owner didn't hurt his chances, either.

When Leo moved from the Kimball House, he rented a room from Sophie Metzger Selig (not to be confused with Sigmond's wife, Sophia Michael Selig), Lucille's now widowed aunt, who had been married to Emil's younger brother Jacob, who died in 1907. Sophie lived at 93 East Georgia Avenue. Within a week of moving in, Leo was introduced to Lucille. By early fall, Leo accompanied Lucille to the theater and other functions hosted by the city's German-Jewish elite.

At twenty, Lucille was an intelligent young woman. She was well-read and loved music of all genres, but her favorite was ragtime. Leo loved classical music and owned a Victrola. Even though they had different tastes in music, they seemed content with each other's company.

On Valentine's Day 1909, Lucille made a declaration of love for Leo: a cut-out heart with his name written on the front in glitter. Because Leo was more reserved, his feelings weren't as clear. The couple continued to date and enjoy each other's company. On 9 June 1909, ten months after Leo arrived in Atlanta, Lucille accepted his marriage proposal. Their photo was taken in Grant Park, a place many sweethearts spent their warm, lovely days, sometimes rowing across the large lake. Leo and Lucille made a dashing couple—he in a dark suit and round spectacles, she in a light-colored chiffon dress. The park would become one of Lucille's favorite places.

The day after Leo proposed, she got on a train for a long-planned trip to Aunt Emma and Uncle Bud's home in Athens, where her visits always brought dances, teas, and card parties. Professors and students from the nearby University of Georgia attended many of these functions. Lucille arrived in the middle of graduation celebrations, so fun was to be had.

While Lucille was gone, Leo let down his sometimes distant demeanor and sent Lucille love letters—or at least what he considered love letters. On 10 June—the day Lucille was to arrive in Athens—Leo wrote that he "assumed" she arrived safely and that he had gone by the house on Georgia Avenue to play poker with her father and others. Leo much preferred bridge. He sighed the letter "Much Love to you, I am dearest, fondly your beau…."[36]

On 12 June, Leo sent another letter, joking with Lucille about a date he made with Harriet Montag to attend the Lyric Theater. He asked if Lucille was jealous. He spoke about the long letter Lucille sent to Josephine and how he would stop by the Selig house that evening to read it before his dinner.[37] His letters—still formal for a newly engaged man—showed his desire for a new life with Lucille.

By the time 14 June arrived, Leo displayed his longing to be with Lucille. His reserve cracked, and he told her of his joy at receiving two letters from her. He asked her to read between the lines of his letter. Could she feel his warmth and the feelings he sent her way?[38]

In the last letter, dated 16 June, Leo asked Lucille to let him know what time her train would arrive in Atlanta so he could meet his "Goddess Athena."[39]

Lucille's family welcomed the couple's engagement. A photo shows Emil, Josephine, Lucille, Leo, Lucille's sisters, and their husbands gathered around the monarch of the Cohen family, Regina, in celebration of this couple's upcoming union. Another striking photo is of Regina; she's in a chair on a porch, with Josephine and Lucille standing behind her. Three generations of women with their own stories. The resemblance is evident.

ᘓ

On Wednesday, 30 November 1910, the most popular song in the country was "All That I Ask of You Is Love" by Henry Burr. On that same day, a secret ten-day gathering on Jekyll Island off the Georgia coast established a foundation that would later become the Federal Revenue System. Additionally, Thomas Edison informed a *Washington Post* reporter that he had invented a "heavier-than-air flying machine."[40] In Atlanta, twenty-two-year-old Lucille Selig was preparing to become Mrs. Leo M. Frank, and she would sign her name this way until her death in 1957.

The ceremony took place at the Selig home and was performed by Rabbi David Marx. Lucille wore a wedding dress of white satin trimmed in princess lace and pearls. A wreath of delicate orange blossoms held her hair in place, and she held a bouquet of roses and lily of the valley. The house was exquisitely decorated with large bunches of smilax and cases of pale pink carnations. The centerpiece on the long dining room table was a flat basket filled with carnations and ferns.

Seventeen-year-old Regina Silverman—Sarah Silverman's younger daughter—played Mendelssohn's "Wedding March" on the piano as Lucille held Emil's arm. Leo and his best man, Milton Rice, stood gazing at the beautiful bride. Regina Silverman accompanied Helen Michael, Aunt Emma and Uncle Bud's daughter, who sang.

In attendance were close friends and family, including Lucille's maternal grandmother, Regina Cohen; Henrietta Cohen Wolfsheimer and her husband, Carl; and their fifteen-year-old daughter, Sarah. Of course, Aunt Emma and Uncle Bud were among the audience. Leo's parents, Rudolph and Ray, had made the trip from Brooklyn.

An intimate reception followed the ceremony. Josephine, wearing lavender chiffon blending into a gray gown, welcomed the gathering of friends and family. Lucille's new mother-in-law stood close by. Ray Frank's gown, gray embroidered chiffon, trimmed with lace and folds of coral velvet, almost rivaled Josephine's gown and flattered Ray's tall, thin figure.

When there was a lull in the festivities, Leo and Lucille emerged in their traveling clothes, ready to depart for some well-deserved private time. Lucille wore a brown velvet toque—a type of hat—trimmed with quills; it was the perfect match for her brown velvet dress. The couple spent several weeks at the Piedmont Hotel in Atlanta before going north on a wedding trip to Atlantic City, New Jersey.

Upon returning from their honeymoon, Lucille and Leo took up residence at 68 East Georgia Avenue with Lucille's parents, Emil and Josephine. The home's location near the corner of East Georgia Avenue and Washington streets kept them close to extended family and friends. Just around the corner was Henrietta and her family, along with Regina, who had moved in with her daughter.

Lucille's parents thought Leo was a special catch, and they treated him like the son they never had. Lucille and Leo seemed happy; she was making a life out of her new role as wife to a successful businessman, and he worked much more than he relaxed. They had plans and dreams.

ରେ

In winter 1913, three years into their union, tragedy hit when Lucille suffered a miscarriage. This must have been a devastating time for Leo and Lucille, who both wanted children.[41] If only Lucille and Leo could have guessed what would befall them in the spring and challenge every ounce of their love, strength, and resolve.

Chapter 7

A Simple People

The name *Mary* comes from *Miriam*, an ancient Hebrew name with two meanings: "beloved" and "bitter or rebellious." The latter refers to Moses's sister, Miriam, whose birth coincided with the Hebrew enslavement in Egypt. When she was seven, she kept watch over her brother Moses after their mother placed him in a basket and set him in the Nile River among the reeds.[42]

Mary Phagan and her family are known and remembered for her brutal murder, yet the stories surrounding the family are rich, exciting, and heartbreaking in ways worth knowing. Skeletons hidden from prying eyes in the proverbial closets show a dynamic set of events before and after Mary's birth. These stories give the reader a three-dimensional look into the Phagans and Bentons and what made this little girl who she was. The families, both influential in their communities, trace their histories to the American Colonial era. While the Phagans and Bentons were not rich, their lives were not the hardscrabble picture the newspaper articles painted at the time of the murder. That's not to say Mary's mother and her second husband didn't struggle—they did—but there is much more to their stories if we only look.

Frances ("Fannie") Elizabeth Benton Phagan gave birth to Mary Anne Phagan on 1 June 1899, after four months of mourning. The previous February, when Fannie was five months pregnant with his second daughter, William Joshua Phagan died of measles complications, most likely pneumonia. Mary represented hope for the whole family, and Fannie must have longed for a good and meaningful life for this fatherless baby. Her brothers and sister doted on their baby sister. Fannie must have known that William's death left her with two choices common to widows of the time: live off the kindness of family or remarry. Fannie chose the kindness of family. She left the Phagans and traveled home to her mother and family in Marietta, Georgia, when Mary was only months old.

The details of the Phagan and Benton families can be traced back for generations. Those family records have been preserved for future generations, and those descendants have fought to keep Mary's story alive, as if to say, "Don't forget what she could have been, if not for this tragedy." Rightly so. More than a hundred years after the murder, there are still places, especially in Georgia, where the mention of Mary's name begins a conversation. Many residents in Marietta grew up with her story because such a crime leaves a legacy, an unwanted identity for the generations that follow. Others, whose families lived in Marietta and Atlanta in 1913, have no idea of their relatives' connections to the murder, the trial, and its aftermath. The details of the mob's so-called justice are largely lost in legend. Her murder overshadowed who she was, her dreams, and her love for family; instead, most remember her for how she lost her life.

Though in different ways, Mary and Lucille experienced the silencing of their stories. Mary's name was plastered in every newspaper across the country at the time. Lucille, too, was thrust into a story she didn't choose. Both, first and foremost, are remembered for what happened one April day in 1913: Mary's life abruptly and violently ended, and Lucille's journey down a dark path from which she wouldn't return. Neither story has a happily-ever-after.

The Phagans

The Phagans' story begins in 1730 in Augusta, Virginia, with the birth of Philip Phagan (also Feagin). Philip, likely of Scotch-Irish descent, married Martha Newman on 20 February 1763, at the age of thirty-three. They had four children, Moses (b. 1765), Martha (b. 1767), Philip Jr. (b. 1778), and Rebekah (b. 1782). After Martha's death at the age of forty-two, Philip married Ann Boseman. They had two children, Margaret (b. 1785) and Lydia (b. 1792). Philip died in South

Carolina in 1797, leaving his plantation to Ann and other tracts of land to his children, including Moses.[43]

Moses found his way to Franklin, Georgia, where he married Phoebe Smith. The couple lived in Habersham County, Georgia, where Moses died in 1830, leaving behind Phillip (named for Moses's father), Margaret, and James. Philip Phagan married Margaret Wilkes Newel on 1 July 1823. He was thirty-four and, like his father, had several children. Among them was a daughter, Ruth Mary Ann, born in 1830. This was Mary's paternal great-grandmother. Ruth Mary Ann gave birth to William Jackson Phagan, called WJ, on 17 November 1854 at the age of twenty-four. WJ had Ruth Mary Ann's surname, Phagan, which means either there was a short-lived marriage or she wasn't married. On 7 July 1859, at the age of twenty-nine, Ruth Mary Ann married twenty-year-old Daniel M. Thacker in Hall County, Georgia. Three years later, Ruth Mary Ann gave birth to Minerva Lindora. Daniel went to fight for the Confederacy and died 3 November 1864 in Richmond City, Virginia, while fighting the Seven Days battle. Ruth Mary Ann was widowed at thirty-four.

In 1872, seventeen-year-old WJ Phagan, Mary's paternal grandfather, married Angelina "Jelina" O'Shields. A year later, they had their first child, William Joshua Phagan, Mary's father. WJ and his wife would go on to have eleven children. There is strong evidence that the siblings always remained close.

William Joshua took to the land and worked right beside his father, a farmer. By this point, the Phagans were living in Marietta, a small town twenty miles north of Atlanta. This town would become very important to Lucille though there is no evidence she ever visited.

The Bentons

The maternal side of Mary Phagan's family had roots in the Georgia colony early in the country's history. Samuel J. Benton and his wife, Anna Pickeron, are Mary's earliest identified relatives. Samuel was born in Georgia in 1770, and he married Anna on 22 October 1796, in Columbia, Georgia, located on the Savannah River, close to

Augusta. The couple had a son, Milton Lovelace Benton, in 1812 when Samuel was forty-two. He died in Jasper County, Georgia, when Milton was five.

Milton married Catharine Backer in Jasper County on 13 December 1832, at the age of twenty. The couple had several children, but one, Samuel J., named after Milton's father and born in 1835, is connected to this story.

Samuel J. Benton was twenty and living in Coweta County when he married Anna E. Guinade in 1855. The couple had two children, William (b. 1856) and Nancy (b. 1860). On 4 March 1862, when he was twenty-seven, Samuel enlisted in the Confederate Army. He died of disease just over a year later in Tupelo, Mississippi. The 1870 census revealed Anna was living with Milton, her father-in-law, and she had two more children, a daughter (b. 1867) and a son (b. 1870), but no new husband. This census calls Milton the "inferred father." In the 1880 census, Anna is referred to as Milton's spouse, and they had two more sons and a daughter. The youngest daughter, Frances ("Fannie"), would become Mary's mother. By this time, the Benton family lived in the community of Olinville on the east side of Marietta's town square.

The Phagans lived nearby, and at some point, William Joshua Phagan and Fannie Benton met and fell in love. The couple married on 27 December 1891 and moved to a farm owned by William Joshua's father (WJ Phagan). William Joshua and Fannie lived there for the next few years and had Benjamin Franklin and Ollie Mae. The family seemed to be thriving.

WJ Phagan's business was trading, buying, and selling homes, an enterprise that kept his family on the move. When he purchased an old plantation home in bad need of renovation in Florence, Alabama, the entire Phagan family—including William Joshua, Fannie, and their children—loaded wagons with feed, tools, and furniture, tied their stock behind the wagons, and like pioneers, headed West in a wagon train in the middle of winter. The mornings were cold, and water had to be heated to pour on the wagon wheels to loosen them from the frozen ground. Years later, after the family returned to Cobb County, Georgia, WJ said it was a wonder the whole family didn't freeze to death.[44] The family finally reached their new home—a house that had been a hospital in the Civil War—and realized the scale of renovations needed was far more than they had expected. William Joshua and Fannie moved into a smaller house on the property located close to the plantation house, keeping the Phagan family intact. Fannie gave birth to two more sons, Charles Bryan and William Joshua Jr., known as Josh.

When her husband died in 1899, life drastically changed for Fannie. Like her mother, Anna, who eventually married her dead husband's father, Fannie would find out what choices women had when their husbands were gone. After Mary was born, Fannie took her children and traveled home to Marietta. Mary would see Olinville as her hometown. The family moved in with Anna, now sixty years old and called Nannie. Fannie was twenty-five.

ꝏ

In 1907, Fannie moved her five children to Egan, a mill town just outside of East Point, to open a boarding house. By 1910, the family lived on Washington Avenue in East Point in 1910. The children, Ben (fifteen), Ollie Mae (fourteen), Chas (thirteen), Josh (twelve), and Mary (eleven) were still at home. According to the East Point Historical Society archives, the family lived on the corner of Martin and Hendrix streets. This possibly could have been where the boarding house was located.

On 25 February 1912, Fannie married John William (Will) Coleman. He would be the first father Mary would know. Will Coleman worked for the Atlanta sanitation department, and the family moved to Bellwood, a mill town on the west side of the city.

Most of what's written about Mary's murder depicts Mary and Will's relationship as close, including the publication of Mary's poem titled "Pa." A letter Mary wrote to Myrtle, her cousin in Marietta, gives us an account of Mary's last Christmas with her siblings and stepfather.

Atlanta, GA
Dec. 30, 1912
My Dear Cousin

I thought I would ans your letter to let you know that we are all well hope you are the same. Well how did you enjoy Christmas? I had a fine time at the Christmas tree. What did old Santa Claus bring you? Well I didn't get very many things but they were nice. Mr. Coleman gave me a pair of kid gloves and Ollie gave me a mesh bag. Charlie came Tuesday and stayed until yesterday and Joshua came Wednesday. Of course we were glad to see them. It does look like some of you all could of come. Well, Myrt I don't know what to think of you for not coming. I think that was a poor excuse. When I come up there I will give you what you need. Me and Ollie & moma & Charlie & Joshua went out at uncle Jack Thurs. and taken dinner. "But gee."[45]

Will Coleman became part of the family the previous February, almost a year before Mary wrote the letter, yet she still refers to him as Mr. Coleman. Also, the letter shows Ollie Mae gave Mary a silver mesh bag for Christmas, which Mary took with her the day she was murdered. It was believed that the bag held $2.50, along with Mary's $1.20 in pay, but the bag was never found.

From this letter, we also see that Ollie Mae and Mary are the only children left at home. Charlie and Josh, now fifteen and fourteen, were no longer living with the family. Mothers today would view this as too young to leave home, but children working in factories grew up fast and went out on their own quicker. Mary had begun work for the National Pencil Company earlier in the year at a rate of ten cents an hour for a sixty-hour workweek.[46]

None of the family had any idea how short their time with Mary would be.

Chapter 8

The Murder

Saturday, 26 April 1913
Morning

The weather was brutally cold, a harsh chill that cut straight to the bone, along with on-and-off rain. At breakfast, Lucille tried to convince Leo to forgo his plans to attend a baseball game that afternoon with her brother-in-law, Charles, and to put off his work at the National Pencil Company so he could accompany her and Josephine to the opera. Leo refused. Opera was not his cup of tea. Baseball, with its strategies, appealed to the engineer part of him, but when Leo got a taste of the weather, he chose to cancel the outing. He was prone to sickness, and sitting in the elements wouldn't be the best idea. Instead, he proceeded with his Saturday ritual of catching the trolley to the factory to prepare sales commission invoices in triplicate for the salesmen and distributors, balancing the books, and creating a financial report to show his boss, factory co-owner Sig Montag. That week, four thousand pencils went to the freight yard to be shipped to F. W. Woolworth and S. H. Kress 5&10 stores. While most employees had collected their pay on Friday (due to the Confederate Memorial Day parade), a few, including Mary, had been laid off the Monday before and likely hadn't gotten the news that Saturday was a holiday. She had been laid off when the brass supply ran out. Mary worked in the "tipping department," where she affixed erasers to the pencils with small brass bands. Those workers who didn't know about the schedule change likely would come to the factory to collect their pay on Saturday.

Once at his office, Leo placed a wire basket of pay envelopes on his desk so he wouldn't get distracted from his work. For a while, his office boy, Alonzo Mann, and a stenographer worked close to him, but they left shortly before noon.

Lucille spent the morning dressing for the opera, taking care to look her best. Lucille and her mother would see the matinee of Gaetano Donizetti's opera *Lucinda Di Lammermoor*, starring Frieda Hempel. Lucille was thrilled to attend. Anyone who was anybody would see this show before it left Atlanta.

ଔ

On the other side of town, in Bellwood—a mill village in northwest Atlanta—Mary Phagan ate a breakfast of cabbage and wheat biscuits in her family's kitchen. These homes were occupied mostly by families that migrated to the city from farms where they had barely eked out a living. Many found life was still difficult; instead of working in the fields, they worked low-paying jobs in dark, dusty factories.

Mary must have been excited about both Saturday and Sunday. As lively as Mary could be, she worked just as hard—too hard for a child of thirteen, almost fourteen. When Fannie had married William Coleman a year before, Mary could have quit her job, but she loved having her own money. That Sunday, she would take the streetcar to Marietta to visit her aunt and perhaps to see her favorite cousin, Myrtle Barmore. The two were great friends and often exchanged letters. For the first eight years of Mary's life, the two played together.

Mary put on her new violet dress, sewn by Aunt Lizzie, and gray heels. She styled her auburn hair in pigtails, securing them with bows that matched her dress. Her beauty often led others to believe she was older than her actual age, but she was undeniably still a child. Mary put on a dark blue hat trimmed with blue ribbons and small red flowers, grabbed her parasol in case the cold mist turned into a full rain, and placed her silver mesh purse over her arm. She said goodbye to her mother, assuring her she'd be home after the parade. Mary closed the door to her house at 146 Lindsay Street at approximately 11:45 a.m.

She walked to the corner of Bellwood Avenue and Lindsay Street, then stepped into Mrs. A. A. Smith's store. Mrs. Smith took one glance at Mary's bare arms and suggested she return home to fetch a cloak. She cautioned Mary that she might catch a cold in the chilly weather. Mary replied that she was going into town for only a short while and would be fine.

Upon entering the English Avenue trolley at 11:50 a.m., Mary gave her fare of a five-cent piece to the conductor, W. T. Hollis. He would sign a statement that no one sat with Mary; however, George Epps, who was fourteen and lived right around the corner from Mary, said he sat with her. According to Epps, the two planned to watch the parade together, but first, Mary was going to collect her pay. Epps said the two planned to meet at Elkin-Watsons, a local drugstore, by two o'clock, and that the last time he saw Mary was about 12:07 when she stepped off the trolley on Hunter Street and headed to 34 Forsyth Street, the National Pencil factory. George collected his newspapers and went to the drugstore, where he waited until four, but Mary never turned up. He left for the Atlanta Crackers game.[47]

W. M. Matthew, the motorman of the streetcar told a Pinkerton detective on 3 May that Mary sat in the third seat on the right-hand side of the streetcar.[48] He never mentioned seeing George Epps on the streetcar with Mary when speaking to the Pinkerton detective.

Afternoon

The four-story National Pencil Company, which had once been a hotel, was near the railroad tracks that separated Atlanta's business and industrial districts. That week, Mary had worked two short shifts due to the brass sheet metal shortage. Her pay suffered, but any amount was better than none.

Leo Frank's office was in the corner of the second floor, the same floor where Mary worked. Her intention was to retrieve her pay as quickly as possible and watch the parade. Many of her friends from work had talked about the movie at the Bijou, so she thought she might see that afterward. Mary entered the National Pencil Company through the street-level front doors. This area was not well lit, and its shadows could leave a person unnoticed.

When Mary arrived, Leo was alone and engrossed in his work. He was so involved that he didn't notice her until she spoke, telling him she had come to collect her pay. Leo asked for her employee number—he knew very few employees by name. He found her envelope with the $1.20. She thanked him and turned to leave. At the door, she paused and asked if the brass sheet metal shipment had come in. Leo told her it had not.

Leo couldn't see the direction she went, but later said he heard her footsteps as she walked away. Leo would later recount that he heard her talking to a girl. Less than two minutes later, Lemmie Quinn, a foreman, came to talk to Leo. Soon after, Leo left for lunch.

Lunch

Lucille and Josephine rushed out of the house on Georgia Avenue so as not to be late for the opera, passing Leo as he came home for lunch. He sat and ate with Emil, Lucille's father. Had he had a moment of spontaneity and gone to the opera with Lucille and Josephine, his life would have been different, but Leo lacked the patience to sit through an afternoon of opera in a language he didn't know. He was practical, perhaps bordering on boring. A mechanical engineer, Leo was quiet, intelligent, and dedicated to work. He loved sports for the strategy involved, but opera was an experience he didn't care for. Lucille must have expected Leo's refusal before she invited him, and there is no indication she was bothered by it. The couple's interests often seemed to diverge.

Lucille kept up with the latest fashion, attended teas, and volunteered, like many wives married to successful businessmen. She was a member of the Atlanta chapter of the Council of Jewish Women, an organization responsible for helping settle immigrants from Eastern Europe, launching a children's dental clinic, and adopting the children's ward at Grady Hospital, among other projects.

Leo approached life with the same structure he relied on as superintendent. He worked on Saturdays to keep things running smoothly. The effort was worth the payoff of his uncle's admiration, even if the routine made Leo seem dull and pragmatic.

After Leo finished his lunch, he went to lie on the sofa in the parlor and smoke a cigarette. He knew it was time to get back to the factory. Before he'd taken his lunch break, he had warned two plant employees on the fourth floor that he planned to bolt the door when he left, and they would be locked inside. One of these employees, Arthur White, had his wife visiting. Arthur told her to leave before she was locked inside, and her exit from the building—and what she saw—would be important in the days to come. Remembering the employees locked inside and the fact that he still had a financial report to complete, Leo went back to work.

On his way to the streetcar stop, Leo spoke to relatives. He would later be questioned about the time of his return to work. With roads along the parade route closed, his streetcar had to shorten its route and stopped at the edge of the business district. The walk to the factory was short, and along the way, he waved to employees in the crowd gathered for the parade.

Uptown, the outgoing governor, Joseph M. Brown, readied to be part of the parade. Come June, he would relinquish the governorship to the governor-elect, John Slaton. On that cold spring Saturday, the citizens of Georgia still liked Slaton. He owned a powerful law firm that represented Fulton Bag and Cotton Mill and other large Atlanta businesses. A rumor was floating around the city that Slaton's law firm would merge with the firm of Luther Rosser, who was known for his skills in ligation and earned $100,000 a year, representing clients such as Georgia Railway and Electric Company (which later became Georgia Power).

Georgia's primary industry had shifted from agriculture to manufacturing, which made cheap child labor appealing. State laws governing children in the workforce were almost nonexistent, but pressure (from those without ties to manufacturing, as well as teachers, pastors, and social workers) was mounting to regulate child labor. Company owners demanded lawmakers reject reforming—or passing—child labor laws, and Governor-elect Slaton had his work cut out for him.

Hugh Mason Dorsey, solicitor general of the Atlanta Judicial Court, must have attended the parade. Most notable people did that day. His sights were set on a political career bigger than Atlanta. What better way to make this happen than being a successful prosecuting attorney? All he needed was a big case that would catch the public's attention. So far, the right case hadn't materialized.

Tom E. Watson likely covered the parade for his publication, the *Jeffersonian*, which he claimed represented the common people. He viewed himself as the voice of the working man.

The parade, including a brass band, school children, and aging Confederate veterans, began at two o'clock. The icy mist turned to a full rain before the parade, with pomp and circumstance, reached Oakland Cemetery.

Nine thousand graves of Confederate soldiers, with only one hundred identified, received a Confederate flag that day. The unnamed soldiers were given floral wreaths. A cannon was fired from the highest point in the cemetery. Seventy-five thousand spectators watched the parade and attended the memorial service.

❧

As the curtain went up at the Atlanta Municipal Auditorium for the opera, parade spectators stood five rows deep on Peachtree Street. Mary Phagan was nowhere to be seen. Neither Lucille nor Leo had any idea their lives had changed forever. There was no turning back.

Late Afternoon and Evening

Newt Lee, the factory's night watchman, used the key that Leo had given him the night before to unlock the front door of the pencil factory at four o'clock on Saturday afternoon. Five o'clock was his usual starting time, but Leo had asked Lee to arrive an hour early because he had originally planned to leave for the baseball game. The gas light on the main floor was burning brightly, just as Lee had left it at the end of his shift that morning. Mr. Frank insisted that the light should always shine its brightest so the police could see inside as they made their rounds at night.

Lee shut the door behind him. "Step here a minute, Newt," Leo called from the second-floor landing. Leo wrung his hands nervously and explained that he hadn't finished his work as he had thought he would. He apologized for asking Lee to come in early and suggested that Lee enjoy the town and return at six. Lee mentioned that he could catch some extra sleep at the factory, but Leo insisted he go out and enjoy his time off. Newt did as he was told. Later, Newt would alter part of his testimony to say that Leo hadn't locked the front door while Lee was walking around the city.

Newt Lee returned to the factory a little before six o'clock. When he tried the front door, it was still unlocked. Leo called from upstairs, inquiring about the time. Lee told him it was two minutes before six. Leo instructed him not to punch in because a few people had worked in the factory that day, and he wanted to change the time slip as he regularly did at the end of each workday. This time Leo took twice as long to change the slip.

"He [Mr. Frank] fumbled it in, while I held the lever for him." Lee finally punched the slip and went downstairs, just outside the front door, where J. M. Gantt met him. Frank had fired Gantt, a bookkeeper, two weeks before because the cash box had been two dollars short. Gantt told Lee he had come to retrieve a pair of shoes he'd left at the factory.

Lee told him he wasn't allowed to let anyone in after six.

Mr. Frank came down the stairs and saw Gantt. He jumped back, frightened, according to Lee's testimony.

Gantt spoke respectfully, asking if he could retrieve his old shoes from upstairs. Frank told Gantt he had seen the shoes in the trash, but Gantt was felt sure they would still be where he had left them.

Mr. Frank lowered his head. "Newt, go with him and stay with him and help him find them."

Gantt found his shoes within minutes and asked Lee if he could use the phone. Lee permitted him to do so, and then Gantt left. He was in the factory for only minutes and always within Newt Lee's sight.[49]

ଓ

Leo called Newt Lee at the factory a little more than an hour later, something he had never done in the few weeks Lee had worked there.

"How is everything?" Leo asked.

"Everything is all right, so far as I know," Lee answered. The two said goodbye. Leo never asked after Gantt.

Lee did wonder why his boss had called.[50]

Night

After Newt and Leo ended their conversation, Leo returned to his chair, where he looked at a newspaper while his father-in-law and others played poker. Leo filled them in on the day's stories. Poker was considered a man's game, so Lucille was likely upstairs or visiting with one of her sisters.

Around the same time, Fannie and Will were becoming concerned because Mary had missed supper. Will went to stand outside the Bijou Theater to see if Mary came out. He did this until ten, the end of the last show, and came home without her.

At the pencil factory, Newt Lee began his rounds. He punched on the hour and half hour, making all his punches. He checked the elevator doors on the office floor like always and found them fastened down as expected.

Several hours into his shift, Lee entered the basement. "I went down to the toilet and when I got through I looked at the dust bin back to the door to see how the door was, and it being dark I picked up my lantern and went there and I saw something laying there which

I thought some of the boys had put there to scare me, then I walked a little piece towards it and I seen what it was and I got out of there. I got up the ladder and called the police station. It was after three o'clock."[51]

Lee got an officer on the phone. "A white woman has been killed up here."[52]

Chapter 9

The Investigation of the Murder Scene

Sunday Morning

Early Sunday morning, 27 April, as the gray of dawn washed over the sky, the bell rang at the Seligs' home on East Georgia Avenue. Lucille pulled on her heavy blue robe as Leo dressed. Detective John Black, a celebrated Atlanta Police detective in a pork-pie hat, and W. W. "Boots" Rogers, an erstwhile Fulton County officer, stood at the door.

Lucille invited the men to wait in the parlor and explained Leo would be with them as soon as he finished dressing.

Leo entered the room minutes later, wearing both a freshly ironed shirt and trousers. He paced the floor, wringing his hands, firing questions at Detective Black about the factory and the night watchman but not giving him time to answer. Leo also said he dreamed the phone rang at four that morning. What had happened at the factory?

Detective Black, already forming a negative view of Leo, explained he was there to take Leo to the factory to see for himself what happened.

Black, using every inch of his height, had a take-charge, authoritative demeanor. His no-nonsense attitude must have made him seem threatening. Leo wasn't caught off guard by the detective's visit because John Starnes, an attaché in the detective department, had called earlier, explaining that someone would be there to take Leo to the factory. Both Leo and Lucille were expecting these visitors. Lucille, knowing her husband, probably understood his nervousness but also knew the detective would question Leo's fidgeting. Black didn't know Leo was a ball of anxiety on most days, that it was just part of his makeup. Black told Leo to finish dressing so they could leave.

Lucille interjected that Leo hadn't had breakfast. Boots Rogers chimed in that he too was hungry. Leo told Lucille he would take some coffee and forgo food. She offered the two men coffee, but Black suggested something stronger, like whiskey, would be better for calming Leo. Lucille went in search but found no liquor.

Leo climbed into the automobile with Black and Rogers, but not before asking Lucille to call Mr. Darley, the forty-seven-year-old factory personnel director and one of Frank's close associates to meet him at the factory. The group set out for the National Pencil Company.

When the on-call officer, W. F. Anderson, arrived at the pencil factory around four that morning, he crawled into the small trap door leading to the factory's basement on the direction of Newt Lee, who had attempted to call his boss at home. Leo never answered. Anderson must have felt some apprehension as he and the other responding officers took the wooden plank ladder down into the bowels of the building. Anderson's flashlight beam landed on a body turned face-down in the rear of the basement, partially hidden behind a partition. Her arms were folded under her, and her dress was pushed above her knees. And, if this chilling sight didn't tell Anderson and his men how brutal this death was, the missing shoe from the small foot announced what she went through before her last breath.

When the body was turned over, the reality of the crime hit home: "Her face was full of dirt and dust."[53]

The girl's right eye was damaged and purple. Scratches and bruises covered her cheeks. Above her ear was a deep gash caked with dried blood, yet it was the cord embedded in her throat that revealed she died from strangulation. The girl's underwear had been ripped and tied around her neck alongside the cord. Her swollen tongue hung from her mouth. A trace of blood came from her nose and ears.

What Officer Anderson and the rest of the men saw in front of them was a Black female, which didn't match Newt Lee's initial description of a White woman. The body was caked with soot.

The morning watch commander, Sergeant R. J. Brown, grabbed a piece of paper from the trash near the body and wiped the soot on the girl's face, revealing she was White. The dark basement—the gas lamps turned to the lowest flame—smelled of cedar and lead from the years of shavings disposed there. The officers began to search for anything that might belong to the girl or her attacker. Later, after interviewing the girl's family, they would discover her silver mesh handbag was missing. It was reported she had a few dollars inside. On her wrist, was a bent gold bracelet spattered with blood. On her left ring finger was a signet ring.

Two civilians were with the police officers on the scene, Boots Rogers, the former police officer who accompanied Detective John Black to get Leo Frank, and *Atlanta Constitution* reporter Britt Craig, who was there because he was waiting at the police headquarters for a ride home and was invited to ride along to the crime scene. Maybe he would get a good story. A trail led from the elevator to the hiding place, making it clear the body had been dragged the length of the basement. Sergeant L. S. Dobbs unearthed the first of two bizarre notes under the sawdust near the victim's head. He read aloud from the lined paper: "He said he would love me laid down play like the night witch did it but that long tall black negro did by his slef [self]."[54]

While Dobbs read, Newt Lee broke in: "That means me—the night watchmen."[55] Later, in interviews and testimony, Lee would say he said, "[White folks] put it off on." The second note was written on a National Pencil Company pad. Again, this note implicated Newt Lee: "Mam that negro fire down here did this when I went to get water and he push me down thro hole a long tall negro black that did [had] it. i right while play with me."[56]

"You did this, or you know who did it," Dobbs said to Lee, who would tell his story at the coroner's inquest several days later.[57]

If not for Boots Rogers, the victim's family would have learned of her murder not from police but from the *Atlanta Constitution*'s extra edition: Britt Craig was busy writing his story for the *Constitution* while the officers and detectives were investigating the basement. Rogers had a sixteen-year-old sister-in-law, Grace Hicks, who worked at the pencil factory. He went to her home on McDonough Boulevard.

By this time, the victim's body had been removed and taken to Bloomfield's Funeral Home. Boots took Grace straight to view the victim. Shocked, she identified the girl as Mary Phagan. Unsure where Mary lived and Leo still unreachable, the officers struggled with how to contact the family. Grace called fellow pencil factory employee Helen Ferguson, who lived in Bellwood, close to Mary. Helen was good friends with Mary and knew the family well. Helen was sixteen, and the *Atlanta Constitution* described her as "a timid little girl in a short dress with hair hanging in two braids down her back and an almost inaudible voice."[58]

Helen had attempted to get Mary's pay envelope for her after work on Friday, but Leo Frank told Helen that Mary would have to come in on Saturday to pick it up herself. There were two men in the office when she spoke with Leo. Helen had retrieved Mary's pay twice before, but she had used Mary's employee number to do so and spoken with the shift supervisor instead of Leo. This time, she couldn't remember Mary's number and went home empty-handed.

Helen told the officers that the Phagans did not have a phone, but she would take the message to them at their home on Lindsay Street. The simple wood-frame homes on Lindsay Street were built close together. Some had front porches and picket fences; most had just two small bedrooms, a kitchen, and a front room.

Like any mother, Fannie was consumed with worry and probably didn't sleep Saturday night. She thought Mary might have taken a streetcar to Marietta to visit her aunt instead of waiting until Sunday morning. Fannie was adamant that Mary would have sent a message to her if she could. Will Coleman called the police that Saturday night, but the officers didn't know about the murder at the time.

At dawn, Helen Ferguson knocked on the Phagans' door and told Fannie what she knew. Fannie collapsed, and a physician was called.

As Fannie and Will tried to come to terms with Mary's death, John Starnes finally reached Leo Frank and told him he was sending a car. Newt Lee, the first of many suspects in the murder, was arrested for the murder of Mary Phagan.

At about five o'clock that morning, Leo Frank and Detective Black sat in the back of Boots Rogers's car as they left for the pencil factory. They asked Leo if he knew Mary Phagan. Leo asked if she worked at the factory and said he couldn't know if she worked there unless he looked at the payroll. Black and Boots suggested they go to Bloomfield's Funeral Home—maybe Leo would remember Mary if he saw her. Leo agreed without hesitation. When the group arrived, Leo hung back in the doorway. When asked if he recognized Mary, he said no. He went on to say if she had been at the factory Saturday, he could check the payroll and confirm whether she collected her pay. There is conflicting testimony on whether Leo ever looked at Mary's body from his position by the door.

The men left the funeral home and went to the factory. Onlookers were already gathering outside, and the men made their way through the growing crowd. N. V. Darley (the personnel director Leo asked Lucille to call) met the group at the door. Leo led the small group to his office in the corner of the second floor. The plating department, where Mary had worked, was also on the second floor. Detective Starnes and Newt Lee, now in handcuffs, joined the group. Once in the office, Leo opened the safe and brought out the time book. He ran his finger down the page and stopped at Mary's name, explaining she had come in to collect her $1.20 pay. He asked if the pay envelope been found on her body, but no one answered. He remembered Mary had come in a little after noon because his stenographer and office boy left at noon, and Mary entered his office soon after their departure.

One of the officers suggested they go to the basement to see where the body had been found. Leo said the group could take the elevator. The cable gave him a bit of trouble and appeared locked. Darley, a large man, yanked the cable, and the men were on their way down. When the elevator stopped, a stench filled the air, a smell none of these men would forget. The smell, though, was not investigated and would turn out to be important evidence. As the men observed the place where Mary's body had been found, one noticed that the lock on the back door had been tampered with. Leo, worried that someone would break in, took Darley with him to find a hammer and nails. Leo was so rattled he couldn't hit the nails properly with the hammer, so Darley took over. Leo's nervous demeanor didn't improve his situation—the officers were becoming deeply suspicious of him. Why? What person wouldn't be overwhelmed by seeing a murdered girl's dead body at the funeral home?

When the men returned upstairs, Newport A. Lanford, the chief of detectives, waited. If Leo had been nervous before, Lanford's arrival must have felt overwhelming. Lucille and Leo's friends and coworkers understood his high-strung nature, but the Atlanta Police Department didn't know the pencil factory's superintendent. Lanford was distinguished in his uniform. He was balding and wore a bushy gray mustache. At fifty-one, he had spent twenty-five years on the force.

Frank and Darley spent the next twenty minutes escorting Lanford around the third and fourth floors of the pencil factory, where most of the German pencil-making machines were housed. They looked in dressing rooms and visited the department where Mary worked, but nothing out of the ordinary caught their attention. Frank had calmed while in his element. The group's last stop was the time clock, where Newt Lee was required to punch in every half-hour. Leo took a long look at Newt's punched slip and stated all was in order. This time slip was placed in Leo's safe.

The detectives asked Frank to accompany them back to headquarters to view the murder notes found next to Mary's body. The group had grown since arriving at the pencil factory. Starnes, Lee, and Black sat in the back of the automobile. Darley and Frank were in the front, with Rogers driving. Leo, who sat on Darley's lap, was visibly shaking. The murder, the visit to the see the body, the detectives and their suspicion surely all weighed heavily on Frank.

At the station, the murder notes were not available—the *Atlanta Journal* had borrowed them. The officers didn't seem bothered that evidence was in the newspaper's hands. Leo and Darley left the station and went to Montag Paper Company to speak with Mr. Sig, the pencil factory's co-owner and Leo's boss, but Mr. Sig had not come into work. Darley went home, and Leo took a streetcar to Washington Street, where Mr. Sig lived. He went to the Montag residence for a short talk; perhaps Leo was seeking guidance. When Leo left the Montag house, he went home, arriving at a quarter to eleven. Lucille must have been waiting with a million questions.

Sunday Afternoon

Leo went back to Bloomfield's that afternoon. Hundreds of people who had read the *Atlanta Constitution*'s scoop on the murder—most strangers to Mary's family—lined up around the block to view her body. Before Mary's burial, ten thousand people would come to view her body, which still bore the mark of the cord used to strangle her. Many came out of pure morbid curiosity.

Frank greeted a few employees, such as Darley and the office boy, Alonzo Mann, and left soon after to go to police headquarters. They now had the murder notes. When Leo looked at them, he had nothing to say that helped the detectives. When he left the station, he stopped by the pencil factory, where he found a large crowd. A storm brewed on the horizon.

Sunday Evening

Upon Leo's return, Lucille gathered her husband, and they left for a party, where they would discuss the murder with close friends and family. They relaxed and let down their guard. After the party, they stopped to see Rosalind, Lucille's sister, and her husband, Charles, who had planned to attend the baseball game with Leo on Saturday before Leo canceled. The four talked a little while, and then Leo and Lucille went home, where Lucille's parents were having a bridge party with the Lippmanns, Wolfsheimers, and Strausses. Leo, sitting to the side, read the morning paper. The day ended with laughter and conversation. This pleasurable, typical evening would be one of the last for Lucille and Leo. They took the gaiety for granted.

Across town, police arrested twenty-seven-year-old Arthur Mullinax for the murder of Mary Phagan.

Chapter 10

Suspects

Newt Lee was the first to be arrested but not the last. The Atlanta police had a dilemma: A young girl had been murdered and found in the factory where she worked. Citizens were concerned about their safety and the safety of their children in the workforce. The newspapers were publishing multiple issues a day with the latest news. The *Atlanta Georgian*, owned by Randolph Hearst, was new to the city. The way Hearst's paper covered the case—not always within journalism ethics—set a fire under the *Atlanta Constitution* and *Atlanta Journal*, the city's leading papers until the *Georgian* came along. The media attention put intense pressure on the police to solve this murder and take the attacker to trial. So amid the influx of tips from the public and the chaotic reporting of the papers, Atlanta's detectives—each aware that solving this murder would be a career-defining achievement—worked tirelessly.

The police were not the only ones intent on solving such a heinous crime. Hugh Dorsey, Atlanta's prosecutor, had his eye on the investigation. In Dorsey's time as prosecutor, a significant win had eluded him. In 1910, he had lost a high-profile case that should have been an easy victory. The powerful people poised to help Dorsey achieve his political goals shook their heads at his failure. He knew he had to prove himself.

ɞ

Arthur Mullinax left his girlfriend's home on Bellwood Avenue that Sunday afternoon as Leo Frank visited the funeral home a second time.

An Atlanta police detective arrested Mullinax and escorted the handsome young man to headquarters.

Arthur lived in a boardinghouse at 62 Poplar Street that was owned by baseball player Jim Rutherford, who adamantly told police that Mullinax was home around ten thirty on Saturday night and that Mullinax was asleep at five o'clock Sunday morning when Rutherford left the house. Rutherford, who played for the Lagrange team, came into town on Saturday afternoon at two o'clock. Arthur wasn't home. At seven o'clock, Rutherford went to the Terminal Station to meet his team manager. While there, he saw Arthur and his sweetheart, Pearl Robinson. Rutherford told police that he saw Arthur and Pearl get off the English Avenue streetcar in front of the Bijou Theater.

"Mullinax has always been a quiet unassuming fellow and was not inclined to stay out late at night," Rutherford explained. "I know he came directly home after leaving Miss Robinson at her door."[59]

E. R. Sentell implicated Mullinax at the police station when he visited Chief Lanford on Sunday. He swore he saw Mullinax with Mary Phagan minutes after midnight Sunday morning. Sentell said he was walking along Forsyth Street when he encountered Arthur and Mary walking across Hunter Street toward the National Pencil Company. He recognized them when they walked under a street lamp.

Detectives grilled Arthur, but he gave a straightforward account of his whereabouts Saturday night. He never changed his story and swore he spent the evening with Pearl. He confirmed Rutherford's statement that he and Pearl had come uptown on the English Avenue streetcar—he was formerly a conductor on this line—to Forsyth Street and crossed to the Bijou Theater. Pearl and Arthur saw two movies and afterward took the streetcar to Miss Robinson's house. There is a good chance Will Coleman was watching for Mary outside the Bijou when Arthur and Pearl emerged. Once the couple arrived at Pearl's house, they talked for fifteen minutes. Arthur then got back on the streetcar and went back to the boardinghouse, where he paid Mrs. Rutherford a dollar for work she did on his clothes, and went to bed.

Arthur Mullinax learned about the murder on Sunday like the rest of Atlanta did—from the newspaper. He insisted his only significant conversation with Mary had been when they were in Western Heights Baptist Church's Christmas show. He had a small part, but Mary played Sleeping Beauty. Mullinax admitted Mary was considered the prettiest girl in the neighborhood.

Mullinax was known to talk to Mary when she rode the English Avenue streetcar he conducted. Mary's stepfather, Will Coleman, stated that he didn't believe Arthur committed the murder, but it took a couple of days before he was cleared. Detectives discovered that the navy had discharged Mullinax's accuser, E. R. Sentell, three weeks before the murder because of poor eyesight.

ꝏ

The next person to be arrested was teenager Geron Bailey. The police felt he'd had the opportunity to encounter Mary on Saturday at the pencil factory, so they arrested him as a material witness around the same time they arrested Mullinax. Geron would be granted his freedom when it was determined he had nothing to do with the murder and was not at the factory on Saturday.

ꝏ

One suspect in Mary's murder gained more attention than Arthur Mullinax or Geron Bailey. Much discussion arose about twenty-six-year-old John M. Gantt, the former bookkeeper whom Frank had fired two weeks earlier and who had come to the factory on Saturday evening to retrieve his shoes. The employees spoke among themselves since Mary's death, and many told detectives that Gantt paid more attention to Mary than a man of his age should. Girls who worked alongside Mary mentioned that Gantt was taken with her, and other co-workers made it clear that Gantt was infatuated with Mary. E. F. Holloway, the factory's timekeeper, reported that Gantt had told him he frequently walked Mary home from work. Holloway informed a reporter from the *Atlanta Georgian* that Mary was "quiet and modest." "I never noticed her talking with any employees," he continued. "She was invariably polite, as though she had been carefully raised in her home. She focused strictly on her own work and was never seen conversing with any men, as far as I know."[60]

Like many other Atlantans, Gantt watched the Confederate Memorial Day Parade on the Saturday of the murder. After the parade, Gantt and some friends walked around the city, not going anywhere in particular. At six that evening, Gantt made his visit to the pencil factory to get his shoes. He retrieved the shoes and left, but not before putting Leo on edge. The whole visit lasted only minutes.

At seven-thirty that evening, Gantt met two friends, Arthur White, the employee Leo locked in earlier that day when leaving for lunch, and O. G. Bagely, an employee at Atlanta Milling Company. Bagely's brother came along with the group to Globe Pool Parlor on Broad Street. Gantt claimed only to watch the pool games, not play. When Gantt left, he claimed he went to his sister's house, where he had a room, and that she met him at the door. Later, his sister, Mrs. F. C. Terrell, would tell the police a conflicting version; she said that Gantt had packed his stuff three weeks earlier to take a job in California, and she hadn't seen him since. She acknowledged that she and her brother had known Mary and her family in Marietta and that Mary had played at her house when the girl was much younger.

Judge Powers issued an arrest warrant for John Gantt. Herbert Schiff, assistant superintendent of the pencil factory, had spotted Gantt on Monday morning at a quarter to nine, boarding a streetcar bound for Marietta.

Atlanta police sent word to Bailiff Hicks of Marietta that they wanted to arrest Gantt, and Hicks arrested him before noon that day as he stepped off the streetcar. The *Atlanta Journal* said that no one knew why Gantt was in Marietta or what he had done all day Sunday.[61] But the next day, Gantt admitted to police that he had bought a farm in Marietta and his parents were already there. He also explained that he slept late on Sunday and later visited Miss Annie Chambers of 18

Warren Place, whom he had been visiting since Christmas. It was there he was told that one of the girls at the factory had been murdered, but her identity was not made clear to him.

Gantt was taken to a holding cell at the Marietta Jail until Atlanta detective Hazelett arrived to take him back to the city. Gantt was asked if he knew Mary Phagan.

"Yes, I knew the girl. I knew Mary Phagan quite well," he said, "but I swear to you I had not seen her since I left the plant as an employee three weeks ago."[62] Gantt said he had never been in love with Mary and admitted to knowing her ten years earlier in Marietta when she was a small child. He did say Mary was beautiful.

The night of Gantt's arrest, Judge Gober, his lawyer—a relative of Gantt's—asked that Gantt be granted an immediate hearing. Chief Lanford announced on Tuesday morning that neither Mullinax nor Gantt would get an immediate hearing and would remain in custody. After the announcement, Judge Gober presented Judge Bell with a writ of habeas corpus, and the petition was set for a hearing on Tuesday afternoon. The police would have to show the evidence against Gantt. The defense would use Gantt's statement and his sister's new statement. Mrs. Terrell had recanted her original statement to police: She admitted Gantt did come home Saturday night and she did open the door for him.

Gantt was released because the court accepted Mrs. Terrell's new statement.

As the Atlanta detectives interrogated their suspects, their thoughts kept coming back to one person: Leo M. Frank.

Chapter 11

The Pinkerton Detective Agency

In the days that followed the discovery of Mary's body at the pencil factory, we can only guess Lucille's state of mind as the case closed in. She must have harbored some worry even if she didn't speak the thoughts aloud. She would have been a good wife and kept their lives running as smoothly as she could. There must have been some discussion of what this child's death meant to the National Pencil Company. Had Lucille suspected more would be made of her husband's presence at the factory on Saturday? After all, she was born and raised in Atlanta. She must have understood Leo's position. More than once, her thoughts had to have lingered on his choice to work rather than attend the opera or, at the very least, the baseball game.

On Monday morning, 28 April 1913, a knock sounded on the front door of the ash green house on East Georgia Avenue. When Lucille answered, she found Detective Black and Haslett on the doorstep. She escorted them into the large home and went to tell Leo.

The detectives told Leo that he was wanted at the police station, and the two detectives were to escort him. This time Leo was allowed his breakfast. When Leo was ready, the three men left the house and walked to Decatur Street, where the police station was located. One can only imagine Lucille watching from the door with thoughts racing through her mind. The police had taken Leo again.

ଓ

While Leo dressed and finished his breakfast, R. P. Barrett, a machinist who had worked eight weeks at the pencil factory, noticed red spots on the metal department's floor, not far from the women's dressing room on the second floor, and only feet from Mary's workstation. A white substance was smeared on the bloodstain in what looked like an attempt to hide the spots. Barrett went to find the janitor, Mell Stanford, who insisted the spot had not been there on Friday at midnight when he left. Barrett found the foreman, Lemmie Quinn, who had come to meet with Leo on Saturday after Mary had left Leo's office. Quinn called the police to inform them of the findings. After he made the call, Barrett went to the bench lathe to finish something he was working on Friday. He noticed half a dozen strands of auburn hair in the cogs of the stall lathe that he felt sure had not been there on Friday. He went to find Quinn again. Employees began to arrive at the factory and hurried to the scene to see the red spots and hair. Later that week, Barrett searched under Mary's machine and found a piece of a pay envelope that had no name or amount written on it.

Police chief James Litchfield Beavers arrived at the factory to take a look at the bloodstains. Mrs. George W. Jefferson worked in the polishing room and was shown the blood spots. She agreed that the spots had not been there on Friday evening. She offered that there were cords in the polish room used to tie the pencils. After these cords were removed from the pencils, they were placed on a nail with knots still in the cords. Maybe the murderer got the cord to strangle Mary from the nail in the polish room.

Fourteen-year-old Magnolia Kennedy, a worker in the metal room, was shown the hair on the lathe. She said it belonged to Mary. Chief Beavers had part of the floorboards torn up and dripped alcohol on the stains. Had the stains been paint spots, they would have disappeared. These turned bright pink. Beavers announced it was blood. He added this to facts he knew. Beavers began to think Mary had been attacked in the metal room and dragged to the opening in the floor leading to the basement.

Quinn stated he had tried to call Mary and three other workers on Friday to tell them to collect their pay that day instead of Saturday. The Phagans had no phone, so he couldn't reach her.

☙

While Chief Beavers and his men decided Mary had been murdered in the metal room, Leo walked with the two detectives to police headquarters. Leo asked why he was being brought in again, but Black didn't respond. After a long silence, Haslett spoke. "Well, Newt Lee has been saying something," he replied, "and Chief Lanford wanted to ask you a few questions about it."[63]

When the men arrived at headquarters, Leo was escorted into an outer room to wait for Chief Lanford's return. Leo chatted with officers while he waited. These were not the actions of a man who had something to hide. Around nine fifteen, Sig Montag and Herbert Haas, the National Pencil Company's attorney, arrived. Forty-five minutes later, attorney Luther Rosser came in. "Hello boys," he greeted them. "What's the trouble?"[64]

ᘓ

Luther Zeigler Rosser was born on 30 December 1857 in Bowdon, Georgia, in Carroll County. His father was a minister, so the family moved around. In 1878, Luther went to Harvard and was listed in the school catalog as a former school principal who became a lawyer. At twenty-eight, he married Julia Ophelia Connally. The couple would have four children, three girls and a boy. Their son, Luther Zeigler Rosser Jr., would marry Hugh Dorsey's sister in 1911, two years before Dorsey and Luther Rosser would go toe to toe in an Atlanta courtroom.

ᘓ

While Mr. Haas spoke with Luther Rosser in the outer room, Chief Lanford arrived and asked Leo into his office without either lawyer noticing.

When Leo was seated, Lanford placed a time slip in front of Leo that read "taken at 8:26" with two lines under the writing. Newt seemed to have punched the time slip three times with intervals of an hour instead of every half-hour as he should have.

Meanwhile, in the outer room, Mr. Rosser demanded to be allowed into Chief Lanford's office. "I am going into that room, that man is my client," he demanded.[65] Rossner was allowed inside.

Leo agreed to give a statement, saying he should do this just like anyone else who was in the factory the day of Mary's murder. When he finished, Chief Beavers entered the office. Rosser had a conversation with the two chiefs, who expressed suspicion of Leo.

"Why, it is preposterous, a man who would have done such a deed must be full of scratches and marks and his clothing bloody," Rosser said.[66]

When Leo heard this comment, he jumped to his feet and removed his undershirt and top shirt, revealing his body.

Rosser insisted that two detectives, Mr. Black being one, accompany Mr. Haas and Leo back to Leo's home and look at the dirty laundry from the past week. Rosser must have thought this would settle the suspicion of Leo and did not join them. The group of men caught the Washington Street streetcar, where Josephine sat after her shopping trip. The group went to 68 East Georgia Avenue. What Josephine must have thought when she saw her son-in-law enter the streetcar with Mr. Haas and the detectives.

Regina and Emil were at the home when the men and Josephine arrived. The detectives, followed by Leo and Mr. Haas, went upstairs to Lucille and Leo's bedroom. Leo took the laundry bag and emptied the clothes on the bed. The detective studied all the clothes but found nothing unusual, so they left.

While Leo was allowing the men to go through the laundry, Lucille arrived home but remained downstairs. When the men left, Leo ate lunch with her, Josephine, and Emil. Minolta Knight, the cook, served them. The group must have discussed the recent events. Lucille would have expressed her concern for her husband, but the reality that Leo seriously could be considered the murderer would have seemed far-fetched to everyone in the kitchen of the East Georgia Avenue house.

ꭥ

Leo went to Mr. Wolfsheimer's house after he finished his lunch. Mr. Wolfsheimer took Leo in his automobile to his place of business on Whitehall, near Mitchell. Leo walked the rest of the way to Forsyth Street. People were still crowded outside the factory. Had Leo taken the streetcar as he typically did, he would have been more vulnerable to questions and comments. By this time, many knew that the police were questioning Leo.

Mr. Herbert Schiff, Mr. Wade Cambell, Mr. Darley, Mr. Holloway, and three foremen, Mr. Stelker, Mr. Quinn, and Mr. Zigarke, were sitting in the outer room of Leo's office. The plant had shut down for the day because the girls who worked there were upset. Quinn took Leo back to the metal room to show him the blood spots found by Barrett that morning.

Leo squatted and examined the spots with a flash lamp (an early flashlight). Leo stated he didn't believe the spots were blood because haskoline—what was believed to be the white substance on the floor—would have taken fresh blood or fresh paint off the floor. At the very least the chemical would have turned the color pink. The spots had to be old.

Leo left the factory and went to Sig Montag's office to deliver the financial reports from Saturday. The two men had a long conversation and decided since the papers were running the story about Leo being detained by the police, Leo should tell his uncle Moses, who was more than seventy years old and in poor health. Moses was also about to take a trip to Europe. Leo didn't want him to discover the police's interest in him from the newspapers or any third party. Leo wrote a telegram to Mr. Adolph Montag, telling him to let his uncle know that Leo had been in police custody that morning but had been released. He reassured his uncle that all was good.

On Leo's return to the pencil factory, Harry Scott from Pinkerton arrived. Leo met him in his private office, along with Darley, factory personnel director, and Herbert Schiff, assistant superintendent. What Leo didn't know was that Scott had worked with Detective Black, and they were friends.

Leo took Scott on a tour of the factory while telling him what he knew of the case. Darley had informed Leo earlier that Mrs. White—who brought lunch to her husband on Saturday—saw a Black man inside the front door of the factory upon her entry at noon. Leo took Scott to the basement when they finished the tour of the upper floors. While downstairs, Leo showed Scott the elevator and where the body was found. Scott went through some of the debris on the floor, placing things in his pocket. One of these items was a piece of cord that resembled the cord found around Mary's neck. Leo then opened the back door, and both men made a search of the alley emerging on Hunter Street. They walked to Forsyth and stopped in front of the factory, where the two talked about Pinkerton's rates. Leo passed this information to Schiff, who telephoned Mr. Montag. It was agreed that Pinkerton's rates were acceptable.

Before parting, Mr. Scott said, "Well, I don't need anything more….The Pinkertons in this case, according to their usual custom in ferreting out the perpetrator of this crime will work hand in hand with city officers."

"All right, that suits me," Leo responded.[67]

Scott left, and Emil joined Leo in front of the factory, where they talked before heading home. The two arrived at six thirty and joined Josephine and Lucille for supper. After supper, Lucille's two sisters and their husbands came over. By this time, Leo's detention at the police station was all over the papers. Around ten o'clock that night, the visitors left and Lucille and Leo went to bed. This would be the last night Lucille would have Leo with her in bed.

Chapter 12

Found Guilty Before Trial

At seven thirty Tuesday morning, Lucille and Leo woke. Lucille dressed for the day, leaving Leo to do the same. No one had come to the door demanding Leo go to police headquarters. Maybe the officials received enough proof that Leo wasn't involved with the terrible deed. Leo came down, and they had breakfast before he left for a typical day at work. She busied herself with her daily routine.

As Leo stepped on the streetcar, he paid the fare for himself and the young man behind him, Dickler, who thanked Leo for his kindness. The newspapers that morning of 29 April had John Gantt's face on the front pages. Pinkerton was mentioned in a piece about the detectives' case against the former pencil factory bookkeeper. Leo didn't seem to be the kind of man to celebrate someone else's misfortune, but the headlines must have relaxed his fear.

Leo entered the factory at eight thirty and went straight to work. About an hour later, he left for his daily trip to Montag Brothers to speak with the general manager. His meeting didn't last long. Leo walked with Mr. Jordan, an employee with Montag Brothers, as they left the building together. On the corner of Forsyth and Hunter streets, Leo met one of Lucille's cousins, and they had a drink at Cruickshank's Soda Fountain.

ᘓ

The same morning around nine o'clock, Detective Black opened the door to Newt Lee's room at 40 Henry Street, not far from the Bellwood section where Mary's house stood. Black looked in a metal drum Lee used for storing his clothes. He found a linen shirt covered in fresh blood. He rolled the shirt up and took it with him. Black was so positive that Leo murdered Mary, he guessed Leo had planted the shirt in Lee's room.

ଓ

Leo bid Mr. Selig goodbye, and before he crossed the street to the factory, he talked with a reporter about the murder investigation:

> No one is more anxious to learn of the whereabouts of Mary Phagan Saturday afternoon and night than I am. The company is exerting every effort to get information and has employed a Pinkerton detective to work the case. Officials of the company also thought it best to retain counsel to assist in the investigation, while every one of the foremen and head men about the factory is endeavoring to find out if any of the employees know anything. I deeply regret the carelessness shown by the police department in not making a complete investigation as to finger prints and other evidence before a great throng of people were allowed to enter the place. The affair is exceedingly embarrassing to me, to know that authorities even felt that they should detain me for a while and question me leaves a bad taste, and I am doing everything possible to locate the guilty man.[68]

He went into the factory and straight to his office to do paperwork that he brought from Montag Brothers.

Around the same time, reporters asked Lucille if she had a statement.

> I do not care to go into any of the details of the crime.... My husband is at the office and is perfectly competent to give out all information. Any knowledge I have of the affair, I got from him. All that I know is that he is doing everything to solve the mystery. He has engaged detectives and is personally investigating many of the clews.[69]

Leo sat at his desk when Detective Black and Scott, from Pinkerton, dropped in to see him.

"Mr. Frank, we want you to go down town to headquarters with us."[70]

Leo put away his paperwork and left with the detectives. He said goodbye to employees and took a handful of his good cigars with him. Reporters and photographers surrounded the factory door. Before entering Chief Lanford's car, Leo stopped to give a statement: "I am not guilty. Such an atrocious crime has never entered my mind. I am a man of good character and I have a wife. I am a home-loving and God-fearing man. They will discover that. It is useless to detain me, unless for investigation and for information I might be able to give."[71] Leo had not been arrested, only "detained."

Soon after Leo left with the detectives, a reporter asked Ed Montag, who was at the pencil factory, if he had a statement. "We've been harassed enough by reporters of newspapers," Montag said. "This plant has had all the notoriety it wants."[72]

Once the group arrived at police headquarters, Leo was escorted to Chief Lanford's office. Lanford began questioning him, and Leo answered without hesitation, even though it was within his rights to ask for his lawyer. Detectives Scott and Black entered the office with a bundle and showed Leo a piece of cloth from what looked like a shirt. This was the shirt Black confiscated at Newt Lee's home. Leo studied the corner of cloth and told the men he didn't believe he had seen that color and type of material before.

Newt Lee was escorted into the office from his jail cell and shown the same piece of cloth. Lee said he had a shirt like that at one time, but he hadn't worn it in two years.

The detectives unfurled the bundle to reveal the fresh blood on Lee's shirt. The shirt also had a distinct odor. This revelation must have scared Lee—how would a shirt he hadn't worn in two years be covered in blood? Decades before DNA testing, finding the source of the blood would be difficult. Doctors had only recently created a test to identify blood type.

Lee was taken back to his cell. Chief Lanford stood in front of Leo and examined his face, head, hands, and arms as if Leo were a barn animal. The chief found nothing incriminating, and Leo had not been officially arrested. Still, neither Leo's attorney, Luther Rosser, nor the pencil factory's attorney, Herbert Haas, had been called.

Around noon, Rosser arrived and spoke to Chief Beavers, who had arrived earlier. When Rosser finished the conversation, he went to where Leo sat.

"He [Beavers] thinks it better that you be detained at headquarters but if you desire, you don't need to be locked up in a cell, you can engage a supernumerary policeman who will guard you and give you the freedom of the building."[73] Still, no official arrest was made.

Leo was taken upstairs to John Starnes's desk for a handwriting sample. Newt Lee had been asked to submit a handwriting sample by copying one of the murder notes when he was first arrested. Starnes was the sergeant who called Leo on Sunday morning. Leo wrote as Starnes dictated the murder notes found by Mary's body. This handwriting sample would be examined and compared to the notes. After Leo finished giving the sample, he was escorted to a small room.

Emil Selig had arrived and was arranging for a supernumerary policeman. Leo was moved to a room at the top of the building, where he read magazines and newspapers. Some friends checked in on him, and he was allowed to speak with them.

At two o'clock, Chief Lanford made an announcement to reporters: "We have evidence in hand which will clear the mystery in the next few hours and satisfy the public."[74] The police went on to tell the reporters that Leo was not under arrest. He was under police guard for his own personal safety and had not been charged with anything.[75]

Lucille arrived in the afternoon with her father, her brothers-in-law, Charles Ursenbach and Alex Marcus, only to be escorted to the office of Probation Officer Coogler, where the group waited to see Leo.

A reporter asked her if she had a statement. Lucille broke down several times while talking with him. "My husband is absolutely innocent and able to take care of himself in this matter.... I would rather that any statement come from him. We discussed the matter hardly at all in our home."[76] This statement seemed a way to fend off the reporters rather than the truth. As hard as Lucille worked to prove Leo's innocence, one has to believe they had discussed the happenings at the factory on that horrible Saturday.

Lucille sobbed off and on while waiting. A while later, Leo sent word for her to go home, that he believed he would be released soon. Later, Leo would testify that he wanted to save Lucille from the humiliation of the situation, "but she was perfectly willing to even be locked up with me and share my incarceration."[77]

At midnight, Leo folded back a thin blanket on a cot and decided to get some rest. Scott and Black came into the room and asked Leo to follow them for a talk. The three men went into another room. The detectives revealed evidence that Newt Lee was allowing couples, presumably employees, into the basement at night to have sex. Leo was shocked and explained he had no idea this was taking place. Had he known, he would have put a stop to it.

The detectives explained that Lee would be brought into the room. "Mr. Frank, you have never talked alone with Newt Lee. You are his boss and he respects you. See what you can do with him. We can't get anything more out of him, see if you can."

"All right, I understand what you mean; I will do my best," Leo answered.

John Starnes brought Lee to the room and handcuffed him to the chair.

When Leo questioned Lee alone, he denied any knowledge about couples meeting in the basement on his shift.

"Now, Newt, you are here and I am here, and you had better open up and tell all you know, and tell the truth and tell the full truth, because you will get us both into lots of trouble if you don't tell all you know," Leo urged Lee.

"Before God, Mr. Frank, I am telling you the truth and I have told you all I know."[78]

By this time, a new day had begun, but Leo's circumstances didn't change.

Lucille wouldn't visit Leo for another two weeks. This absence would be thrown in her face as evidence that she had reservations about her husband's innocence.

Chapter 13

She Was Taught to Fear God

When Mary didn't arrive at the small house on Lindsay Street after the parade as expected, Fannie didn't worry. Fannie knew Mary wanted to see the movie at the Bijou because her friends had told her it was good. Fannie felt sure Mary was with some of her girlfriends. When Mary didn't come home for supper, Fannie became concerned. Mary always let her mother know where she was and what she was doing. She wasn't allowed to roam the streets of Atlanta without her mother knowing her destination. For this reason, Will went to the Bijou Theater that evening and stood outside until the last show was let out at ten o'clock. When he didn't see Mary, he inquired around town and found no one had seen her. Fannie waited at home with a friend in case Mary came in. There was the possibility Mary met up with her aunt, who had attended the parade, and traveled back to Marietta that evening without a chance to send word of her early departure. Fannie must have known in her heart that Mary would have gotten word to her somehow.

Upon Will's return without Mary, he called the police, who didn't yet know about a body in the pencil factory. He was told there were no reports of girls Mary's age and description in trouble. The couple went to bed. This must have been a sleepless night for Fannie.

At five in the morning, a knock sounded on the front door.

"There's Mary now," Fannie said as she sat up in bed.

"No, it isn't either," Will replied.

Fannie went to the door. Helen Ferguson greeted Fannie with the news her daughter had been murdered.

"What do you mean? I don't understand you. Tell me how. Maybe you're mistaken—maybe it isn't Mary."[79]

Helen told the truth. Fannie's youngest child was dead.

Later Fannie was asked if Mary was friends with George Epps and if she had plans with him. Mary had never been friendly with Epps, and Fannie said Mary had detested him. She did not believe Mary ever accused Mr. Frank of misconduct to George Epps. Fannie admitted it was possible Mary hadn't told her things that happened at the pencil factory because she was worried Fannie might make her quit. One of Mary's friends, Pluma Watkins, said all matter of things, including that the foremen cursed the girls.[80]

ࡇ

The rumble of a vigilante mentality began in Bellwood on Sunday, 27 April, as word spread that Mary had been murdered and her body found in the pencil factory. Emotions ran high in Mary's neighborhood. Men gathered on street corners near her house talked about getting their hands on the killer before the police could.

Fourteen-year-old George Epps told as much to a newspaper reporter. "I wouldn't have liked to be held responsible for the fate of the murderer of little Mary Phagan if the men in this neighborhood had got hold of him last night," he said.[81] The murder was all anyone could talk about. The brutal event hit too close to home for the hardworking people.

The women in the neighborhood worried about their girls, who, like most children in mill families, worked in the factories of Atlanta to help their households make ends meet. Most worried justice would not be done for a mill family. Fear spread among the women that allowing their girls to walk to work on the streets of Atlanta in broad daylight was dangerous.

"In half the homes the boys and girls do what they can to help in support of the family," Epps said. "This means that our children are not safe on the streets even in the daytime."[82]

When word reached WJ Phagan, Mary's paternal grandfather, he cried out for vengeance:

> I hope the murderer will be dealt with as he dealt with that innocent child. I hope his heart is torn with remorse in the measure that his victim suffered pain and shame, that he suffers as we who loved the child are suffering. No punishment is too great for the brute who foully murdered the sweetest and purest thing on earth—a young girl. Hanging cannot atone for the crime he has committed and the suffering he has caused.[83]

The day after learning that her youngest child had been brutally murdered, Fannie agreed to talk to an *Atlanta Georgian* reporter. She was devastated, and many of those close to her warned she would be unable to attend the funeral services the next day. Fannie, though, had a message for Atlanta mothers. One must believe that by giving this interview, she shined a light on who her daughter was and what she meant to her family. Speaking to the reporter also gave Fannie a chance to rail against the child labor system in Atlanta.

"There are so many unscrupulous men in the world," Fannie told the reporter. "It's so dangerous for young girls working," she continued. "Their every step should be watched. Mothers should question them and ask them about their work and associates and surroundings. They should continually tell them what they ought to do and how they ought to act under certain circumstances."[84]

Fannie declared she never would have allowed Mary to work so young, but she had five children. All had to work to support the family. This type of hardship was common for mill-working families, who all needed a roof, food, and clothes.

Fannie said that her marriage to William Coleman gave Mary a chance to quit, but by then Mary enjoyed having her own money and wanted to continue working. Fannie had taught Mary not to act silly or flirt with men. Mary took this lesson seriously and did as she was told. Fannie knew her daughter had to be forced into the situation that resulted in her murder. The *Atlanta Georgian* quoted Fannie extensively:

"When a girl is pretty," she declared, "naturally she is attractive to men. Mary was pretty too: beside that, she was always happy and in good humor. She had never stayed out any night before in the two years she had been at work. I could trust her anywhere. I knew because she was always so straightforward, and what I thought when she didn't come home was that she had met up with her aunt from Marietta, who was in town, and gone home with her and had no way to let me know."[85]

Fannie sobbed at the thought her girl was in the hands of a murderer—while Fannie believed she was at the parade and movies or later with her aunt.

"Even with the greatest care," she told the reporter, "it looks like things will happen anyway—we don't know how or why."[86] Many readers likely identified with her efforts to raise her children in a safe and loving home. With the loss of her husband, taking the children from Alabama back to Georgia, opening a boarding house, even marrying Will Coleman, her thoughts were on her children, including her beloved daughter.

Fanny continued: "Often I watched Mary on the [street] car when men would look at her...but she never paid attention to them. I think she must have made the man who killed her mad and that's why he did it."[87] Fannie goes on to warn other girls that they are susceptible to the same treatment as Mary. She expressed her frustration that these girls had no one to help or protect them.

The grieving mother's interview is more than a recounting of what happened to Mary that day. Fannie used this as a chance to raise concern about putting girls in jobs meant for adults. She reminded the women reading the newspaper that without protections or regulations, their daughters, too, could fall victim to predators in the workplace. These girls, like Mary, were at the mercy of men in authority who didn't have their best interests at heart. This interview called out the factory owners in Atlanta: "If you could only have seen her.... She looked so beautiful and so young and so bright!... I am sorry for all other young girls working everywhere! To think they're all open to the same things and there is nothing to protect them."[88]

The more Will Coleman heard about the circumstances of Mary's death over the next couple of days, the more he believed in Newt Lee's guilt. He was convinced that Mary never left the factory that Saturday after collecting her pay.

"If the negro watchman did not kill the child, how would it have not been impossible for him to hear her screams going on in the building?"[89] Will posed a valid question, but he wasn't aware of all the facts. "A livery stable man next door heard them, and it would have been much easier for the watchman to," he continued. "If the black did not do it himself, then he must have known something about it, and who the person was who did it."[90] Coleman believed Mary left Frank's office and went to the dressing room for a drink of water before leaving. Frank, not knowing where Mary had gone, could have locked her in the factory when he left for lunch. Coleman, unaware that Newt Lee wasn't at work, assumed he watched Mary enter the dressing room and attacked her there. While Newt Lee couldn't have been the attacker in this scenario, someone else certainly could have committed the crime this way.

☙

The information Mary's sister, Ollie Mae, gave to Pinkerton detective L. P. Whitfield shed light on Mary's relationship with her sister and what had taken place when Mary was at work. Ollie, at nineteen, was close to her younger sister. The two girls were the only siblings left at home. Benjamin, the oldest, had joined the navy and was on a battleship in New York. The other brothers worked at mills and lived elsewhere. Ollie had quit her job at M. Rich & Bros. two weeks before.

Ollie and Mary shared a tiny bedroom in the house on Lindsay Street, and they talked every night. Mary shared her concerns, and Ollie tried to provide her with guidance. Mary told her sister everything, including that she had seen pencil factory employees, during the dinner hour, hugging and kissing. These couples tried to hide themselves behind boxes. Mary looked through the crack and saw the couples having sex. Ollie swore to Whitfield that Mary had no sweetheart and that George Epps wasn't telling the truth. Mary had stated on more than one occasion she did not like him.[91]

The day Mary disappeared, Ollie was in Marietta, a trip Mary intended to take the next day. Mary's older sister wasn't home when her mother and stepfather were worrying about Mary missing, and she wasn't there when Helen Ferguson came with the news. When she did hear the news, Ollie was crushed. She hadn't been there when her sister needed her.

"Oh, I am so lonely without her. I never had but one sister," she told a reporter.[92]

Laid to Rest

A crowd had gathered at the train station in Marietta the morning of the funeral, 29 April, when the family and Mary's white casket arrived. Fannie was helped into a cab when she saw her daughter's casket lifted from the train. She cried out and fell into Will's arms. Some time passed before the couple could leave for the church. The service was held at the Second Baptist Church of Marietta, located on Atlanta Street, across the road from the Marietta Cemetery. A thousand people crowded the front yard of the church. Some of the family was there waiting, including all of Mary's brothers and Ollie. Benjamin had come from New York. He wore his naval uniform, which made him look more like a child than his nearly twenty years.

In the chaos of the previous two days, the family had neglected to choose pallbearers, so they were selected on the church grounds: L. M. Spruell, B. Autrey, Ralph Butler, and W. T. Potts. These men hoisted the little white casket on their shoulders and walked Mary's body into the church. The choir sang "Nearer, My God, to Thee." The crowd followed the procession into the sanctuary. Within five minutes, all the wooden pews were filled, and Reverend T. T. G. Linkous of "the Christian church at East Point" took the pulpit. When the choir began to sing "Rock of Ages," Fannie wailed. No one, including her husband, interfered with her grief. Reverend Linkous asked everyone to pray and searched for the right words to express his own loss and sadness. "The occasion is so sad to me," he said, "—when she was but a baby, I taught her to fear God and love Him—that I don't know what to do."[93] He cried openly, continuing his prayer for the police and the rancor that those who loved Mary harbored in their hearts. He raised his hand over his head. "May God aid officers of the law in detecting and bringing behind bars such a man."[94] The family on the front row watched the reverend. Fannie stopped crying for a minute, and WJ Phagan, Mary's paternal grandfather, exclaimed, "Amen!"[95]

Reverend Linkous went on to say he believed in forgiveness but admitted he didn't know how it would be applied in the case of Mary's murder.

Miss Lizzie Phagan, Mary's aunt, who made the new dress she wore when murdered, shrieked and fainted. She was carried from the church.

"The reverend concluded, 'All I can say is God bless you.'"[96]

Mary's casket, sitting in front of the pulpit, was opened, and the crowd filed by to see Mary for the last time. When a friend burst into tears and cried out her thoughts, the *Constitution* quoted a man who watched her cry: "'The [racial epithet] knows all about it,' growled a sunburnt farmer, a wry, humorless smile disfiguring his face. 'And I could make him [Newt Lee] talk. Oh yes. If we had that scoundrel in Marietta, we'd know how to get him to talk. We'd make him be polite. He'd talk just as pretty as you please for us. Either that—or something else.'"[97]

The vigilante mentality began to grow.

As the casket was carried from the church, Fannie followed, supported by her husband on one arm and the reverend on the other. The casket was loaded in the hearse and family in wagons for the short drive across the road to the grave site. The thousand people crowd walked across the railroad tracks to the Phagan plot where Mary's paternal grandmother was buried.

Reverend Linkous said a few words as the casket was lowered into the ground. With the first shovelful of dirt, Fannie cried out, "She was taken away when the spring was coming—the spring that was so like her." Fannie walked up to the edge of the grave and waved her white handkerchief. "Goodby, Mary. Goodby. It's too big a hole to put you though. It's so big—b-i-g, and you were so little—my own little Mary!"[98]

Chapter 14

The Coroner's Inquest

On 30 April 1913, Leo still waited at police headquarters to be released. Lucille hadn't seen him in twenty-four hours. She attempted to visit over the next few days even though she had been treated rudely on her first try. Family and close friends, such as Dr. Marx, The Temple's rabbi, kept her at bay, reminding her that Leo sent his wishes for her not to come. But Lucille wanted the city to know Leo was incapable of committing such a crime and that she stood beside him. Her close-knit family provided her a place to lean. Her brothers-in-law, father, and Dr. Marx regularly spoke with Leo and reassured her things were going well. Staying put was the best thing she could do. Dr. Marx would later admit this tack was probably not the wisest choice, but who could have known? Still, there must have been that hollow place in her chest, waiting for the decision on whether he could come home. Little did Lucille and Leo know powerful people were invested in the outcome of the murder trial in the making.

The sensational case that would launch Hugh Dorsey's political career had evaded him. Dorsey watched the investigation with keen interest, and he itched to plant himself in the middle.

Hugh Mason Dorsey was born 10 July 1871, in Fayetteville, Georgia, just south of Atlanta, to Sarah Matilda and Judge Rufus T. Dorsey. When Hugh was eight years old, his family moved to Atlanta, where his father and another judge, William Wright, formed the firm Wright and Dorsey. Hugh attended local Atlanta schools and earned a bachelor's in arts from the University of Georgia in 1893. He then left for the University of Virginia, where he studied law. When he finished, he was admitted to the bar in Fayetteville.

At the time of the coroner's inquest, Dorsey, age forty-two, had been married almost two years to Adair Wilkinson of Valdosta, Georgia. The couple would go on to have two sons, Hugh Mason Jr. and James Wilkinson. In a small city like Atlanta, everyone knew everyone. Hugh Sr.'s sister, Sarah, married Luther Rosser Jr., the son of Leo's chief counsel, Luther Rosser Sr., who, at fifty-six years old, was fourteen years older than Dorsey. Atlanta's political landscape was a small world.

Dorsey's ambition was to be more than a solicitor in a circuit court. In the days since the murder, he began making his move to wrest control of the case from the police department, which he felt was failing miserably. On that point, he was right: Atlanta police were less than lackluster in their investigation of the murder, but his actions were designed to appear as if his only concern was justice for Mary's family. He focused on finding Mary's killer and bringing him to trial, but he was not beyond twisting witness testimony to suit himself—even if it implicated an innocent person. He approached the days after the murder with care. He was smart enough to know the coroner's inquest had to be finished and its verdict rendered before he could take complete control. The newspapers noticed Dorsey's aggression concerning the case.

On the second day of the inquest's testimony, before his conference with police officials, Dorsey called their investigation "hesitating." He went on, "All leads given the police have not been followed closely and there is much more to this thing that has not been brought out. Unless some decisive action is taken quickly the mystery will remain unsolved."[99] When Dorsey finished talking with the officials, he stood in front of reporters and said he had been on the fence about taking on the Phagan case, but he would reach a decision by the next day so the case could be presented to the grand jury. In his opinion, the handwriting evidence had been botched because the police had allowed Lee to copy the note instead of dictating it to him. With this choice, Lee could have altered his handwriting.

ଋ

Paul V. Donehoo, Fulton County coroner, was charged to preside over the inquest, which began on 28 April 1913, the day Leo Frank was arrested. Donehoo was legally blind but made up for his lack of sight with a logical mind and an understanding of human character and motivation. A six-man jury of prominent White men from the community was chosen: Homer C. Ashford (foreman), Glenn Dewberry, J. C. Hood, Clarence Langford, John Miller, and C. Y. Sheets. The jury would listen to testimony and decide if those accused would be held over for the grand jury to make the decision on whether to indict.

No witnesses appeared the first day; instead, the jury was taken to the pencil factory to look at the basement and the metal room on the second floor where the blood drops and strands of hair had been found earlier that morning. At noon Donehoo dismissed the proceedings until Wednesday morning at nine o'clock (30 April), at police headquarters, when the jurors would begin to hear witness testimony.

Mullinax and Gantt were no longer being investigated, so Leo Frank and Newt Lee were the only suspects. Mullinax's accuser proved to not have his facts straight, and his poor eyesight cleared him. Gantt's sister had changed her initial testimony and swore he was at her house that night. Both suspects were released soon after their arrests.

Wednesday morning brought George W. Epps, the fourteen-year-old boy who said he rode the streetcar with Mary that Saturday morning. He claimed the two were friends. George lived at 248 Fox Street, and his backyard connected to Mary's. The *Atlanta Georgian* called the two sweethearts, but Fannie, Mary's mother, stated several times the two were no such thing. George testified that "'She [Mary] said she was getting afraid," he told the inquest. "She wanted me to come to the factory every afternoon in the future and escort her home. She didn't like the way Frank was acting toward her." Later, Epps would retract this statement. George testified that Mary and he planned to meet at the drugstore to watch the Confederate Memorial Day parade. He said he waited until four o'clock and finally gave up, leaving for the Atlanta Crackers baseball game. After the game, he went straight home and arrived around seven. "Yes! I went to her house when I got through with my papers. She hadn't got back. The folks were looking for her."[100]

Another witness to take the stand on 30 April was F. W. Berry. He identified the handwriting of the notes to be almost the same as the notes Newt Lee wrote for the detectives. Mr. Berry had worked at the Fourth National Blank for twenty-two years and was, at the time, an assistant cashier. Throughout his time of employment with the bank, he had to study handwriting daily. In the detectives' minds, this experience made Berry a handwriting expert. On the stand, Berry was given a stack of handwriting samples and asked to pick out the one that most closely resembled the notes found by Mary's body. He did this and stepped down.

Detective Starnes was called to the stand. He looked at the notes Berry had chosen. Starnes said he had given one note to Lee to copy, and another detective gave Lee the other note. Starnes pointed out Lee had misspelled the same way as the original notes, yet he had been instructed specifically to copy the notes.

When Starnes stepped down, R. P. Barrett was called to the stand. He testified that he lived at 180 Griffin Street and was a machinist at the pencil factory. He knew Mary and worked close to her. He explained finding the bloodstains on Monday morning and estimated they were four or five inches in diameter.

Next to testify was Newt Lee, whose testimony remained unchanged. Lee insisted he found Mary's body face up; the officers said they found it face down when they were called to the factory. Lee was asked several times if he turned the body over. He swore he never touched the body. When Donehoo asked Lee how he knew Mary was dead, he answered, "I knew she was dead because she was there. There ain't no white woman going to be there if she ain't dead. She was all dirty and bloody I knew she was dead, boss."[101]

John M. Gantt took the witness stand to speak about his visit to the pencil factory on Saturday evening to retrieve his shoes. His testimony was the same. He did point out that Leo was nervous. When asked why he was let go from the pencil factory, Gantt said it was a disagreement. When pressed about this so-called disagreement, Gantt admitted that two dollars were missing from the cash box. Leo Frank explained it would come out of his pay or Gantt would lose his job. Gantt chose job loss.

L. S. Dobbs, one of the first officers to arrive at the murder scene, was called to the stand. He testified about seeing Mary's body. He held a deep suspicion of Lee and accused him of knowing more about the situation. Lee became agitated. Dobbs pointed out that Lee felt the notes found near the body implicated him. Dobbs described how Mary's body was dragged through the basement. It was along the drag path the officers found Mary's shoe and hat.

ଔ

On 1 May, Donehoo issued a "commitment" against Leo Frank and Newt Lee that held in custody and charged them with being suspects in connection to Mary's murder.

> To the Jailor:
>
> You are hereby required to take into custody the person of Leo M. Frank, suspected of the crime of murdering Mary Phagan, and to retain the said Leo M. Frank in your custody pending the further investigation of the death of said Mary Phagan, to be held by Coroner of said county.[102]

Donehoo's commitment led to the official arrest of the two. Leo had been "detained." Frank and Lee were moved to the Fulton County Jail, known as "the Tower," on Pryor Street. The jail's nickname, "the Tower," came from the building's turret, which could be seen across the city.

ଔ

Donehoo adjourned the inquest until two o'clock on Monday. The purpose was to obtain clearly defined evidence. On Saturday, 3 May,

Donehoo and Detective Harry Scott went to the fourth floor of the pencil factory. For the purpose of reenacting Mary's screams, they stationed two men on the second floor, where the police thought Mary was murdered. Donehoo and Scott faintly heard the screams. Then, the detective and coroner went to the basement, listening for the screams on the second floor. This time, they heard nothing, yet employees at neighboring businesses claimed to hear screams the day Mary was murdered and came running out of their buildings.

Detective Scott and Black took statements from Arthur White and Harry Denham, the two men who were working on the fourth floor the day Mary was killed.

Arthur White:

> About 11:25 a.m. Emma Clark and Corinthia Hall, two employees, came up to the fourth floor of the factory, saying that they came up for a coat. They told me that my wife was down stairs. I think they came down to the clock, met my wife, gave her some money and she then went out in town. She returned to the factory at about 12:25 p.m. and talked with me on the fourth floor until 12:50 p.m. when Mr. L. M. Frank came upstairs and told Mrs. White that he was going to lock up the factory. Mr. Frank went down stairs ahead of Mrs. White.[103]

This verifies Leo's statement about locking the doors when he left for lunch. Denham's statement was similar to White's. Denham stated he had gotten to work at 7:30 a.m. and left at 3:10 p.m. He added one fact that verified Leo's statement: "Mr. Frank also asked us if we would finish by one o'clock and we replied that we could not. He then stated that he would lock us inside of the factory."[104]

Pinkerton detective L. P. Whitfield interviewed people who worked in businesses across from the pencil factory. No one saw anything unusual the day Mary was murdered.

Adam Woodward, who worked at Wood's Feed and Sales Stables at 33 S. Forsyth Street, told the coroner he did not hear screams from the pencil factory as some reported he had stated. Instead, he had heard a shout in the evening and thought it came from some soldiers who were being chased by Officer Taylor.

A suspect was brought to the attention of the detectives that would change the course of their investigation.

Chapter 15

Feuding Officials

The first sign of discontent within the investigation came with Hugh Dorsey's securing an affidavit from Monteen Stover, a girl formerly employed at the pencil factory and who went to collect her pay on Saturday, 26 April, between 12:05 and 12:10 p.m. The Pinkerton detectives had already interviewed her, and her timing of events remained the same. When she walked into Leo's office, it was empty. The *Atlanta Constitution* reported, "The building seemed empty of human occupants, she declares, and no sounds came from any part…she says she went through both outer and inner office in search of Frank."[105]

Stover insisted she remained for five minutes, leaving at 12:10 p.m. This would have placed Monteen in Leo's office at the exact time Leo said Mary entered the office to collect her pay.

Colonel Thomas Felder appears on the already crowded scene of those swearing to get to the bottom of Mary's murder with ongoing news that the famous Detective William Burns would come to Atlanta to help solve the murder. The front page of the *Atlanta Constitution* declared they had created a fund to help pay for Detective Burns's fee. When asked by reporters what he thought of Burns's agreement to come to Atlanta, Dorsey told them he was fine with Burns investigating, too. The fund raised five thousand dollars, and Felder declared to a reporter, "We will catch the guilty man and we won't be long about it."[106]

William John Burns was known as America's Sherlock Holmes. He rose to prominence when he investigated the 1910 *Los Angeles Times* bombing that was orchestrated by the Iron Workers Union and killed twenty people. Burns and his team tracked down Jim McNamara and Ortie McManigal in Detroit. He also found that the

Iron Workers Union Leadership approved more than one hundred bombings. In 1921, Burns would become the director of the Bureau of Investigation, the BOI, which would later become the Federal Bureau of Investigation.

Burns, who was in Europe on a high-profile missing person case, sent his right-hand man, C. W. Tobie, to begin asking questions about the murder. Burns promised to be in Atlanta shortly after 1 June.

Chief Lanford, feeling the pressure to produce results from the department's investigation, announced that he had documentary evidence that would convict the murderer. He refused to release the evidence to Dorsey.

The same day, the headline of the *Atlanta Georgian* read, "Best Detective in America Now on Phagan Case Says Dorsey."[107]

Dorsey stopped short of revealing who this new detective was, but the damage was done. Lanford, still smarting from Dorsey's criticism, bristled and told the *Constitution* that he thought the "world's most famous detective" was none other than a capable attaché to the solicitor's staff.[108]

The two men saw the murder differently. Dorsey believed Mary was taken to the basement of the pencil factory, awake, and then killed. Lanford believed Mary was struck on the back of the head on the second floor.

The newspaper described the investigation as "multi-cornered." Dorsey and the mystery detective were in one corner. Chiefs Lanford and Beavers, along with their detectives, stood in another. The Pinkerton Detectives were in the third corner, and the last corner was occupied by William J. Burns and his team.

Not long after C. W. Tobie arrived in Atlanta, he spent eight hours briefing with Dorsey, who welcomed him to the investigation. Tobie agreed to make copies of his daily reports for Dorsey and his men. Chiefs Beavers and Lanford were furious, and Harry Scott from Pinkerton was distrustful of the whole arrangement. Burns had stolen one of the Pinkerton's highest-paying clients.

Tobie must have found it hard to work with the negative feelings coming his way. He avoided the press and went to Marietta to get to know Mary's friends and family. When he came back to Atlanta, the *Constitution* found him and questioned what he had learned. Tobie had just come from visiting with Fannie Coleman and had learned that on the day of the murder, Mary got up early to help Fannie with housework. Mary ironed the summer dress she intended to wear to Sunday school the next morning. The dress was left spread across the chair and was still there on the morning Tobie interviewed Fannie. A tribute to the daughter who would never come home. Also, Tobie met with a number of girls who worked with Mary. They had pooled their resources and provided Mary with the first flowers sent to the funeral home.

"She was the best girl that any of us knew," the factory girl told the detective.[109]

Little did C. W. Tobie know that he would get himself tangled in the hard feelings between the Atlanta police and Pinkerton Detective Agency. Tobie didn't improve the relationship when he suggested to reporters that clues had been overlooked. His investigation drew most of the same conclusions the Atlanta detectives and the Pinkerton Detective Agency had drawn. The real loser in this whole unfortunate set of circumstances was Leo, who was a chess piece in an intensely competitive game.

In Beavers's and Lanford's opinions, Thomas B. Felder waltzed into Atlanta, stirring up trouble by insisting that Burns come to town and save the factory girls from a repeat of the crime. Lanford and Beavers saw his actions as belittling. The police chiefs were confident Felder's interest in Mary's murder was self-promotion, which was revealed when Felder was pushed into releasing the names of those who had contributed to the fund to help pay Detective Burns to investigate Mary's murder. Two prominent Jewish citizens, William J. Lowenstein and Joseph Hirsch, were on the list. Lanford and Beavers saw this as proof that Felder was working for Leo Frank. They accused

Felder, who in turn accused Lanford, of undermining the prosecution of Frank.

The battle in the newspapers between the Atlanta police and Felder began.

Chapter 16

"White Folks, I'm a Liar"

James Conley, known as Jim, was arrested the afternoon of 1 May, after Holloway, the day watchman at the pencil factory, saw him on the second floor washing what looked like bloodstains out of a shirt. He was taken to headquarters to be questioned.

Conley wasn't new to interrogation. Besides numerous arrests for drunkenness, three months before, Jim had been arrested for shooting at (but missing) his common-law wife, Lorena Jones. He went to jail, but he was out long before 26 April.

Conley was born in Atlanta, and his parents worked at Capital City Laundry on Mitchell Street. He attended Mitchell Street Elementary, located at 249 West Mitchell Street, a newly built schools for Black students. Jim was tutored by Alice Carey, the school's principal, and when Jim left school, he was able to read and write.

When he was a teen, Jim worked for a year or so at Wood's Feed and Sales Stables on South Forsyth Street, where he groomed horses. His next job was as a delivery boy for Orr's Stationery Company, and later he worked as a buggy driver. In 1911, he was hired at the National Pencil factory as the elevator operator. He managed to hold onto this position despite his drinking problem until right before Mary's murder. He lost the position and became the janitor. Holloway told the *Atlanta Georgian* that Jim was found on the top floor of the factory, passed out drunk, by some boxes he was supposed to be breaking down.

Detectives John Black and Harry Scott questioned Jim when he was arrested that morning. Jim made the following statement.

> My full name is James Conley. I reside [at] 172 Rhodes Street with Lorine Jones, who claims to be from Marietta, Ga. This

woman is not my wife and I have been living with her a little over two years. I have been having intercourse with Lorine Jones. I have been employed as elevator man and roustabout at the National Pencil Co factory in Atlanta for the past two years.... On Saturday, April 26, 1913, I arose between 9 a.m. and 9:30 a.m. and ate my breakfast. At 10:30 a.m. I left the house, 172 Rhodes Street, and went to Peters Street and visited a number of saloons between Fair and Peters and Haynes and Peters Street. I purchased a half pint of rye whiskey. I visited the Butt-in Saloon and went back to the pool tables and saw three colored men shooting dice, and I joined them and won 90 cents from them. I then purchased some beer, paying 15 cents. I then walked up the street and visited Earley's beer saloon, purchased two beers and wine, paying ten cents for same. This was all the money I spent on Peters Street, and I arrived home at 2:30 p.m. and I found L. Jones there and she asked me if I had any money. I replied yes, and gave her $3.50 (one dollar in green back, and the rest silver money.) I drew $3.75 from the pencil factory on Friday.... At 3:30 or 4:00 p.m. Saturday, April 26th, I purchased 15 cents worth of beer and then returned to the house, and sent the little girl out to get ten cents worth of stove wood and five cents worth of pan sausage. I remained home Saturday night and 12 o'clock noon, Sunday, April 27th, I walked up Mitchell Street and got a cigarette, remaining there until 12:45 p.m., and returned home, remaining until 6:30 p.m., when I went to my mother's house, 92 Tattnall Street, and got my lunch, and then returned home and I remained at home until Monday, April 28th. On April 28th I reported for work at the pencil factory at 7:05 a.m.

Signed James Conley[110]

Both Black and Scott had their sights on Leo and didn't give Conley much thought. Jim had the detectives convinced he was illiterate though many of his friends, family, and co-workers knew this wasn't true. Time would reveal his discrepancy. One can't assume that Jim's lie was because he was somehow involved in the murder. He was smart and didn't want to draw suspicion to himself. Many young Black men made this choice to stay under the radar of the law. And with good reason.

☙

As recently as 1908, five years before Mary's murder, the Georgia legislature established a commission to investigate Georgia's convict leasing system. The commission met in room 16 at the state capitol in the evenings. They heard more than 120 witnesses testify over three weeks and learned that the state government didn't know where most of the convicts ended up or how many were being held against their will. The system resembled present-day human trafficking syndicates.

The details were horrific. Young Black men infected with tuberculosis were left to die on the floor of a storage shed at a farm near Milledgeville. Witnesses reported that the convicts lived and slept in the same clothes for months at a time. One Black man broke his arm and was back to work in a few months with a dislocated arm. Workers from the Chattahoochee Brick Company testified to the commission that conditions at the brick company were much worse than at other places.

When James English, a majority stock holder in the brick company, appeared before the commission, he vehemently denied abusing. He claimed that as an absentee owner, he had not been in the factory for three years. In October 1908, Governor Smith ordered a special session of the legislature, which voted two-to-one to abolish the convict leasing system by March 1909.

Two years before this took place, when Jim was around twenty, the 1906 Race Massacre—four days of all-out war on Black Atlantans—took place. There were twenty-five documented deaths, but hundreds of deaths were not accounted for. Jim, like many young

Black men at the time, must have learned from these events to be as invisible as possible when around White people.

☙

Based upon Jim Conley's first interview, he had no big worries. Though the detectives thought him inconsequential—and Dorsey shared this sentiment—he remained in custody for two more weeks.

On 16 May, two Pinkerton detectives, W. D. McWorth and L. P. Whitfield, interviewed Mrs. J. A. White. Leo had reported to Harry Scott that Mrs. White had seen a Black man at the pencil factory when she came to visit her husband on the Saturday Mary was murdered. For some reason, the Pinkerton detectives waited to talk to her. When the two detectives interviewed her, Mrs. White told them she went to the pencil factory to see her husband, Arthur White, twice that day. She entered the factory for the second time at twelve thirty and went to the fourth floor, where her husband was working. When she came back downstairs at one, a Black man was sitting on a box near the elevator. The detectives asked if she could identify him, but she said she wasn't sure—the area was dark. Whitfield asked her if she would go to police headquarters to see if she could pick the man out of a line-up. She explained she would have to come in later because she had a baby and could not carry the child because of her health.

The two detectives went to headquarters to speak with Detective Black, who said he had interviewed Jim Conley but that he was illiterate and couldn't have written the murder notes. The Pinkerton detectives went to Conley's home to speak to Lorena. She told the detectives that when she left the house at three o'clock to buy snuff, Jim was home, sitting in front of the fireplace. When she returned, Jim was no longer there. She stepped to the washstand to get some Vaseline, and he jumped out from behind the washstand. She screamed, and Jim said he hid to scare her. Lorena admitted he owned four shirts.

The next day McWorth went to the pencil factory to interview Barrett about the hair found on the lathe. While there, he spoke with Mr. Darley, factory personnel director, who said on the Monday, Tuesday, and Wednesday after the murder, Jim went about his job without saying a word to anyone and looking worried. Herbert Schiff, assistant superintendent at the factory, stated to McWorth that while the police detectives were in the building on the morning of 28 April, Jim was found in the shipping room behind some boxes. Schiff told him to leave and Jim said he would give a million dollars to be a White man so that he could walk by the detectives. Lemmie Quinn told McWorth that he had received two complaints from two of the girls working there that Conley was too familiar when he talked to them.

McWorth and Whitfield then asked after the pay Jim received for that week. Schiff said he drew $3.73. The two detectives then searched the basement from corner to corner, hoping to find Mary's missing mesh purse. They found nothing. When Quinn and Darley were asked about Conley's character, both told stories that were told to them by young girls working at the factory. It seemed many didn't trust him, and one, Helen Ferguson, was so afraid of him that she left the building by the back door.

While these stories didn't prove Conley committed the murder, they suggested he needed to be investigated further. At some point—this is where stories diverge—Detectives Black and Scott found out that Jim could write. Leo stated that when he found out the police were interested in Conley, he had told them Conley could read and write. He also sent a message to them that he had proof in his desk at the pencil factory that Jim could write. The detectives discovered, one way or the other, that Jim could write. It seems that Jim had signed a contract to buy a watch from a local jeweler. The payment was to be taken from his pay each week.

On Sunday, 18 May, Detectives Black and Scott brought Jim Conley in for questioning. It began with Black locking the door and throwing the key out the open transom above the door. Outside the door stood Britt Craig, the *Atlanta Constitution* reporter. Black began, "Well, Jim, we've got the deadwood on you. Better cough up and tell us something."[111]

Jim swore he didn't know a thing.

"Listen, can you write?" Scott asked. He held a piece of paper.

"Naw, sir, I can't. I never could," Conley answered. Scott asked if he would swear he couldn't write, and Conley said he would.

"Do you know what the penalty for perjury is?"

"Naw sir—what is it?"

"Twenty in the gang—maybe more."

Scott unfolded the watch contract with Jim's signature and placed it in Jim's hands.

Jim paused, as if at a loss for words. "White folks, I'm a liar."[112]

Instead of taking Jim back to where he had been held, the detectives sent him to a basement isolation cell. He was left there an unknown amount of time to think about the interview with the detectives.

ଓ

On 24 May, as the grand jury deliberated whether Leo and Newt Lee would be indicted and held over for trial, Jim Conley sent word to see Chief Lanford. Within minutes he was sitting in the chief's office. He made the following statement, witnessed by G. C. February, the notary public in Fulton County.

> On Friday evening before the holiday, about four minutes to one o'clock, Mr. Frank come up the aisle and asked me to come to his office. That was the aisle on the fourth floor where I was working, and when I went down to the office he asked me could I write and I told him yes I could write a little bit, and he gave me a scratch pad and told me what to put on it and told me to put on there "dear mother," "a long tall, black negro did this by himself," and he told me to write it two or three times on there. I wrote it on the white scratch pad, single ruled. He went to his desk and pulled out another scratch pad, a brownish looking scratch pad, and looked at my writing and wrote on that himself, but when I went to his office he asked me if I wanted a cigarette, and I told him yes, but they didn't allow any smoking in the factory, and he

pulled out a box of cigarettes that cost 15 cents a box, and in that box he had $2.50, two paper dollars and two quarters, and I taken one of the cigarettes and handed him the box and I told him he had some money in the box, and he said that was all right I was welcome to that for I was a good working negro around there, and then he asked me where Gordon Bailey (Snowball they call him) was, and I told him on the elevator, and he asked me if I knew the night watchman and I told him no sir, I didn't know him, and he asked me if I ever saw him in the basement and I told him no sir, I never did see him down there, but he could ask the fireman and maybe he could tell him more about that than I could, and then Mr. Frank was laughing and jollying and going on in the office, and I asked him not to take out any money for that watchman I owed, for I didn't have any to spare, and he told me he wouldn't, but he would see to me getting some money a little bit later. He told me he had some wealthy people in Brooklyn, and then he held his head up and looking out of the corner of his eyes and said "Why should I hang?" and that's all I remember him saying to me. When I asked him not to take out any money for the watch, he said you ought not to buy any watch, for that big fat wife of mine wants me to buy her an automobile but he wouldn't do it; I never did see his wife. One Tuesday morning after the holiday on Saturday, before Mr. Frank got in jail, he come up the aisle where I was sweeping and held his head over to me and whispered to me to be a good boy and that was all he said to me.[113]

ಣ

Later that day, the grand jury came back with an indictment for Leo, but they would wait until Monday to decide about Newt Lee. Newspapers reported Newt Lee would be released on Monday and would not be held over for trial. Lee would not be indicted, but he would remain in jail until the trial. Conley's statement, which the authorities didn't entirely believe, had captured Dorsey's attention. Here was an employee accusing Leo Frank of asking him to write the notes the day before the murder. This established intent. This didn't fit with the story Dorsey and detectives had carved out of evidence, but it was close. The authorities were convinced Jim wasn't telling the whole truth, but they didn't believe he had killed Mary. They believed he helped Leo Frank hide the murder. They were so focused on Leo's guilt that Jim's changing story was explained as fear of his boss.

E. F. Holloway, the timekeeper and foreman at the pencil factory, shared his thoughts on Conley with a reporter.

> Jim Conley, when he came to work here about one year ago, was a pretty good negro.... Then Jim got drunk. He had been running the elevator and we were afraid to trust him afterward. We then put him to work sweeping in the trimming department. Here Conley was closely associated with the girls... Jim got so bad he used to carry whiskey with him in his pocket. Several times he was caught by employees taking a drink. This was not known by management until after the murder of Mary Phagan.... About one week before the crime was committed the forelady of the trimming and finishing department, Miss Eulah May Flowers, went to the top floor of the building to look over the stock of boxes. When Conley was not sweeping he was supposed to fill the box bins with boxes. When Miss Flowers moved toward the bin to look in she stumbled over a form. She screamed and fell back. It was Conley. He was dead drunk. Miss Flowers tried to wake him up, but was unable.... Thursday after the murder, when the plant was shut down because we all were called to the investigation I testified and went back to the factory. As I entered the metal department I heard a splashing in the cooling tank. There was Conley washing his shirt. When I entered he was very much startled and tried to hide the shirt by trying to drop it through a crack in the floor.... Now I don't say

> Conley was degenerate enough to commit a crime so terrible when he was sober, but I am thoroughly convinced that he strangled Mary Phagan when about half drunk.
>
> I'll go further and say that during the last three months that Conley was here, I was suspicious of him and tried to watch him as closely as possible.[114]

❧

Meanwhile, three days had passed since Jim Conley had made what is called his second statement. Detectives Scott and Black played a version of good cop, bad cop. Harry Scott accused Jim of murdering Mary and said that was why he wasn't telling the complete truth. John Black brought him drinks and food in an attempt to get him to share more with him. They were looking for a better story that would convict Leo Frank. On 28 May, Conley was taken from his cell to Chief Lanford's office, where E. F. Holloway was waiting. Conley was shown a copy of the newspaper with Holloway's thoughts on Jim's guilt. This must have scared Jim much more than Holloway's presence. The headlines screamed of his guilt. Jim asked to meet with Black alone. It seems his plying Jim with food had worked. Conley made what would be referred to as his second statement.

> I make this statement, my second statement, in regard to the murder of Mary Phagan at the National Pencil factory. In my first statement I made the statement that I went to the pencil factory on Friday, April 25, 1913, and went to Frank's office at four minutes to one which is a mistake. I made this statement in regard to Friday in order that I might not be accused of knowing anything of this murder, for I thought that if I put myself there on Saturday, they might accuse me of having a hand in it, and I now make my second and last statement regarding the matter freely and voluntarily, after thinking over the situation and I have made up my mind to tell the

> whole truth, and I make it freely and voluntarily, without the promise of any reward or from force or fear of punishment in any way….

Jim begins the statement in the same way he did his original interview and the previous statement and then it begins to change.

> I met Mr. Frank, at the corner of Forsyth and Nelson Streets going to Montags, and he told me to wait a few minutes, and he asked me where I was going, and I told him I was going to the Capitol City Laundry to see my mother, and he didn't say nothing, only he said to wait a minute until he come back, that he was going to see Montags, and I stood there until he come back, he was gone about 20 minutes, I guess. He come back and told me to come to the factory, that he wanted to see me, and I went to factory with him, walking behind him, and he stopped at the Curtis Drug Store at Forsyth and Mitchell Streets and he got a drink, and I waited on the outside until he come out and then he told me to come on and I went to the factory with him. He had a box with him, which he carried with him to the Montag's; it has an opener to it, and after we got to the factory, Mr. Frank took the box and put it there at the trash barrel, which was just to the right of the steps as you go in, he put a box there for me to sit on. There was some great big boxes back further. He told me to sit down there until I heard him whistle…. Then he told me not to let Mr. Darley see me, and after Mr. Frank went up the steps, in a few minutes here comes a young lady downstairs, that was Miss Mattie. I think she had on a dark red suit and a rain cloak and a parasol in her hand, but I didn't notice her hat. Then here come Mr. Darley down and he had on a gray suit of clothes, didn't have any hat on his head, and he stopped Miss Mattie at the front door, and when he stopped her I saw Miss Mattie with a handkerchief wiping her eyes, it seemed to me like she had been crying, and then I heard Mr. Darley say to her, "Don't worry, I will see that you get that

next week," and they stood there and talked awhile, but I could not hear anything else they said, then she went on out the door and Mr. Darley came back up the steps, and Mr. Darley stayed up there a good while, then he come down and left and I did not see him anymore. Then here comes Mr. Holloway down, about five minutes after Mr. Darley had gone; Mr. Holloway went out on the sidewalk and stood there three or five minutes and then he come and went back up the steps and then here come another colored fellow, a pegged-legged one, and he went up the steps, he had some bills in his hands and Mr. Holloway come back down with the pegged-legged one and went out on the sidewalk and looked at the fellow's wagon, but what he said to him I don't know.... Mr. Frank whistled for me twice...and when he whistled I went on up the stairs and double doors on the stairway were closed and I opened them and they shut themselves, and Mr. Frank was standing at the top of the steps.... Mr. Frank grabbed me by my arm and he was squeezing my arm so tight his hand was trembling...he carried me through the first office and into his private office...then he saw two ladies coming and he said to me, "Gee, here comes Miss Emma Clark and Miss Corinthia Hall" and he come back in there to me...he motioned to the wardrobe and I was a little slow about it and Mr. Frank grabbed me and gave me a shove and put me in the wardrobe and he shut the doors and told me to stay there until after they had gone...he jerked the door open and I was right there in front of the door, and then Mr. Frank said to me to sit down in a chair... "Jim, can you write?"... "Yes sir, I can write a little bit, Mr. Frank".... He give me a pencil that he got off the top of his desk...he told me what to put there... "dear mother, a long tall black negro did this by hisself".... Then Mr. Frank reared back in his chair and asked me if I wanted to smoke and I told him "Yes, sir," and he taken out a cigarette for himself and handed me the box

> and I taken out a cigarette...and I handed the box of cigarettes back and he told me that was all right to keep them, and I told him he had some money in the box and he said that was all right, I could have that... Mr. Frank looked around at me and held up his head toward the top of the house and said "Why should I hang, I have wealthy people in Brooklyn." ...then Mr. Frank told me he was going to take that note I had written and send it off in a letter to his people when he wrote, and recommend me to them....[115]

Jim goes on in his statement describing what he did after he left the factory. He ends with an explanation of washing his shirt. This statement suggests Leo's nervousness. Still, it didn't give proof that Leo Frank had killed anyone or that Jim Conley knew of the crime. Chief Beavers and Chief Lanford, along with Harry Scott, escorted Jim Conley to the Tower to have him speak with Leo Frank. Of course, they understood they couldn't make Leo agree to see them.

Leo was visiting with a friend when word came to his cell that the group of officers and Jim Conley wanted to meet with him. Leo must have remembered how things went when he met with Newt Lee at Black and Scott's request. Rosser, Leo's lawyer, was in Rabun County, representing Georgia Railway and Electric Company in a court fight to open the Tallulah Gorge Power Plant. Leo told the messenger he would not meet with the group.

The group had to find another way to get more proof that Leo killed Mary. The next afternoon, the same officers decided to bring Jim from his cell and grill him again. This would be the worst interrogation yet. This questioning took place in Lanford's office. At dusk, Conley gave another affidavit that would come to be known as his third affidavit.

> On Saturday, April 26, 1913, when I come back to the pencil factory with Mr. Frank I waited for him downstairs like he told me, and when he whistled for me I went upstairs and he asked me if I wanted to make some money right quick and I told him "Yes, sir," and he told me that he had picked up a

girl back there and had let her fall and that her head hit against something, he didn't know what it was, and for me to move her, and I hollered and told him the girl was dead, and he told me to pick her up and bring her to the elevator and I told him I didn't have nothing to pick her up with and he told me to go and look by the cotton box there and get a piece of cloth, and I got a big wide piece of cloth and come back there to the men's toilet where she was, and I tied her up, and I taken her and brought her up there to a little dressing room, carrying her on my right shoulder, and she got too heavy for me and she slipped off my shoulder and fell on the floor right there at the dressing room and I hollered for Mr. Frank to come there and help me, that she was too heavy for me, and Mr. Frank come down there and told me to pick her up, damn fool, and he run down there to me and he was excited, and he picked her up by the feet, her head and feet were sticking out of the cloth and then we brought her on to the elevator, Mr. Frank carrying her by the feet and me by the shoulders, and we brought her to the elevator and then Mr. Frank says, "Wait, let me get the key," and he went into the office and got the key and come back and unlocked the elevator door and started the elevator down. Mr. Frank turned it on himself and we went on down to the basement and Mr. Frank helped me take it off the elevator and he told me to take it back there to the sawdust pile, and I picked it up and put it on my shoulder again, and Mr. Frank, he went up the ladder and watched the trap door to see if anybody was coming, and I taken her back there and taken the cloth from around her and taken her hat and shoe which I had picked up upstairs right where her body was lying, and brought them down and untied the cloth and brought them back and throwed them on the trashpile in front of the furnace, and Mr. Frank was standing at the trap door at the head of the ladder. He didn't tell me where to put the things. I layed her body down with her head towards the elevator, lying on her stomach and the left side of her face was on the ground and the right side of her face was up, and both arms were laying down with her body, by the side of her body. Mr. Frank joined me back on the first floor. I stepped on the elevator and he stepped on the elevator when it got to where he was, and he said "Gee, that was a tiresome job," and I told him his job was not as tiresome as mine was, because I had to tote it all the way from where she was laying to the dressing room, and in the basement from the elevator to where I left her. Then Mr. Frank hops off the elevator before it gets even with the second floor and he makes a stumble and he hits the floor and catches with both hands, and he went on around to the sink to wash his hands, and I went and cut off the motor, and I stood and waited for Mr. Frank to come from around there washing his hands, and then we went on into the office, and Mr. Frank he couldn't hardly keep still, he was all the time moving about from one office to the other, then he come back into the stenographer's office and come back and he told me "Here comes Emma Clark and Corinthia Hall," I understood him to say, and he come back and told me to come here and he opened the wardrobe and told me to get in there, and I was so slow about going he told me to hurry up, damn it, and Mr. Frank, whoever that was come in the office, they didn't stay so very long, till Mr. Frank was gone about 7 or 8 minutes, and I was still in the wardrobe and he never had come to let me out, and Mr. Frank come back and I said, "Goodness alive, you kept me in there a mighty long time," and he said, "Yes, I see I did, you are sweating," and then me and Mr. Frank set down in a chair. Mr. Frank then took out a cigarette and he gave me the box and asked me did I want to smoke and I told him yes, sir, and I taken the box and taken out a cigarette and he handed me a box of matches and I handed him the matches back, and I handed him the cigarette box and he told me that was all right, I could keep that, and I told him he had some money in it and he told me that was all right, I could keep that, and Mr. Frank then asked me to write a few lines on that paper, a white scratch pad he had there, and he told me what to put on there, and I asked him what he was going to do with it and he told me to just go ahead and write, and then after I got through writing Mr. Frank looked at it and said it was all right, and Mr. Frank looked up at the top of the house and said, "Why should I hang, I have wealthy people in Brooklyn," and I asked him what about me, and he told me that was all right about me, for me to keep my mouth shut and he would make everything all right, and then I asked him where was the money he said he was going to give me and Mr. Frank said, "Here, here is two hundred dollars," and he handed me a big roll of greenback money and I didn't count it; I stood there a little while looking at it in my hand, and I told Mr. Frank not to take another dollar for that watch man I owed and he said he wouldn't—and the rest is just like I have told it before. The reason I have not told this before is I thought Mr. Frank would get out and help me out, but it seems that he is not going to get out and I have decided to tell the whole truth about this matter. While I was looking at the money in my hands, Mr. Frank said: "Let me have that and I will make it all right with you Monday if I live and nothing happens," and he took the money back and I asked him if that was the way he done and he said he would give it back Monday.[116]

Finally, the authorities had what they felt they needed to convict Leo Frank for the murder of Mary Phagan.

Chapter 17

A Grand Performance

Leo's days in the Tower had a routine, and he must have found some comfort in this. Still, he was accustomed to being busy, so he read all the papers and the multiple editions that came out each day. Keeping up with this investigation gave him a feeling of control. As Sheriff C. W. Mangum made his rounds on Friday, 30 May, Leo spoke to him. "I don't know who is guilty but I do know that the man who murdered Mary Phagan ought to be hanged."[117]

Sheriff Mangum told a reporter that Leo looked him square in the eye and talked like an innocent man.

☙

That same day, around the dinner hour, Chief Beavers and Chief Lanford put Jim Conley in Lanford's car, pulled the curtains so no one would notice who was inside, and headed to the pencil factory. The employees were sent home. Herbert Schiff, E. F. Holloway, and Detectives Campbell and Scott joined the tour of the factory. Conley was asked to reenact what he said happened the day Mary Phagan was murdered. Jim began at the top of the stairs on the second floor where Leo was to have whistled for him to come up from his perch by the front door. He repeated word for word what his statement said. Jim lay down in the metal room, showing the group where he first saw Mary dead. Jim described how he wrapped her body in a cotton bag on Leo's orders. Both men carried her into the elevator and went down to the basement.

It is at this point that the group should have realized something was wrong with Jim's story. Earlier, he had admitted that while waiting for Leo to call him, he had gone to the basement, where he defecated in the elevator shaft. He revealed this detail when detectives were questioning him after he made his last statement. Part of the group was present the Sunday after Mary's murder; their elevator trip to the basement disturbed the feces, releasing a horrible smell. If, as Jim claimed, he and Leo took Mary's body down the elevator on Saturday afternoon, they—not the Sunday group—would have disturbed it. However, Beavers and Lanford either failed to make the connection or chose to ignore the discrepancy.

Chief Beavers asked Jim to lie on the basement floor and show the group how he placed Mary's body. Conley did so almost exactly the same. This suggested, at the very least, Jim had been in the basement with Mary's body.

"There is no doubt that the Negro is telling the truth and it would be foolish to doubt it. The Negro wouldn't go through the actions like he did unless he had done this just like he said," Harry Scott said in front of reporters in the group.[118]

Jim was so detailed in his performance that he stopped the elevator six inches before they reached the second floor on the way back up. He demonstrated how Leo tripped and fell as he attempted to exit. Conley's details—how the drops of blood in the metal room got there and the cord around Mary's neck—convinced many of the group that he was telling the truth.

After Conley got out of the elevator, he took the group to the sink where Leo had washed his hands, then led Jim into his office and told him to sit down. He described how Leo twisted his chair and rubbed his hands together, "acting like white folks does when they is scared, turned red in the face, and kept looking around."[119]

Leo then told Jim to get in his wardrobe, and Conley remained there while Emma Clark and Corinthia Hall came into the office. While this detail seemed like something only Jim could know if he was in the closet listening, much of the evidence had been paraded through the newspapers. Jim could have added this to his story easily.

While this reenactment took place, a large crowd of employees gathered outside the building. Most of them believed Jim had committed the murder and was trying to blame an innocent man, Leo Frank. Chief Beavers led Jim out of the back, but some of the crowd saw them and yelled, "There's the Negro now; get him."[120] No one moved toward the car as it drove away on its way back to the Tower.

Jim Conley's story was a sensation after the newspapers printed the story of his dramatic performance. Everyone wanted to hear the story. Jim would be held as a material witness instead of charged as one of the murderers.

After Jim's performance at the factory, he held court in his cell at the Tower, regaling reporters and the curious. As the *Constitution* reported:

> James Conley sat on a bunk in his cell at the Tower last night and for an hour freely discussed his grim connection with the Mary Phagan tragedy. He was a willing talker, ready answerer of questions and throughout the interview he seemed to find relief in relating the narrative of his complicity in Atlanta's most hideous crime. "I was intending not to tell the whole business. I was fixin to take care of Mr. Frank like he told me to in the first place. I was going to keep my mouth shut and say nothin', until some of those folks down at the pencil factory opens up and begins trying to make out that I killed the little girl, and that I'm trying to save my own neck by fixn' it on Mr. Frank.[121]

What Jim didn't know was an *Atlanta Georgian* editor had taken an interest in Jim having a decent lawyer—not because he believed Conley's story but because he *didn't*. He approached William Smith and offered to pay Smith's forty-dollar fee if Smith could get Conley as a client. So the editor asked Lorena Jones, Conley's common-law wife, to come see him.

Friday evening, as Jim talked to the reporters, Lorena and lawyer William Smith entered the Tower just in time to hear Jim say, "He ain't paid me nuthin yet, like he promised to do…."[122]

Once Smith began representing Conley, he told Jim to stop talking to people about what happened. Some of Leo's friends were in the group listening outside his cell. Smith knew all Jim's showboating would cause him trouble.[123]

ௐ

On Saturday, Dorsey was having similar thoughts about Conley. He called for Jim to be brought to him so he could be cross-examined. Dorsey was well aware that Jim Conley was becoming his star witness. Conley was shown an intricate diagram of the pencil factory, drawn by an *Atlanta Georgian* staff artist. Jim walked Dorsey through the various events he described at the factory they day before. Hugh Dorsey accepted his story but understood Conley's storytelling skills could cause problems for the prosecution. He sent Jim back to his cell and called William Smith for a meeting.

Before this tour of the factory, detectives had attempted to bring Conley to meet with Leo about Conley's statement, but Leo remained silent and refused all interviews without his lawyer. Rosser was still in the North Georgia Mountains litigating for his client.

When Jim was taken back to his cell after meeting with Dorsey, he agreed to an interview with a reporter. Conley had a lot to say about how he would pay the price for his part in helping hide the murder: "Yes sir, I guess maybe it's over with me. I suppose they're going to hang me or send me to the penitentiary for life, but I done told the truth."

When the reporter asked what he would say to Leo Frank if he could, Jim said, "I am ready right now to face Mr. Frank. I'll look him right in the eye and I'll say, 'You know I didn't kill that girl, Mr. Frank, and you know I'm telling the truth to these white folks.'"

When asked how long Jim knew Leo Frank, he answered, "I guess I must a known Mr. Frank for about two years. Yes sir, he was always a good boss to me. There was never no trouble about my getting money if I needed it."

The interviewer pointed out that Jim was telling a story that might cost his boss his life. Jim replied, "Well, I had to do it. That's all there was to it. I had to tell the truth."[124]

☙

When Hugh Dorsey met with Conley's lawyer, Smith readily agreed to have his client moved to the county jail instead of staying in the Tower. He meant to keep Conley safe from his own tendency to talk too much. Both men agreed they believed Jim's story but knew he could hurt the case and himself. Moving him to police headquarters would allow them to control his visitors.

Smith began to notice that the *Atlanta Georgian* seemed to favor Leo's position rather than Conley's. He understood the *Georgian* was not paying for Conley's representation because they wanted him to get a fair shake; they wanted Smith to provide inside information about the case. Smith went to the *Atlanta Georgian*'s newsroom and met with the editors to explain that giving them information about his defense of Conley would violate attorney-client privilege. Smith gave up all the money promised him, walked away, and represented Jim for free.

At this point, William M. Smith was thirty-three years old and known for helping those who couldn't afford him. He had been on the Atlanta bar for eleven years and often represented Black clients. This did not garner him a lot of respect among more successful White lawyers. At the time there were only ten or so Black lawyers in Georgia. Smith had some noteworthy cases. In 1911, he represented an older Black woman against Georgia Railway and Electric Company for damages to cover her injuries that were received on a streetcar when a fight broke out between a White conductor and a Black man who had refused to pay his fare. Georgia's Supreme Court ruled in the woman's favor, which was almost unheard of at the time.

Jim Conley was moved from the Tower back to the county jail and lost his audience.

Meanwhile, Chief Lanford was infuriated that Sheriff Mangum would not allow newspapermen or visitors to see Leo unless Leo approved. Lucille began visiting Leo once a day.

ꝏ

On Sunday, 1 June, during the Atlanta Crackers baseball game at Ponce De Leon Baseball Park in Atlanta, a tornado hit and wrecked the stands, sending spectators into the field. The tornado was described as having formed on the field, at first just spinning dirt but turning angry and destructive.[125]

The *Atlanta Constitution* reported that Jim Conley had requested to be moved to the jail at the police headquarters. The papers reported Leo Frank's friends tried to intimidate him by stopping at his cell and jeering that they could shoot him through the bars of his cell.[126]

A *Constitution* reporter asked Chief Lanford what he thought of the move. The chief replied,

> I don't want a repetition of the circumstances under which we have to deal with Superintendent Frank. Sheriff Mangum allows friends of Frank to visit him by the score, but flatly refuses to allow men working on the case to see him or talk with him. The sheriff says that Frank does not want to see the detectives and that he will not admit any one to see Frank without his consent. We have made three attempts to obtain an interview with Frank for Conley, who says he is sure he can make Frank admit the truth of his (Conley's) affidavit, but have been refused upon the same grounds—that Frank does not want to see Conley.[127]

What Lanford doesn't say to the reporter is that Leo's lawyer, Luther Rosser, was in Northeast Georgia fighting a case. Leo had the right to turn down the interview because his lawyer couldn't be present. When the reporter questioned Sheriff Mangum on the subject, he stated that he did not believe the stories about Leo's friends threatening Conley. He went on to say Conley was not disturbed by anyone during his stay at the Tower. He then addressed his choice of not allowing the detectives and Conley to see Leo. "The prisoners in the Tower will be convicted in the courts," he said, "not in the jail. If the judge or anyone else who had authority cares to admit interviews without Frank's consent, it is another matter."[128] Sheriff Mangum intended to uphold the letter of the law.

Chapter 18

The Cook Is Arrested

Twenty-year-old Minola McKnight worked as a cook for Emil and Josephine Selig on Georgia Avenue. Her husband, Albert, about twenty-five years old, worked at Beck & Gregg Hardware in Atlanta. The hardworking couple seemed stable; they paid their bills and showed up to their respective jobs every day. They lived in a small house on Pullman Street where many other working-class Black families lived. On Monday, 2 June, Minola was arrested at the Seligs' house just after noon. Minola sobbed that the police were going to hang her for something she knew nothing about. The detectives followed Dorsey's orders and held her under a charge of suspicion. Albert had been brought into the police station at the same time, where he said Minola told conflicting stories about what time Leo was home for lunch the day Mary was murdered. One of those stories was that Leo didn't come home for lunch until well after 1:30 that afternoon.

Conley had accused Leo of getting him to help hide Mary's body between 1:10 and 1:50 p.m. Five witnesses—Lucille, Josephine, Emil, Corinthia Hall, and Minola—were prepared to testify under oath that Leo was home for lunch on that Saturday by 1:30 that afternoon.

During Minola's interview, Detectives Starnes and Campbell told Minola they wanted her to sign an affidavit that stated Leo came home much later. When Minola was told what Albert said, she accused him of lying. She denied ever saying anything other than Leo came home at 1:30. Albert, who was present for the interview, attempted to force her to say she had told more than one story. She resisted. Even as the detectives booked Minola and placed her in a jail cell, she swore Leo Frank was innocent and home for lunch when she said.

The next day, Tuesday, Minola was brought to an office next to Campbell and Starnes's office on the third floor of police headquarters. Again, Albert was there, but this time, he brought a lawyer, George Gordon, to represent Minola. Two White businessmen, Ernest H. Pickett and Roy L. Caven, sat in the office with Minola. Both men had a stake in her signing an affidavit. According to an *Atlanta Constitution* reporter, "Both men are employees of Beck & Gregg Hardware. The head of which, L. H. Beck, is foreman of the grand jury which indicted Leo Frank." He went on to say, "Solicitor Dorsey will not explain the nature of a big picture." This would indicate Albert was pressured to discredit his wife since he worked Beck & Gregg. And with the connection to the grand jury foreman, this situation points directly back to Dorsey.[129]

Albert and George Gordon left these men to grill Minola and went into the hall. Detectives Campbell and Starnes left Pickett and Caven—who were only employees of Beck & Gregg Hardware and not part of the police department—to interview Minola in the office where she was being held. When the detectives returned two hours later, Minola was ready to give a statement. Had someone not leaked her affidavit to the papers, no one would have known what took place with Minola. The newspapers saw Minola's affidavit as hearsay and admissible in court.

Minola McKnight's affidavit:

> On Saturday morning, April 26, 1913, Mr. Frank left home about 8 o'clock and Albert, my husband, was there Saturday, too; Albert got there I guess about a quarter after 1, and was there when Mr. Frank come for dinner, which was about half-past one, but Mr. Frank did not eat any dinner and he left in about ten minutes after he got there.
>
> Mr. Frank came back to the house at 7 o'clock that night, and Albert was there when he got there. Albert had gone home that evening, but he come back, but I don't know what time he got there, but he come sometime before Mr. Frank

eat supper that night about 7 o'clock, and when I left about 8 o'clock I left Mr. Frank there.

Sunday morning I got there about 8 o'clock and there was an automobile standing in front of the house, but I didn't pay any attention to it, but I saw a man in the automobile get a bucket of water and pour into it. Miss Lucille was downstairs, and Mr. and Mrs. Selig were upstairs. Albert was there Sunday morning, but I don't remember what time he got there. When I called them down to breakfast about half past eight I found that Mr. Frank was gone. Mr. and Mrs. Selig eat breakfast and Miss Lucille didn't eat until Mr. Frank come back and they eat breakfast together. I didn't hear them say anything at the breakfast table, but after dinner I understood them to say that a girl and Mr. Frank were caught at the office Saturday.

I don't know who said it, but Miss Lucille and Mr. and Mrs. Selig and Mr. Frank were standing there talking after dinner. I didn't know the girl was killed until Monday evening. I understood them to say it was a Jew girl, and I asked Miss Lucille, and she said it was a Gentile.

On Tuesday Mr. Frank says to me: "It is mighty bad, Minola I might have to go to jail about this girl, and I don't know anything about it."

I heard Mrs. Razin, Mrs. Frank's sister, tell Lucille that it was mighty bad, and Miss Lucille said "Yes, it is. I am going to get after her about it." I don't know what they were talking about.

Sunday Miss Lucille said to Mrs. Selig that Mr. Frank didn't sleep so good Saturday night. She said he was drunk and wouldn't let her sleep with him, and she said she slept on the floor on the rug by the bed because he was drinking. Miss Lucille said Sunday that Mr. Frank told her Saturday night that he was in trouble; that he didn't know the reason why he would murder, and he told his wife to get his pistol and let him kill himself. I heard Miss Lucille say that to Mrs. Selig. It got away with Mrs. Selig mighty bad: she didn't know what to think. I haven't heard Miss Lucille say whether she believed it or not. I don't know why Mrs. Frank didn't come to see her husband, but it was a pretty good while before she come to see him, maybe two weeks. She would tell me, "Wasn't it mighty bad that he was locked up?" and she said, "Minola I don't know what I am going to do."

When I left home to go to the solicitor general's office, they told me to mind what I said. They paid me $3.50 a week but last week she paid me $4. One week Mrs. Selig gave me $5, but it was not for my work, and they didn't tell me what it was for. They just said, "Here is $5 Minola." But of course I understood it was a tip for me to keep quiet. They would tell me to mind how I talked and Miss Lucille gave me a hat.

Question: "Was that the reason you didn't tell the solicitor yesterday all about this—that Miss Lucille and others had told you not to say anything about what happened out there?"

"Yes, sir."

Question: "Is that true?"

"Yes, sir."

Question: "And that is the reason why you would rather have been locked up last night than tell this?"

"Yes, sir.'

Question: "Has Mr. Pickett or Mr. Cravens, or Mr. Campbell or myself, [presumably Detective Starnes], influenced you in any way to make this statement?"

"No sir."

Question: "You make it of your own free will and accord in their presence and the presence of Mr. Gordon, your attorney?"

"Yes, sir."

This was signed by Minola McKnight on June 3, 1913.[130]

After her release that evening, a reporter from the *Atlanta Georgian* interviewed her at her home on Pullman Street, only blocks from Lucille's home on Georgia Avenue. Albert was the only other person present. The reporter wrote that her first comment about the affidavit was "a complete and absolute denial of its truth."[131] Despite the affidavit stating that she had made her statement in Mr. Gordon's presence, Minola told the reporter she did not even know who he was. "I ain't got no lawyer 'cept God. He's my lawyer," she said.[132]

"Did you sign any affidavit in the office of Chief Lanford?" the reporter asked.

"No sir. I never had a pen or pencil in my hand," Minola replied.

"Have you read what this affidavit says as it was published in the papers?"

"It was read to me: I can't read."

"Is there anything in there that you said?"

"No sir, It's most all a pack of lies."[133]

Chapter 19

Speaking Out

Lucille was infuriated when Minola told her employers that the detectives forced her to give the affidavit. The part about her being forced to sleep on the floor because Leo was drunk enraged her, not to mention her statement that Leo threatened to commit suicide. Lucille sat down and penned a letter to the three newspaper editors for the *Georgian*, *Constitution*, and *Journal.* One has to imagine she was warned to leave well enough alone. The letter ran on 5 June in all three newspapers.

> Dear Sir:
>
> The action of the solicitor general in arresting and imprisoning our family cook because she would not voluntarily make a false statement against my innocent husband brings a limit to patience. This wrong is not chargeable to a detective acting under the necessity of shielding his own reputation against attacks in newspapers, but an intelligent, trained lawyer whose sworn duty is as much to protect the innocent as to punish the guilty. My information is that he had no legal right to have her arrested and imprisoned.
>
> The following statement from the *Atlanta Journal* undertakes to give the history of the arrest up to the time the woman was carried to the police station in a patrol wagon, weeping and shouting in a hysterical condition:
>
> "The negress was arrested at the Selig residence shortly after noon Monday upon the order of Solicitor General Hugh M. Dorsey.

> She was carried to the solicitor's office and that official with Detectives Campbell and Starnes examined her for more than an hour. The woman grew hysterical during the rigorous examination and finally was led from the solicitor's office to the police patrol, weeping and shouting, 'I am going to hang and don't know a thing about it.'"

They tortured her for four hours with the well-known third degree process...and with the result stated in the *Atlanta Constitution* of June 4 as follows:

> "Her husband, who was also carried to the police station at noon, was freed a short while before his wife left the prison. He was present during the third degree of four hours under which she was placed in the afternoon. He is said to have declared, even in the presence of his wife, that she had told conflicting stories of Frank's conduct on the tragedy date.
>
> "After she had been quizzed to a point of exhaustion, Secretary G. C. February attached to Chief Lanford's office was summoned to note her statement in full.
>
> "It was the longest statement made by the woman since her connection with the mystery. It will be used at trial. The negress was calm and composed upon emerging from the examination."

That the solicitor sworn to maintain the law, should this falsely arrest one against whom he has no charge and whom he does not even suspect, and torture her contrary to the laws, to force her to give evidence tending to swear away the life of an innocent man is beyond belief.

Where will this end? My husband and my family and myself are innocent sufferers now, but who will be the next to suffer? I suppose the witnesses tortured will be confined to the class who are not able to employ lawyers to relieve them from the torture in time to prevent their being forced to give false affidavits but the lives sworn away may come from any class.

It will be noted that the plan is to apply the torture until the affidavit is wrung from the sufferer. Then it ends, but not before.

It is to be hoped that no person can be convicted of murder in any civilized country on evidence wrung from witnesses by torture. Why, then, does the solicitor continue to apply the third degree to procure testimony? How does he hope to get a jury from knowing the methods to which he has resorted?

Of course, if he can torture witnesses into giving the kind of evidence he wants against my innocent husband in the case, he can torture them into giving evidence against any other man in the community in either this or any other class. I can see only one hope. And that is to let the public know exactly what this officer of the law is doing, and this, as I do trust, to the sense of fairness and justice of the people.

It is not surprising that my cook should sign an affidavit to relieve herself from torture that had been applied to her for four hours, according to the *Atlanta Constitution* "to a point of exhaustion." It would be surprising if she would not, under such circumstances give an affidavit.

This torturing process can be used to produce testimony to be published in the newspapers to prejudice the case of anyone the solicitor sees fit to accuse. It is also valuable to prevent anyone stating facts favorable to the accused because as soon as the solicitor finds it out, he can arrest the witness and apply the torture…

My husband was at home for lunch an in the evening at the hours he has stated on the day of the murder. He spent the whole Saturday evening and night in my company. Neither on Saturday, nor Saturday night, nor Sunday, nor at any other time did my husband by word or act or in any other way, demean himself otherwise than as an innocent man. He did nothing unusual and nothing to arouse the slightest suspicion. I know him to be innocent. There is not evidence against him, except that which is procured by torture.

I have been compelled to endure without fault, either on the part of my husband or myself, more than falls to the lot of most women to bear. Slanders have been circulated in the community to the effect that my husband and myself were not happily married and every conceivable rumor has been put afloat that would do him and me harm with the pubic in site of the fact that all our friends are aware that those statements are false and all his friends and myself know that my husband is a man actuated by lofty ideals that forbid his committing the crime that the detectives and the solicitor are seeking to fasten upon him.

I know my husband innocent. No man could make the good husband to a woman that he has been to me and be a criminal. All his acquaintances know he is innocent. Ask every man that knows him and see if you could find someone who knows him and see if you could find someone who knows him that will say he believes him guilty.

Being a woman, I do not understand the tricks and arts of detectives and prosecuting officers, but I do know Leo Frank and his friends know him and I know and his friends know that he is utterly incapable of committing the crime that these detectives and this solicitor are seeking to fasten upon him.

Respectfully yours,
Mrs. Leo M. Frank[134]

This move on Lucille's part forced Dorsey's hand. He wasn't used to being questioned by the newspapers or a suspect's wife. Minola's loud claims did nothing for Dorsey or the case. He addressed Lucille's letter with a statement of his own:

> I have read the statements printed in the Atlanta newspapers over the signature of Mrs. Leo M. Frank and I have only to say, without in any wise taking issue with her premises, as I might, that the wife of a man accused of crime would probably be the last person to learn all the facts establishing his guilt, and certainly would be the last person to admit his culpability, even though proved by overwhelming evidence to the satisfaction of every impartial citizen beyond the possibility of reasonable doubt.[135]

He goes on to plead his case against Leo in the paper, explaining the grand jury indicted Leo for the crime. He talks about how the "suffering to the relations who are innocent of participation in the crime but who must share the humiliation flowing from its exposure."[136]

Dorsey never addresses the accusations of forcing Minola to sign the affidavit. Instead, subtly undercutting Lucille, he sows doubt as to whether she even wrote the letter—as if she wouldn't articulate such strong views. After all, the prevailing belief at the time was that women, particularly well-bred ladies, did not hold strong opinions, and if a lady dared to disagree with a man of high esteem, she would never do so publicly. He continues to downplay her letter, imply her opinions are unreasonable, and assert that she can't fully know the evidence against her husband. He makes a point of Leo's grand jury indictment but doesn't mention that the foreman of that grand jury, the hardware store owner and Albert's boss, sent his employees to grill Minola. Lucille's valid points clearly struck a nerve with Dorsey.

In the middle of this back and forth in the newspapers, Leo's mother, Ray Frank, arrived in Atlanta to stay with the Seligs and her daughter-in-law. The *Atlanta Georgian* acknowledged her arrival in the paper.

On 8 June, Lucille responded again with a letter to address Dorsey's statement.

> I think fairness to Mr. Frank requires that the public should clearly understand Mr. Dorsey's position as stated by him in his card in the *Constitution* of June 6, and repeated in papers

yesterday in reply to my statement that he proposes to use testimony which comes from witnesses as the result of torture. [Lucille goes on to quote the first part of Dorsey's statement and then concentrates on the part she feels is key.] "that I welcome all evidence from any source that will aid an impartial jury, under charge of the court, in determining the guilt or innocence of the accused."

That is to say, he thinks it unnecessary to waste time in disputing the fact that detectives are procuring testimony from witnesses by torture. He considers this point immaterial. He believes he is thoroughly justified in using tortured testimony, if it is turned over to him for he says: "I welcome all evidence from any source."

The *Journal* and the *Constitution* stated that he had my cook arrested and carried to his office and quizzed to such an extent as to drive her into hysterics, and that after this he sent her screaming to the police station in the patrol wagon. After she left his office, she was taken to detectives' torture chamber, and according to the *Atlanta Constitution*, she had the third degree applied to her to the point of exhaustion after which she made an affidavit, which the detectives or someone immediately gave out to the papers....

I do not wish to be in any manner bitter toward Mr. Dorsey, even in my feelings because it is so perfectly clear his actions is dictated by a serious mistake of judgment, and my only purpose is to let the community understand as thoroughly as I can, in the interest of fairness to my innocent husband, that Mr. Dorsey is proposing to use third-degree torture chamber testimony in an effort to take his life, and he thinks it is perfectly proper for him to do so....

I know I cannot keep up with all the false affidavits and false rumors and innuendos that have been so industriously put in the newspapers, but I feel that I should call attention in this instance to Mr. Dorsey's position, which he so boldly justifies.

Mrs. Leo M. Frank
Atlanta, GA
June 7, 1913[137]

Lucille had found her voice, and she would use it throughout the ordeal she and Leo faced.

Chapter 20

No Thimble-Rigging

In the first week or so of June, Rosser must have felt he could celebrate. Lucille's letters were garnering attention. For the first time since Dorsey became involved with the murder case, his choices were under scrutiny. Lanford's and Beavers's preoccupation with throwing mud at Felder and Burns distracted them from any new investigations.

Luther Rosser decided to address the situation head-on. He wrote his own letter to the newspapers that was published in the 11 June issue of the *Constitution*.

> Editor *Atlanta Constitution*
>
> Felder and Lanford in an effort to make progress in their feud, charge each other with giving aid to Leo Frank. Lanford charges that Felder was employed by Frank and is seeking for that reason to shield him. Felder charges Lanford and his associates are also seeking for some reason, to shield and protect Frank.
>
> Both charges are untrue and, at a time when no harm could come to an innocent man, might well be treated as antidotes to monotony.
>
> Unfortunately, however, the present situation is such that fair-minded citizens may be misled by these counter charges.
>
> Felder does not nor has he at any time directly or indirectly, represented Frank. For Lanford to change the contrary does Frank a serious injustice.
>
> If Chief Lanford had been in some normal mood, he would have known that every act of Felder has been against

> Frank. The engagement of the Burns agency ought to have satisfied Lanford. No detective agency of half prudence would have double-crossed the Atlanta department in the Phagan case. Nor did Felder have excuse for suspicion against Lanford. There was reason to suspect his fairness, his accuracy and soundness of his methods, but not his reckless zeal against Frank.
>
> Had Felder been in a calm mood, I am sure he would never have charged the chief and his associates with intention to help Frank.
>
> Lanford at once, as soon as Felder charged him with favoring Frank, settled in his mind the guilt of Frank, and from that moment has bent every energy of his department, not in finding the murderer, but in trying to prove to the public that Felder was wrong in charging him with trying to shield Frank...[138]

Rosser goes on to point out Lanford made poor choices in his investigation and how they affect Leo. Then he switches the subject to Jim Conley and takes apart the state's star witnesses.

> Conley is very ordinary ignorant, brutal negro, not unacquainted with the stockade. His actions immediately after the crime were suspicious. So much so that they attracted the attention of the employees of the factory and occasioned general comment. In spite of those facts, Conley was not taken into custody until several days after the crime and not then until the employees of the factory caught him suspiciously washing a shirt and as a result reported him to the police. He was not brought before the coroner's jury, and practically no notice was taken of him in that investigation. So swiftly were Lanford and his associates pursuing Frank that they ran over this negro standing in their path with the marks of guilty clearly upon him...

Rosser goes on to point out that Lanford and the detectives didn't give a lot of attention to Conley until he made what he called his last statement that matched the detectives' and prosecution's views of what happened the day of Mary's murder. Then they showed their interest in this man who had made several statements before this last one. Rosser then launched into what Jim's final statement indicated.

> But what a statement: So full of contradictions, so evidently made for self-protection and where was so easily apparent the guiding hand of detective. If Lanford meant to be fair, if he was only seeking the truth, why did he rush into print with the assertion that this statement was the truth and therefore of necessity the last? Might he not in decency have left this negro to his own will, unbiased by the opinion that the statement was true and the last to be given? Who knows but that this negro might have given numerous other statements if he had not been so heavily handicapped by Lanford's opinion?
>
> The truth is, this negro is not to give any other or further statement if the detective department can prevent, unless made under their supervision and direction...
>
> No one has been rude enough to bring this negro before the grand jury, nor, indeed, to make any charge against him.
>
> After the statement of this negro and in view of all the evidence which so strongly points to him as the slayer of little Mary Phagan, is the grand jury to leave him without charge or investigation to be wet-nursed by Lanford until Frank's trial?
>
> Or is it the purpose to keep the negro's case from the grand jury in the nature of an offered reward to spur him on to swear his worst against the white man?
>
> Would it not be just and decent to bring this negro's case before the grand jury and let that body hear his confession, so that it can then decide whether the negro should then be indicted?

> In the shadow of this great crime let there be no thimble-rigging: let no single fact be concealed: let no man's place or reputation stand in the way of the fullest, fairest, fairest investigation.
>
> Respectfully,
>
> Luther S. Rosser

ଓ

When Judge Roan, who would preside over Leo's trial, read Rosser's statement, he called Hugh Dorsey and informed him that Conley should be moved from the county jail at police headquarters, where Dorsey could control who talked to him, back to the Tower. The law said that Conley was a material witness, so he needed to be in the county jail where Sheriff Mangum would protect him from those who wanted to influence his testimony. Of course, this meant Dorsey couldn't keep Conley quiet. Rosser must have been happy, Dorsey not so much. Dorsey and William Smith showed up in Judge Roan's office to file a petition saying Jim Conley should be released since he was not a material witness. This move must have dumbfounded Judge Roan, who decided he would set a hearing two days later to decide the matter. As strange as Dorsey's request was, he was thinking on his feet.

On Friday morning, 13 June, all the lawyers involved in the case and reporters met in Judge Roan's courtroom. The *Atlanta Constitution* reported that Dorsey had every intention of rearresting Conley if Roan released him during the hearing. Dorsey wanted to prevent Jim Conley from being taken back to the Tower. If Dorsey rearrested Jim upon his release, he could charge him with suspicion of Mary's murder and hold him in the county jail at police headquarters. And sure enough, the *Constitution* ran a story on page two of the Saturday paper with the headline "Conley Released Then Rearrested." The *Constitution* went on to explain that as soon as Judge Roan ordered Jim Conley to be released, the city detectives rearrested him and held him on a charge of suspicion of murder: "By this the detective department and Solicitor Hugh Dorsey won their first point, as had the negro been ordered held by the state, he would have been transferred to the Tower and placed in the custody of the sheriff, where the detectives could not have reached him at their own free will."[139]

The re-arrest came as no surprise to anyone. Rosser was aware of Dorsey's intention from the beginning, and William Smith, Conley's lawyer, was aware of what would happen before the group showed up in the courtroom for the hearing. He did not want his client to be free to roam and get into trouble. Rosser didn't view Conley as a material witness; he viewed him as guilty of the murder and strongly protested, denouncing Jim Conley's affidavits as unbelievable. Rosser pointed out that Lanford was not the right person to have custody of Conley. He suggested that the sheriff of Fulton County was an unbiased officer of the law.

The sheriff was indignant that anyone would suggest Conley had been intimidated or threatened while in the cell in the Tower. He challenged the reporters to "[p]rove all this stuff about intimidation of Conley or of any other man, white or black."[140]

Employees of the pencil factory still spoke out in support of Leo's innocence. R. P. Barrett, the foreman of the metal room where Mary worked and the man who found the hair and blood, wrote to the *Atlanta Georgian*, explaining why he believed Jim Conley killed Mary Phagan. Barrett made the point that if Jim found Mary's body on the floor of the plating department near the ladies' toilet, why had there been no blood there? He said Conley's story looked shaky.

While this scuffle around Jim took place, Atlanta's early summer weather turned upside down. The *Atlanta Georgian* reported that readers should get out their winter coats because the highs would be fifty—not in the low eighties. Leo remained quiet and enjoyed visits from family and friends. Lucille was among them. On one Sunday and Monday, the *Atlanta Georgian* reported that Leo received more than thirty visitors. After they left, Lucille dined with Leo for their afternoon meal. Both Leo and Lucille were convinced that a trial would set the story straight.

On Sunday, 15 June, Hugh Dorsey embraced the idea of appointing a legislative committee to investigate the penal system. He stated juries in Georgia had difficulties convicting a man even when his guilt was evident:

> I think one of the difficulties lies in the fact that the members of the average jury know that the conditions which surround a convict in Georgia tend to make a man worse and not better, and that juries are consequently reluctant to deliver even a guilty man into the hands of justice that will merely inflict punishment on him without much likelihood of doing him any good.

The ever-present thoughts of his appearance are reflected in this statement.

On Monday, Frank A. Hooper, a well-known criminal lawyer assisting Dorsey, announced that the Mary Phagan murder case was ready for trial and that the crime had been investigated from every angle. Hugh Dorsey left for a weeklong vacation, proving that the prosecution was confident and relaxed.

Lucille broke her silence and gave an interview to reassure those following the case that she had absolute confidence in her husband's innocence. This interview showed she had reconciled with the fact that they had to walk through the process of the law. She reiterated that nothing about Leo or his nature could be compared to the kind of person it took to commit the murder.

> In all the year and a half of our engagement, in the happy knowledge and consent of both our parents, I was Leo's "best girl" and he was my one and only beau. If I went to a party, it was conceded that I should go with Leo, and if Leo went, he invariably went with me. You know, the people of my faith do those things in that way—with us, betrothal is all but as sacred as marriage itself.
>
> Leo Frank and myself have been man and wife for two years and a half. I state it as a circumstance showing how

sweet and mutually happy our home life has been, and not as a thing I should mention ordinarily, that during all the two and a half years of our wedded life not once has Leo been away from me at night, save when once a month he attended the meetings of Jewish Order of B'nai Brith, of which he was president in Atlanta until he was arrested.

He might have gone out in the evenings, perhaps without my knowledge, to places he should not have gone, so far as my free consent may have figured as a factor in his going. I merely cite it as a truthful circumstance that he has not elected to go. He seemed rather to prefer staying home with me. Naturally, that made me very happy—for I am, after all, a woman, like other women, and a woman never gets to the point where she does not dearly love for her husband to show her that he is still her sweetheart.

We have lived here in this house with my father and mother. To them, Leo has been devoted and always most considerate. They love him as a son; they took him close to their hearts before the wedding bells had ceased to ring—for that is the way our people do in those matters.

We have no children of our own, unfortunately, but there are several nieces and nephews in the family and to every one of them Mr. Frank is affectionately attached. I have seen him play with a two-year-old child for hours, not once, but many times.

She talks about his involvement with the Hebrews' Orphan Home by working with Mr. Milton Klein providing outdoor recreation.

Is a man who loves children as Leo Frank loves them likely to have a hand in the slaying of an innocent child, not yet budded into youthful womanhood, as Mary Phagan is said to have been?

> If there is one person in all the world he has been more devoted to than to me, it is his aged and blind uncle, M. Frank.

Moses Frank, an aging man with no children, was the uncle who talked Leo into coming to work for him at the pencil factory. By all accounts, both Leo and his sister were close to this uncle. Lucille goes on to address Jim Conley's role in the case.

> I think my knowledge of Leo Frank and the kind of man he is is worth more than the word of a shiftless negro who has lied persistently and vigorously ever since he was arrested as a suspect—but while my voice will be hushed in the court room, his will be heard by both the judge and the jury trying my husband for his life.

Lucille spoke out for all women even if she wasn't aware of the truth her words rang. Women had few rights in 1913. They couldn't vote, buy or own land, testify for or against their husbands in court, and or watch a court trial unless they had an intimate connection to someone involved in the case. Despite Lucille's bitterness about Leo's arrest, she had to believe that justice would win out. "We await the trial of Leo Frank in confidence," she said. "We have come to think that, after all, we shall get fair treatment—and as that is all we have asked for, we are more and more optimistic every day as to the conclusion."[141]

Chapter 21

Moving Toward Trial

After Dorsey sidetracked Conley's transfer back to the Tower, pencil factor owner Sig Montag and attorney Herbert Haas understood that the prosecution was on its toes and more of a challenger than they first thought. The two men decided to hire Reuben R. Arnold to work alongside Luther Z. Rosser, not because Rosser wasn't extremely capable but because Arnold was good at conflict resolution. Rosser was straightforward and charged into arguing a case like no other lawyer in Georgia could. Arnold was discreet and could be trusted with anything involving his client. He grew up in a world of privilege, living in his father's grand home on Peachtree Street just north of Atlanta.

In June 1913, Arnold was forty-five and had made his own fortune in a law firm whose largest client was the *Atlanta Journal.* He also had a good relationship with Georgia senator Hoke Smith and became one of his trusted lieutenants.

When Dorsey left town, the newspapers announced Arnold was joining Leo's defense team. "After studying the evidence as critically as I can," Arnold told the *Atlanta Georgian*, "I am satisfied that I hazard not a thing in saying that there is no room to believe Mr. Frank guilty of this horrible murder."[142]

On the Wednesday before Dorsey left for his vacation, twelve books of one hundred pages each—evidence, interviews, and reports on the murder—were delivered to the solicitor's office. Discussions of moving the trial to a larger venue began; Dorsey felt many of the public would attend, and more seating would be required. At the same time, the grand jury called Chief Lanford to testify about the "third degree" Lucille had decried in her letters concerning the conduct of the detectives and prosecution. Her voice had brought into question whether the investigation of Mary's murder was biased due to how officers and detectives treated suspected witnesses.

As Dorsey prepared to leave for vacation, he told a reporter that he had asked Fannie and Will Coleman if they approved of his leaving his assistant, Frank A. Hooper, in charge of the investigation while he was gone. The couple approved. Again, Dorsey's actions seemed to milk his concern for Fannie and Will Coleman and their feelings about the investigation. Hadn't Hooper already announced to a reporter that the prosecution was ready for trial?

Chief Lanford attempted to downplay the way detectives "interviewed" witnesses. The *Atlanta Constitution*, reporting on Lanford's testimony to the grand jury, wrote, "In Conley's case, Chief Lanford told the jury the Negro's confession had been secured through clever detective work in confronting him with damaging discrepancies in his stories of innocence."[143]

Lanford went into great detail about the detectives' technique of grilling a suspect or witness. He seems intent on convincing the working-class citizens, the readers and followers of the Mary Phagan murder case, that officers don't treat witnesses and suspects as Lucille described in her letters.

☙

Because Dorsey had requested a change of venue before leaving on his trip, the trial was set to begin on 30 June in a cramped courtroom of the poorly ventilated Thrower Building. On 24 June, Rosser and Arnold came before Judge Roan in his chambers with a scheduling problem. In mid-July, the two lawyers would be in a Swainsboro courtroom for the murder trial of Dr. W. J. McNaughton and Mattie Flanders, both accused of poisoning Mattie's husband, Fred, whose property and life insurance were worth ten thousand dollars. This would not be the only link Dr. W. J. McNaughton would have with Leo Frank.

Hugh Dorsey, now back from his trip, said the trial should be over by mid-July. He said the defense was stalling. Judge Roan pointed out that if the trial took place as planned on 30 June, they would be in the

Thrower Building, but if they delayed a month, the trial could be held in the more spacious courtroom of the Atlanta City Hall, on the corner of Pryor and Hunter streets and across from the Fulton County Courthouse. Delaying wasn't a perfect solution, but the room in City Hall had numerous large windows for ventilation. Also, Judge Roan admitted that he promised his wife that he would take her to the seashore for the week of Independence Day. He complained of fatigue and said he could use some time off.

Dorsey relented. The trial would begin 28 July. Now Frank's attorneys, Luther Rosser and Reuben Arnold, had some time to work on the state's star witness's testimony. Their goal remained that Conley should be indicted. The attorneys also hoped to gather a body of evidence so large they could upend the prosecution.

Rosser and Arnold worked on their strategy to get Conley indicted. If they needed to become to meet that goal, that's what they'd do. At the very least, they would gather evidence to prove Leo's innocence when the trial began on 28 July.

The "night extra" edition of the 9 July *Atlanta Georgian* revealed new evidence: Miss Mattie Smith, who worked at the pencil factory, said that she had seen a Black man sitting on the first floor of the pencil factory between nine and ten that morning. Conley had denied being there at that time. A few feet from where Conley himself said he was sitting, someone found a torn piece of a pay envelope behind a radiator with Mary Phagan's employee number on it. The paper went on to say that a motive of robbery was still under consideration.

What the *Georgian* neglected to explain was that the torn pay envelope was not new evidence. The prosecution and defense were aware of it, but both determined it was unreliable. The torn envelope was just part of evidence found on 15 May by Pinkerton detectives.

W. D. McWorth wrote in his report:

> At 3:15 p.m. I was joined by L. P. W. at the trap door I found what I took to be blood stains and also several pieces of cord used to bundle pencils, and which was entwined in the pipes a radiator adjoining the trap door. I also picked up a roll of

> paper and on examining it, found it to be the end of an envelope. I could see the number 186 stamped in the left hand corner and a name written in lead pencil. I gave the paper to L. P. W. to take into the daylight, and he returned, saying that the name on the envelope was M. Phagan. Below the name could be seen the tops of figures, the plainest of which was the last, an aught [0]. This would have matched $1.20 of May's pay the day she was murdered.[144]

Dorsey and Lanford disregarded this evidence because the Atlanta police detectives had not seen it as relevant. They also felt these two Pinkertons, McWorth and L. P. W., sympathized with Leo. It seemed from the beginning that the police believed the murderer planted this evidence to point at another suspect.

Judge W. D. Ellis indefinitely postponed the application for a writ of habeas corpus to allow Newt Lee, still held at the Tower as a material witness, to go free. Lee was said to be unconcerned. "It don't make no difference to me whether I am inside or outside the jail," he said to a reporter. "It's just as the white folks say. I don't know what all this is that's going on."[145]

Dorsey was asked about allowing Lee to go free. "I have advised against this action, and I have no idea that it will be successful…," he said, "permitting him to go free would be taking serious chances of losing him as a witness when the case comes to trial."[146] Dorsey again was placing a controlling hand on his witnesses for the prosecution.

A few days after the announcement that new evidence had been found, the *Atlanta Georgian* again reported sensational news: a new eyewitness, Will Green, had been found. Green, who was Black, boasted to someone that he had seen Conley kill Mary Phagan. The *Georgian* gave his story:

> I was in Atlanta for a few days. I was shooting craps on the first floor [of the pencil factory] with this negro that Saturday. This fellow was half drunk and was losing money to me. He got mad and cursed his luck.

> Before long a little girl went upstairs. This negro said he was going to take her money away from her when she came down. I thought he was fooling at first, but when she came down he started for her. I yelled at him not to do it, but he kept right on. Then I skipped out, for I didn't want to get mixed up in any trouble. I stayed around town until the next Monday, and then I read all about how a little girl had been killed in the National Pencil factory, and I knew that she was the one I had seen come downstairs at the factory.
>
> I got out of town right away and went back to St. Louis. They were surprised to see me back there, and I told a few of them how I happened to come back. That's how they found out that I had seen what I did.[147]

The paper claimed that police had hunted Will Green since May when his story first came out. Frank Morrow, whom Will Green had taken care of for several months in St. Louis, wired Atlanta as soon as Green told him the story. The Atlanta police paid little attention to his wire because they had received many tips of no value. By the time they got around to investigating the tip, Green had vanished from St. Louis. Morrow sent word to the Atlanta police that he believed there was still a chance to catch up to Green, who had gone to Birmingham. While the defense wanted to interview Green, the prosecution doubted his story because it had arrived to them as hearsay. But the story was enough to make the *Atlanta Georgian*'s readers wonder if Conley could be the real murderer. All the defense needed was a confession from Conley. Soon they got something close to one.

William H. Mincey, a salesman for American Insurance Company, made a startling statement in an affidavit. On the afternoon of the murder, Mincey met Conley near Electric and Carter streets. According to the *Georgian*, Jim was sitting with his head in his hands and seemed drunk.

"How about that insurance?" Mincey says he asked Conley.

"Get away from here. I don't want no insurance," Conley is said to have replied. Mincey pushed Conley to buy insurance.

"I tell you I don't want no insurance. I'm in trouble. I don't want you to bother me," Mincey swears Conley retorted. Mincey continued to push him to buy insurance, and Conley grew angry.

"You go away. I'll be in jail in a few days and I won't want any insurance." When Mincey didn't leave, Conley jumped to his feet.

"I've killed a girl to-day: I don't want to kill nobody else!"

Mincey chalked the comment up to a drunk man's bragging and went about his business. When he saw in the paper that Mary had been murdered, he thought of Conley and went to the factory to speak with E. F. Holloway, the day watchman. He asked him how many Black men worked at the pencil factory. Holloway replied seven or eight.

"You should have every one of them arrested at once," Mincey told him.[148]

Holloway had said Conley hadn't been in the factory that day, not knowing at that time that Conley had indeed been there. Mincey went to the police, but they didn't want his story. Later, women who had been standing nearby when Mincey had the conversation with Conley admitted they heard him tell Mincey he had killed a girl.

The *Atlanta Georgian* kept their pro-Leo Frank stance by either building up the defense's case or attacking the prosecution's. Frank's attorneys, Rosser and Arnold, sponsored a letter-writing campaign asking the grand jury to take up the evidence against Conley. The grand jury that had indicted Leo had cycled off, and a fresh jury was seated. They were flooded with letters requesting Conley be indicted. The defense's efforts seemed futile because no grand jury had ever gone against the solicitor's wishes. Dorsey wanted no part of indicting Jim Conley, but things were about to change.

W. D. Beattie, the new jury foreman, visited Dorsey's office on Friday, 18 July, and asked Dorsey to call the jury into session so they could consider the new and overwhelming evidence against Jim Conley. Dorsey rejected the request. Beatie bypassed the solicitor and called a meeting of the grand jury for Monday morning at ten o'clock. This would be seven days before Leo's trial began. No grand jury had ever done such a thing.

The newspapers reported that Dorsey told Beattie that the attempt "to indict Conley is wrong and should not be made."[149]

The grand jury's Monday meeting sent many connected to the prosecution's case into a frenzy. William Smith, Conley's lawyer, told the *Constitution* that his client probably would be indicted following the meeting. In a long statement to the press, he asked, "What more could the grand jury ask? Conley is giving the state a square deal. Conley is remaining a voluntary prisoner, and no honest citizen doubts that he would be held to account for his part in the terrible tragedy." He went on to point out that if the grand jury doesn't want to be perceived as pleasing "Frank and his friends, they had better leave this alone for the present."

Smith then asked, "Does the grand jury think their legal judgment or their personal integrity above that of our solicitor general, or do they doubt the professional or private character of Hugh Dorsey?" William Smith's words must have mattered to the grand jury and the public. He wasn't flashy like some lawyers, but his character provided him with some clout.

"It is the supreme test of a man's good character, and I glory in the fact that Hugh Dorsey has those high and honorable traits of his good father and mother that enable him to know the right, and knowing the right, to dare to do it."[150]

The July days had settled into Georgia with record-setting temperatures. Atlanta peaked at ninety-seven. On that Saturday, the newspapers were abuzz with the grand jury's upcoming meeting while further south, temperatures were hitting 104 and 107 degrees. Dorsey made a statement to the newspaper concerning the grand jury and the foreman who overruled him.

> Its only purpose will be to exploit the evidence and embarrass the state, and I hope the grand jury when it meets will decide to leave the matter alone.

> The indictment of Conley at this time will be a useless procedure that will not stop the trial of Frank. It will only have a mild but undesirable effect on the state's case.
>
> Conley is in jail and is going to stay there for some time. He is where the authorities can put their hands on him, and he can be indicted much more properly after the Frank case has been disposed of than before, and by delay there is no danger of a miscarriage of justice.[151]

On the same day that the grand jury foreman called the meeting, the Pinkerton detectives stated they had changed their opinion in the murder case: They believed Jim Conley was guilty and Leo Frank was innocent. "The Pinkertons at the coming trial—or any others that may result from the case—will give fair and impartial testimony," Harry Scott told a reporter. "Whether it affects Frank or the negro is no concern of ours. We were employed to apprehend the murderer."[152]

The prediction in the Sunday newspapers was the grand jury would indict Conley the following Monday, and Dorsey would not convince them otherwise. Leo's attorneys had to speak up about the special grand jury session. They began their statement with a disclaimer, explaining they would never make a statement to the newspapers except when they felt the situation warranted the attention. "Clearly counsel on both sides," they said, "should refrain from any comment of or criticism on any action of the Grand Jury to be taken at its meeting next Monday, which might tend to hamper or limit the Grand Jury in their action upon the Conley case." The defense was thrilled the letter-writing campaign had successfully applied pressure on the grand jury. Events were working in Leo's favor, and the attorneys wanted to give verbal support to the jury. "The Grand Jury is an independent body," they said; "it is under the control of no one."

The defense raised the point that the solicitor general was only an adviser of legal principles to the jury; Dorsey's office could not decide who would or would not be indicted. Then Rosser and Arnold replied to Dorsey's statement of the day before. They used Dorsey's own words—"mild but undesirable effect on the state's case against Leo M. Frank"—to drive home their point against the solicitor.

> Ought the Solicitor General for one moment to be influenced in his advice to the Grand Jury by any consideration of the effect upon anybody's ease?... The solicitor has closed his eyes to these plain truths and has rushed into print, day by day, proclaiming the guilt of Frank and the innocence of this negro apparently for no purpose but to convict Frank, innocent or guilty, for the gratification of his professional pride.[153]

This comment hit the proverbial nail on the head and gave voice to suspicions that Dorsey invested so much time in the Phagan case to serve his own aspirations. So went the sparring between the prosecution and defense just one day before the grand jury would consider indicting Conley and one week before Leo's trial would begin.

In the same issue of the *Georgian*, there was a column by a writer who called himself "An Old Police Reporter." He addressed Mincey's story that Conley confessed to the murder after Mincey badgered him to buy insurance. "An Old Police Reporter" commented that the most interesting development in the Phagan case for the whole week was not the grand jury's meeting to consider Conley's indictment but the insurance salesman's affidavit.

"If what Mincey says is true—if his evidence can be made to 'stand up' in court—then he is far and away not only the most important witness yet discovered, but his testimony could serve to clear up the mysterious Phagan case in its most obscure phases," he wrote.

The writer went on to point out that if Dorsey can cast doubt on Mincey's affidavit or on Mincey himself, the grand jury may sway with the prosecution. Either the prosecution or defense would lose. Where did this leave the clients, Conley and Leo?[154]

Only time and a trial would tell. Because no matter what the grand jury decided about Conley's indictment, Leo Frank would be tried for the murder of Mary Phagan.

ↄↄ

Monday brought the searing heat that pushed temperatures to ninety-nine. The grand jury met, and only Hugh Dorsey appeared before them. When the session ended over an hour later, the Dorsey appeared and spoke to reporters.

"I am requested by the Grand Jury to say no action will be taken at this time on the James Conley matter, and that the body will not pay any attention whatever to anonymous communications." "Anonymous communications," of course, referred to the letter-writing campaign. Dorsey also brought up a recent Supreme Court ruling that defined the solicitor general's role in indictments:

> He is to determine whether or not to commence a particular prosecution, or to discontinue one already begun. The Solicitor General draws the bill of indictment and examines the witnesses, not with a view to the interest of any client, but alone to sub-serve public justice.
>
> The whole prosecution from the time the case is laid before him is under his direction, supervision and control.—102 Georgia, page 271[155]

Ruben Arnold was asked about the decision made by the grand jury. "The indictment of Conley is a matter of indifference to us," he replied.[156]

The defense and prosecution moved on to jury selection that would begin so all would be ready for the beginning of the trial the next Monday. Dorsey made it known that he would fight the defense's request for the jurors to be pulled from the grand jury and not the petit jury box. The difference between the two was stark: Registered voters made up the petit jury pool. The grand jury was made up of influential citizens. The judge rejected the defense's request. The solicitor pointed out that the move showed the defense's desperation, not to mention that it reflected their position of privilege.

The courtroom on the first floor of the old Chamber of Commerce building was prepared for the trial. Janitors doubled the number of seats and benches so at least part of crowd that was sure to attend could be seated. Also, they placed twelve large electric fans throughout the room for some movement of the hot air.

On Thursday, Dorsey and Hooper, his assistant, interrogated Jim Conley and Newt Lee for about two hours. This was the first time these the two suspects were brought together. Nothing much was gained from these interviews, but Conley did declare that Lee knew nothing about the murder.

The Sunday afternoon before the trial, Jim Conley was preparing his testimony at police headquarters. There had been several late-night meetings, referred to as "midnight séances," with Conley going through a sort of boot camp. Detectives Black, Starnes, and Scott, along with Chief Lanford and Dorsey, went through every piece of Conley's upcoming testimony with him. Smith trained Conley in public speaking and even went as far as to copy Luther Rosser's style so Conley would be prepared for questioning by the defense lawyers.[157]

That Sunday afternoon, Lucille, Ray, and several friends gathered for a party of sorts at the Tower. Lucille brought fresh peaches and finger foods as if they were at a party in their own home, friends and family confident that Leo would be vindicated. Leo might have needed his own training instead.

Illustration showing Cohen & Selig store, Whitehall Street, Atlanta, Georgia, ca. late 1800s.

Courtesy Chuck Marcus

The graves of Sarah and Harry Silverman,
Oakland Cemetery, Atlanta, Georgia.

Courtesy Jerry C. Hite

Lucille Selig Frank.

Courtesy William Breman Jewish Heritage Museum

The graves of Jonas and Reginia Cohen,
Oakland Cemetery, Atlanta, Georgia.

Courtesy Jerry C. Hite

The graves of Josephine and Emil Selig. The ashes of Lucille Selig Frank were buried between her parents, Oakland Cemetery, Atlanta, Georgia.

Courtesy Jerry C. Hite

Reuben Arnold, Leo Frank's trial attorney, 1913.

Courtesy P. F. Collier and Son Corporation

COLLIER'S FOR DECEMBER 19, 1914

Mrs. Leo M. Frank,
Wife of condemned man

Mrs. J. W. Coleman,
Mother of Mary Phagan

Mary Phagan,
the murdered girl

Judge L. S. Roan,
Who presided at Frank's trial

Solicitor General Hugh M. Dorsey,
Who prosecuted Frank

Top L to R: Lucille Frank and Fannie Coleman (Mary's mother); Middle: Mary Phagan; Bottom L to R: Judge L. S. Roan, who presided over Leo's trial and Hugh Dorsey, Solicitor General.

Courtesy P. F. Collier and Son Corporation

What is believed to be Leo Frank's wedding ring.

Viewing the ring courtesy Chuck Marcus; photo courtesy Jerry C. Hite

Leo Frank.

Courtesy Library of Congress

Funeral flowers being delivered to Leo Frank's childhood home,
Brooklyn, New York, 1915.

Courtesy Library of Congress

The jury that convicted Leo Frank, 1913.

The Leo Frank Case *by Leonard Dinnerstein*

Luther Rosser, Leo Frank's trial attorney, 1913.

Courtesy P. F. Collier and Son Corporation

Leo Frank during trial.

Courtesy P. F. Collier and Son Corporation

The grave of Herbert Clay, one of the masterminds of Leo's kiddnapping and lynching. His grave is within sight of Mary Phagan's grave. Marietta Cemetery, Marietta, Georgia.

Courtesy Jerry C. Hite

The grave of Frances (Fannie) Coleman, mother of Mary Phagan, Marietta Cemetery, Marietta, Georgia.

Courtesy Jerry C. Hite

The grave of Mary Phagan,
Marietta Cemetery, Marietta, Georgia.

Courtesy Jerry C. Hite

Part of Mary Phagan's memorial at her grave,
Marietta Cemetery, Marietta, Georgia.

Courtesy Jerry C. Hite

The Phagan burial plot,
Marietta Cemetery, Marietta, Georgia.

Courtesy Jerry C. Hite

Historical marker at the grave of Mary Phagan,
Marietta Cemetery, Marietta, Georgia.

Courtesy Jerry C. Hite

Jewish section of Oakland Cemetery,
Atlanta, Georgia.

Courtesy Jerry C. Hite

Chapter 22

The Trial Begins

Deputy Sheriff Minor came to collect Leo from his cell early. "How are you feeling this morning, Mr. Frank?" he asked.

"Tip-top…," Leo replied.[158]

A little after seven o'clock, Leo and Newt Lee were taken to the courthouse before the crowds gathered. As he arrived at the courthouse, Leo stopped to speak to a reporter:

> I am very sure of acquittal. I am glad the trial is about to begin after the long wait. I have no fear of the outcome. I am not only innocent of the terrible crime, but I am innocent of any knowledge of it, save as the information has come to me since the officers came to my house that morning three months ago.[159]

Then he was escorted to an anteroom of the second-floor courtroom to wait for the trial to begin. Leo paced. Charles Ursenbach, Leo's brother-in-law, brought him a big breakfast from home and talked with him while Leo ate with gusto. The celebration the evening before might suggest that Leo and Lucille felt the trial was a formality, that jurors would see through Dorsey's prejudice, that the lawyers would reveal details about Dorsey's treatment of witnesses—but most of all, they would see Jim Conley for who he was, Mary Phagan's murderer.

After nine, Lucille and Ray, Leo's mother, appeared. Leo perked up with a smile. Lucille took Leo into her arms, kissing him in front of everyone. His mother tweaked him on the chin, and he laughed.

As the beginning of the trial neared, a great crowd gathered in front of the courthouse and made passing by Pryor Street and Hunter difficult. Streetcars struggled to maneuver through their routes. Spectators jammed the halls of the courthouse, attempting to be one of those allowed inside. Deputies had to cut a path through to get the lawyers and newspaper reporters inside. Upstairs, witnesses and the 144 men in the jury pool waited.

As Leo was escorted into the courtroom that hot morning, it was the first time in months he had seen a crowd. He looked around at the faces, acknowledging one of the women who worked at the pencil factory. He took his seat in front of Judge Roan's bench, next to the table where his lawyers sat. "He was dressed with scrupulous neatness in a gray suit of pronounced pattern which was all conspicuous," reported the *Atlanta Constitution.*[160] Many of his friends, who were allowed to sit close by, inside the rail, came and grasped Leo's hand. The spectators stirred as they strained to see the man at the center of so much attention.

The spectators were even more interested in Lucille as she entered with Ray. She had been seen in public only rarely since Leo's arrest and wore a stylish dress with a stunning dark hat that set her apart from most in the courtroom. An *Atlanta Constitution* reporter described her as "an extremely attractive-looking young woman."[161]

The reporter went on to describe how she kept her stare on Hugh Dorsey. "Her gaze was one of calm estimate," he wrote. "She seemed to be attempting to fathom his thoughts and divine his purposes."

Ray and Lucille sat directly behind Leo. Both seemed calm, hiding the stress that they had been dealing with for three months. The reporter couldn't resist one more comment about Lucille: "Mrs. Frank is a beautiful woman just past the bloom of girlhood and whose attractive face would cause a second look from any man."[162]

Judge Leonard Roan sat in his high-backed leather chair behind his bench. Dorsey, dressed in a regular suit with black brogans, proved he was there to represent the citizens, the working people of Atlanta and Georgia, as a whole. At least five others, including William Smith, Frank Hooper, and assistant solicitor Ed Stephens occupied the table directly in front of the judge's bench and witness stand with the jury box to their right. The surprise visitor at the prosecution table was Will Coleman, Mary Phagan's stepfather.

Rosser and Arnold wore white linen suits, though true to who he was, Rosser wore no tie. Herbert Haas, Stiles Hopkins, a partner in Rosser's firm, and Rosser's son, Luther Jr., crowded around the defense table. Oscar Simmons and Paul Goss joined them for the purpose of choosing a jury and carried thick notebooks of information to help make those decisions.

First would come the swearing-in of the many witnesses. Since Dorsey had chosen to keep Conley at police headquarters, Minola McKnight and her husband, Albert, were the star witnesses in this process. When Albert was called, he was discovered to be absent. Bailiffs were sent to find him. Minola was sworn in, and, again, she denied her affidavit and said it had been forced. Next, jurors were chosen. As each one was picked, he was taken to the jury room, which was inaccessible from outside but large and airy. The windows were some twenty feet above an alley. Deputies were stationed in the alley to keep anyone from getting into the room. For lunch, the jury would be led to a restaurant across the street from the courthouse. At night, they would be taken, under heavy guard, to the Kimball House Hotel. Once chosen, the juror could not go home or communicate with anyone other than fellow jurors. Ten deputies and ten county police were on duty in the streets each day.

The jury would be chosen from 144 men. Rosser had twenty challenges. Some feared that this process would be lengthy, but by one thirty, the jury had been chosen in the case of *The State of Georgia vs. Leo M. Frank*: A. H. Henslee, F. V. L. Smith, J. F. Higdon, F. E. Winburn, A. L. Wisby, W. M. Jeffries, Marcellus Johemming, M. L. Woodward, J. T. Osburn, D. Townsend, W. S. Medcalf, and C. J. Bosshardt.

Court recessed for lunch.

ᘓ

Fannie Coleman, Mary's mother, took the stand as the first witness that afternoon. She wore her mourning dress of black satin and a large black hat, complete with veil. Dorsey began simply, by asking her name and when she had last seen Mary alive. What had Mary had to eat that morning? What was Mary's age?

Dorsey bent down, picked up a suitcase, and placed it on the table. An assistant took the clothes Mary had been wearing out of the suitcase and placed them in front of Fannie. Fannie had shaded her eyes throughout the testimony because the sunlight through the window shone in her eyes.

"What did she wear when you saw her last time?" Dorsey asked.

"Lavender dress trimmed in lace," Fannie replied. She took her hand away from her eyes and spied the clothes. A long sob escaped her.

Ray Frank covered her face and hung her head. Leo, on the other hand, kept from looking at Fannie even though he was right there in front of her. Either the emotion of Mary's mother was too much for him or he was unwilling to look at the clothes. The *Constitution* believed it was the latter. Deputy Sheriff Minor brought Fannie a glass of water that seemed to help.

Dorsey felt her response was enough of an answer. He passed cross examination to Rosser, who was aware of his disadvantage. Both Lucille and Ray reacted emotionally when Fannie broke down. The jurors soaked up the scene.

"What trimming was on Mary's hat?" Rosser began.

"Pale blue ribbon and some small pink flowers."

"How far do you live from the car line?"

"Two blocks."

"Is there a store there?"

"Yes."

"Who kept the store?"

"Mrs. Smith."

"Do you know that Mary caught a car immediately, leaving home at 11:45 o'clock?"

"Yes, she caught a car in five or seven minutes."

"Do you know the boy who was with her?"

"Yes, Epps," Fannie said.

Dorsey objected, asking the purpose of the question be made clear.

"It is necessary for me to know the relation between little Mary Phagan and this boy," Rosser answered.

"I don't know what's on his mind...," Dorsey declared. "We ought to know if he intends to endeavor to impeach this witness."

"We are simply trying to find how Mary Phagan regarded this boy," Rosser said.

Judge Roan allowed Rosser to continue his line of questioning.

"Isn't it true that Mary told you that she detested Epps—that she didn't like him?"

Dorsey objected. Rosser withdrew the question.

"Didn't you tell L. P. Whitfield that Mary told you she detested Epps?"

Again, there was an objection from Dorsey, who claimed the question was immaterial and hearsay.

"I am going to show the improbability of Mary Phagan making an engagement to meet this boy Epps," Rosser explained. The judge allowed the question.

Fannie said she believed Mary had made this remark.

Next on the witness stand was George Epps. Head cleanly shaved, he was barefoot and held a crumpled hat. Dorsey questioned the boy about his age and where he lived. Then he asked Epps when he last saw Mary alive. Epps said that he last laid eyes on Mary on the streetcar riding into the city.

"What time did you leave her?" Dorsey asked.

"Seven minutes past twelve," Epps answered.

"Did you ever see these clothes?"

"She had them on when I left her."

"Where did she say she was going?"

"Right to the factory to draw her pay."

"Did you expect to meet her again?"

"She said she would meet me at 2 o'clock to see the parade. I left her at Forsyth and Marietta Streets at 7 minutes past 12. She was going to the factory then."

"What did she say about Frank?"

Rosser was on his feet with an objection. Judge Roan agreed with Rosser, and Dorsey turned Epps over to the defense.

"How do you know the time?" Rosser asked.

"I saw a clock on Oliver Street, right after I got on the car. It was about 10 minutes to 12," said Epps.

The defense went on to ask Epps when he remembered seeing the clock. His answer was the day he testified at the coroner's inquest.

"Where were you about 12 o'clock?" Rosser asked.

"I don't know exactly where the car was," Epps replied.

"How do you tell time when you can't see a clock?"

"I tell by the sun."

"Can you come pretty close?"

"Yes."

"Are you sure Mary Phagan got off the car with you?"

"I am certain. She got off when I did."

Rosser asked Epps about the timeline he had given. He repeated the same story each time he was asked. He waited for Mary at Elkin Drug Company from two o'clock until four o'clock and never left his post. When Mary hadn't shown by four, he went to the ballgame and finished selling his newspapers.

Epps was excused from the witness stand.

Newt Lee was called to testify next. He told the same story that he had told several times before. His answers were on point. At 5:12 p.m., the court was adjourned for the day. He would return to the stand on Tuesday morning when the court was back in session.

Leo and Lee were taken back to the Tower. Day one of the trial was over.[163]

If one entered the courtroom on the second day, they would have seen a subtle contrast from the day before. Sheriff Mangum and Deputy Minor brought Leo to the courthouse around seven forty-five. He was dressed to perfection, wearing a blue mohair suit and a gray tie. When asked how he was, he answered as he had the prior day: "I am feeling well and confident. Nothing has taken place to disturb me in the least. I hope that the trial will move as rapidly toward its conclusion as the first day's session gave promise. I have nothing to conceal and nothing to fear."[164] But, instead of the hearty breakfast he consumed the first day of trial, the second morning was a bottle of milk and two pieces of toast.

Large crowds filled both sides of Pryor Street, near Hunter Street, by nine o'clock that morning. Lucille and Ray, along with other family members, used the side door into the courthouse to avoid attention from the crowd outside. When Leo was escorted into the courtroom that morning, the *Atlanta Georgian* described his face as a mask. The same reporter went on to describe Lucille: "There isn't anything the least bit 'weepy' or downcast about her. She's a woman—the accused man's wife—but she plainly is a most extraordinary woman, nevertheless." Of Leo, he wrote, "Of all the defendants I ever saw arraigned, Leo Frank, I think looks the least the part of a murderer!"[165]

Newt Lee took the stand to continue his testimony from the first day. He didn't give an inch on his story. Rosser's efforts to make Lee's testimony untrustworthy managed to show only a few discrepancies between his original story and the one he told at the coroner's inquest. Newspaper reporters thought the consistency made Newt Lee look like a reliable witness. Leo's lawyers tried to use the testimonies of Lee and L. S. Dobbs, one of the first police at the pencil factory that morning, to reinforce their contention that Conley was the real murderer.

This strategy showed the defense's hand. When the *Atlanta Georgian* called Rosser's cross-examination of Lee "merciless," Leo lost some public sympathy. Nevertheless, Rosser pointed out that Lee, according to his own words, hadn't been checking the entire basement on his rounds. Almost without exception that night, he went only twenty feet from the ladder to check for fire in the dustpan. The one time he went to the back of the basement, he found Mary's body.

Lee explained that he went to the back of the basement to go to the closet (bathroom). When he opened the door, his lantern shone on what looked like a girl's feet. He claimed that as he moved closer, he didn't think the girl was white because of the soot and her curly hair. Then he saw white spots on her face and blood on the side of her head. Rosser pursued this line of questioning suggest that Lee couldn't have identified Mary as White. After all, the officers had to rub her skin with paper and roll one of her stockings down to see the color of her skin because she was covered in soot.

Leo had watched all of Lee's testimony with intense interest. He hadn't taken his eyes off the night watchmen, except when Lucille whispered to him.

Dorsey produced a large, detailed diagram of the pencil factory, showing their theory of how and where the murder happened. He asked Lee about the late-night conversation between Lee and Leo in an office at police headquarters when Leo became agitated with Lee for not admitting to knowing more about the murder. Leo warned Lee, "If you keep that up, we will both go to hell."[166] Dorsey ended his questioning, and Lee was asked to step down from the witness chair at 11:40 a.m. His last statement did nothing to help Leo's case.

As the day went on, it was evident the jovial confidence shown by Leo's family and friends had worn thin. They had begun the first day with great hope after waiting three months for justice. The testimony thus far hadn't changed anything for Leo. If anything, it had hurt Leo's defense. The courtroom spectators felt the testimony was predictable, nothing they hadn't read in the papers before the trial began. Many of them identified with Mary's family, hardworking people who just wanted to make ends meet. They saw Dorsey as an official standing up for working-class people. Mary's stepfather had a seat at the prosecution table, and her siblings and mother were present, even after the first day when her clothes were displayed. On the second day, spectators looked stern. They seemed to understand that this trial would be long and laborious.

Lucille sat behind Leo again. She counseled freely with Leo's lawyers, leaned in and whispered in Leo's ear, smiled at him, and even ran her hand over his shoulder. Her affection for him was obvious. She was stoic during testimony as if she didn't understand that the end of the trial could leave her a widow. Twice, she embraced Leo and kissed him when he was led out of the courtroom for a recess. She left the courtroom with her body straight and head high, like "a woman out for an afternoon of shopping."[167]

L. S. Dobbs followed Lee. He was asked what he saw that Sunday morning and gave the same testimony from the coroner's inquest. When Rosser questioned him, he asked if it was possible for Lee to see Mary's body from where he stood near the ladder that night. Dobbs answered that Lee could see part of the body. Rosser inquired about what was found in the trash heap. Dobbs confirmed Mary's hat and one of her shoes were found there. Rosser brought up the trim from Mary's hat, but Dobbs said neither he nor the others saw the trim that night, but Mary's bloody handkerchief was found on a sawdust pile ten feet from her body.

Next on the stand was J. D. Starnes, who was asked about his phone conversation with Leo that morning. Dorsey's line of questioning asked for a comparison of Lee's calmness and Leo's nervousness. Arnold objected, but the witness was allowed to answer. Rosser gained ground and began a counterattack to tear apart Dorsey's case. Rosser dismantled Starnes's testimony about the blood spots close to the girls' dressing room on the second floor. Had the officers proved they were blood instead of paint? Rosser also got Starnes to admit that the type of cord that the prosecution contended was used to strangle Mary was found throughout the factory, not just on the second floor. Starnes stepped down.

Before court was adjourned for the day, Judge Roan asked the counsel if they had anything else. Dorsey wanted to enter material into evidence: The murder notes, the length of cord, Mary's clothes, and

Bert Green's factory diagram. Rosser objected to the diagram and argued that it wasn't admissible. The diagram indicated that Leo met Mary in his office and accompanied her to the metal room, then took her body to the basement. Rosser turned to Dorsey and said he was surprised that the prosecution would try to pull something over on him.

Dorsey withdrew the diagram. Court was adjourned for the day.

ଓ

By the third day of the trial, everyone had settled into a routine. Leo arrived from the Tower, had breakfast, and made an entrance into the courtroom where Lucille and Ray, always faithful, sat close to him. Spectators lined up to get into the courtroom, and those who didn't get in that day remained on the sidewalk and in the road under the open windows, hoping to catch that piece of evidence that wowed the case. The first two days didn't come close. Rumors had spread that Conley wouldn't testify. He was hidden.

The days were hot and sometimes exceeded one hundred degrees. Even though the courtroom was outfitted with fans, the air hung thick around the gallery, made much worse by the 250-plus people seated inside.

With the key players in place, Boots Rogers, who drove Detective Black to pick up Leo that early Sunday morning after Mary's murder, took the stand. The audience took a collective breath. Maybe this would be the testimony that moved the case along. Whether the break in the monotony favored the prosecution or defense didn't seem to matter.

Rogers's testimony was a letdown as far as new information, but he provided some comic relief. Rogers testified that when Detective Black suggested Leo needed a drink of whiskey to calm his nerves, Lucille went in search of some, only to return with the news her father had drunk it all the night before to aid his acute indigestion. Rosser said that some nights, he had done the same thing. Leo laughed, breaking his stoic expression. Rogers explained that Leo had been nervous that morning; his hands shook, and his voice was unnaturally high. He mentioned that Leo said he didn't know the name Mary Phagan. When questioned about Leo viewing Mary's body at the funeral home, Rogers said he wasn't sure if Leo could see the body, much less her face, from his position at the door.

Rogers's comments about Leo's nerves echoed Lee, Gantt, Dobbs, and Starnes, who had voiced similar opinions. By this point in the trial, nervousness was Leo's only offense. Many people are nervous; it doesn't make one a murderer.

Sixteen-year-old Grace Hicks took the stand next. She was a pretty, soft-spoken girl with ribbons at her throat and sleeves. If not for being Boots Rogers's sister-in-law and working at the pencil factory, Grace wouldn't have been sitting in the witness chair. Girls and women at that time were thought to be fragile and rarely were considered level-headed, mature, or hardworking. Grace worked twelve to fourteen hours every day in a dark, dirty factory for very little money. There was nothing fragile about her.

Once she was seated, Dorsey asked Grace to tell the jury about how she came to identify Mary's body that night. She described how Boots hurried to her home and picked her up in the early morning hours, delivering her to Bloomfield's Funeral Home, where she viewed Mary's body. It was the shade of hair that told Grace it was Mary. The solicitor used questions about the layout of the metal room to support the theory that Mary was attacked near the girls' dressing room. Dorsey asked about Grace collecting Mary's pay.

"Saturday at twelve o'clock is regular pay-day," she answered, "but the week of April 26th most of the employees got paid off on Friday night between six and seven o'clock. I hadn't worked there since Wednesday. Mr. Quinn called me up and told me that pay-day would be Friday."[168]

When it was Rosser's turn to question Grace, he was surprisingly gentle. He inquired about the blood spots in the metal room. Grace said the spots could be paint.

> There is paint in the polishing room, just across from the dressing room. No paint is kept in the metal room. I have seen drops of paint on the floor. I have seen it leading from the door straight across from the dressing room out to the cooler where the women come out to get water. The floor all over the factory is dirty and greasy. And after two or three days you can't hardly tell what is on the floor after it gets mixed with dirt and dust.[169]

"And do you girls have a place to comb your hair?" asked Rosser.

"Yes, we have one, but many of us girls comb our hair right where we happen to be working," answered Grace.

"And are there any of the girls in the factory who have hair the color of Mary Phagan's?" Rosser asked.

"Yes, there's Magnolia Kennedy. Her hair is almost the same color."

"You worked there a year?"

"I worked there five years. Mary worked there a year."

"In those five years how many times did Mr. Frank speak to you?"

"Three times."

"How many times did you see him speak to Mary Phagan?"

"None."

"Did he ever speak to the girls when he came through the metal room?"

"No."

Grace stepped down. She had testified for an hour.[170]

Newspaper reporters in the courtroom kept a close watch on Rosser. They described him as a force to be reckoned with when he browbeat a resistant witness. Many people believed Rosser would tear apart Conley's testimony if he ever took the stand.

Leo, on the other hand, was seen as too confident and this put observers off. They had a different view of Ray Frank, who spent her days in court watching Leo, her emotions clear on her face. As one *Georgian* reporter described, "When the prosecution scores, another line is added to the face that has been wrinkled by the three months of waiting and horror. When the defense seems to have an advantage, there is a joy expressed as great as the power of Niagara." He continued, "But Mary Phagan is dead; she sleeps peacefully beneath a flowered sod. The mother of Leo Frank is alive and be her son innocent or guilty, the mother is the pitiful figure in the black and baffling mystery."[171]

By this point, both families had lost. Fannie lost her baby, her youngest, and might never recover from the trauma. Ray stood to lose her son to a hangman's noose and firmly believed Leo was innocent. Fannie and Will Coleman believed Dorsey had found and would punish their child's murderer, Leo Frank. All indications show that Hugh Dorsey believed Leo was the murderer. Years later, he would argue the guilt of Leo Frank with a colleague at a dinner, where he vehemently defended the case and its verdict.

Dorsey was confident when Detective John Black took the stand that he would testify that he searched Lee's house only after Leo had informed him that several punches on the time slip were missing; however, the prosecution saw Black's testimony as a failure. Time and again, Black contradicted himself under Rosser's relentless cross-examination. He folded and refolded a large white handkerchief, often running it across his forehead while answering the questions. Before leaving the stand on that Wednesday, Black admitted he was confused and couldn't remember what he had just testified to.

Next, Fannie was recalled to identify Mary's bloodied handkerchief. "Mary carried a little sliver mesh bag the day she left her home, made of German silver," she testified. "This looks like the handkerchief that she carried."[172]

J. M. Gantt was called to the stand in the afternoon. He testified to Leo's nervousness and described the shoes he had come to retrieve. Then he added some testimony that wasn't in the coroner's inquest. He described an encounter with Mary at the factory.

> One Saturday afternoon she came in the office to have her time corrected, and after I had gotten through Mr. Frank came in and said, "You seem to know Mary pretty well," No,

> I had not told him her name. I used to know Mary when she was a little girl, but I have not seen her up to the time I went to work for the factory. My work was in the office and she worked in the rear of the building on the same floor in the tip department.[173]
>
> Court was adjourned until Thursday morning.

ଓ

Almost an inch of rain fell in the previous twenty-four hours, and thundershowers loomed on that muggy Thursday morning. The air was thick, making the predicted high of ninety-one degrees feel suffocating despite the cloud cover. Still, the relentless heat didn't deter the crowds. Spectators, eager for a glimpse of the proceedings, gathered in droves, hoping to secure a seat in the courtroom gallery. Some considered themselves fortunate to find perches on buildings across the street, where they could peer into the courtroom windows.

Among the onlookers was Mrs. Callie Scott Appelbaum, who had recently been acquitted of her husband's murder, a trial also presided over by Judge Roan. Her not-guilty verdict had cast doubt on prosecutor Hugh Dorsey's ability to serve justice. Although women were largely discouraged from attending the trial—except those intimately connected to the case—Mrs. Appelbaum made an attractive exception, turning heads with her beauty and fashionable clothes. Her presence, a silent yet powerful statement, suggested lingering trauma from her own trial or perhaps was an intriguing defense strategy. Her public declaration of Leo's innocence had added an extra layer of complexity to the atmosphere, but Dorsey was unflappable.

The courtroom buzzed when the next witness, Pinkerton detective Harry Scott, took the stand. All eyes were on him, and the tension was palpable, like the impending storm outside.

"What, if anything, did Frank tell you about Gantt?" Dorsey asked.[174]

"He stated in the first conversation that Gantt knew Mary Phagan very well and was intimate with her," Scott replied.

"Did Frank say anything about Gantt's attentions to Mary Phagan?"

"Not that I recall."

"May I refresh the mind of the witness?" Dorsey asked Judge Roan.

Rosser objected.

"Your honor, it is in your discretion to allow me to 'lead' a witness, and if there ever was a time when a witness needs to be led this is one. This detective is in the employ of the defense," Dorsey argued.

"You don't mean to insinuate that I'm holding anything back!" Scott erupted.

"The state has been trapped," Dorsey said. "The witness told me something and now he doesn't seem to remember it and I'm not trying to impeach him, I'm simply trying to refresh his memory."

Judge Roan allowed him to ask the question.

"Mr. Scott, did Frank or did he not discuss Gantt's relations to Mary Phagan?"

"Yes."

"What did he say?"

"He said Gantt paid a great deal of attention to her."

For the defense, one of the most damaging parts of this line of questioning came when Dorsey asked Scott about a conversation he had with Mr. Haas, the lawyer for the pencil factory.

"Did you or did you not make reports or statements to the defendant of what you did?" Dorsey demanded.

"I made them to Herbert Haas, Luther Rosser and Sig Montag," said Scott.

Later, Dorsey asked if Frank's attorneys had suggested to Scott that he suppress evidence. Rosser objected, and Dorsey withdrew the question.

"What was said about the matter?" Dorsey revised his question.

"During the first week in May, Pierce and I went to Herbert Haas's office to discuss the handling of the case and we told him we had strong suspicion against Frank."

Rosser objected but Scott was allowed to finish.

"Mr. Haas said that he would rather we would submit what evidence we might get to them before turning it over to the police, so that they would know in advance what the evidence was and we told [him] that we would quit the case before we would handle it in that way."

When Rosser cross-examined Scott, Scott's anger flashed again. "Did you swear you told all you knew at the inquest?"

"Yes: I did my best in a general way."

"You never hid anything?"

"No: that's not my business nor my reputation."

During the heated cross-examination, Rosser skillfully pressed Detective Scott, drawing out a crucial admission. The courtroom must have held its collective breath as Rosser probed Scott to admit that Haas had explicitly instructed the Pinkertons to find the murderer, regardless of who it might be. Scott relented.

Rosser's revelation was a small coup, but would it be enough to repair the damage caused by the entirety of Scott's testimony?

After Scott stepped down, the courtroom's attention shifted to Monteen Stover, a former pencil factory employee. As she took the stand, a hush must have fallen over the room. Everyone was aware Miss Stover's testimony was crucial.

With a steady voice, she recounted her visit to the factory on that fateful Saturday.

"Were you in the factory April 26?" Dorsey asked.

"Yes. At 12:05."

"How long did you stay there?"

"Five minutes."

"Why did you go there?"

"To get my pay."

"Was Frank there, or was anybody in the building?"

"Mr. Frank was not there and I saw no one in the building," she said. Miss Stover went on to say she left at 12:10.[175]

Leo had insisted he was in his office at that time, the same time Mary Phagan was believed to have arrived. The contradiction hung heavy in the air. Stover's testimony directly challenged Leo's alibi. For five crucial minutes, Leo's office was empty, casting doubt on his account of events.

One detail stood out even more starkly. Miss Stover wasn't asked if she noticed anyone else in the lobby as she entered. Mrs. White claimed to see a Black man, who was allegedly stationed there only minutes later. This inconsistency added another layer of mystery to the trial.

The weight of Stover's testimony settled over the courtroom.

A new piece of evidence was brought to light when R. P. Barrett, a machinist at the pencil factory, took the stand next and testified he found a piece of a pay envelope near Mary's machine. Barrett was one of the employees who discovered the so-called blood spots in front of the dressing room. Dorsey attempted to establish with this testimony there was a good possibility that the murder occurred on the second floor in the metal room.

When Rosser cross-examined Barrett, he was able to get him to admit the pay envelope could have been anyone's because there was no name or pay amount written on it.

Mell Stanford, the janitor responsible for cleaning the factory floors on the night before the murder, took the stand. He recounted how he had used a small broom to sweep the metal room between nine o'clock and midnight. He stated there were no spots on the floor in front of the dressing room that night.

In the quiet courtroom, Stanford described how, on Monday, he discovered a large cane broom standing about six feet from the alleged blood spots in the metal room. He stated he believed they were blood. The weight of his words must have added to the tension in the room.

Mrs. George W. Jefferson, another employee of the pencil factory, took the stand. She calmly recounted the chilling moment when she and Barrett first noticed the blood spots on the floor in front of the dressing room. Her voice steady, she described the cords, similar to the one found embedded around Mary's neck, as hanging on the wall in the polish room, four to five feet from the blood spots. When asked about the size of the spots, Mrs. Jefferson illustrated their size, comparing them as smaller than the palm of her hand.

Next, William Gheesling, the undertaker responsible for embalming, provided a somber account of the condition of Mary's body, his testimony adding a grim layer to the day's proceedings. The last witness of the day, E. F. Holloway, a factory foreman, took the stand. Holloway had been employed at the pencil factory for three years. His responsibilities were attending to the elevator, freight, and more general business. Once again, Dorsey faced disappointment as Holloway's testimony failed to deliver the critical blow he sought.

"What do you do upon leaving—in reference to the elevator?" Dorsey asked.

"Nothing in particular," Holloway replied.

"Did you leave the elevator unlocked on Saturday, April 26?"

"Yes."

Dorsey's voice cut through the courtroom, his frustration and determination evident as he addressed the judge. Once again, the prosecution had been trapped. "On May 12, before Detectives Campbell, Starnes, John Black and my stenographer, Mr. Holloway swore that he had locked this power box on Saturday, April 26, and that he always kept it locked."

Holloway kept his resolve but countered. "I said I had locked it on Friday."

Dorsey pressed on, attempting to corner Holloway into confirming that the elevator had indeed been secured. Yet, Holloway remained resolute. He recalled having unlocked the elevator Saturday morning because White and Denham were working on the fourth floor. Then, he left for the day at 11:25 a.m.

Even as Dorsey reminded him of the affidavit, he had previously signed attesting to the elevator's locked status, Holloway refused to yield. Dorsey ended the questioning. Yet, setbacks such as these did little to deter the determined prosecutor, who remained undeterred in his pursuit of proving Leo guilty.[176]

ꟽ

Women and girls began insisting on having a seat in the courtroom gallery, an unusual occurrence the *Atlanta Constitution* noted with surprise. On Friday, at least a quarter of the audience were women and girls, including one who looked to be under fourteen.

As Lucille attended court each day, life went on around them. Teas, porch parties, and house parties still filled the society section of the newspaper. In her life before the trial, Lucille had attended and enjoyed many of these functions. The contrast of life before the murder and after must have struck her countless times during that first week of the trial. Now, she was sought out, not for invitations to parties, but for comments on the trial. A photo appeared in the *Atlanta Constitution* of Lucille and Julian Boehm, a family friend, leaving the courthouse after a day of testimony. Lucille, fashionably dressed in a skirt, white shirtwaist, and elaborate hat, was smiling. Whether her smile was forced, a response to Julian, or an expression of confidence in the day's testimony, we will never know.

With all parties in place at their tables, Lucille and Ray behind Leo, and the jury in their box, Dorsey called N. V. Darley, factory personnel director, to the stand. Darley, a co-worker and friend of Leo's, was a bit of a wildcard, and Dorsey knew it. Darley was the one Leo asked Lucille to call that Sunday morning when he left with Detective Black and Boots Rogers. Reluctant to testify for the prosecution, Darley was a gamble for Dorsey, but Dorsey knew that if Darley said anything to implicate Leo, the jury would believe it.

Dorsey began by asking Darley about his position at the factory and who he answered to. Darley explained that, like Leo, he answered to Mr. Montag and that their positions and responsibilities were parallel. When Dorsey pressed him about Leo's nervousness, Darley admitted Leo was shaking all over the morning after Mary's murder. He recounted how Leo told him that he was nervous because he had no breakfast or coffee that morning, and the officers had rushed him to Bloomfield's Funeral Home. There, in a dark room, they turned on a light and showed him Mary's brutalized body. Leo was adamant in his belief that the murder was committed in the basement.

During cross-examination, Darley highlighted that Leo managed to complete detailed financial work that Saturday, something an extremely upset person would struggle to do. Darley confirmed he saw the financial report, which typically took all Saturday afternoon to finish, on Leo's desk that Sunday morning. This detail was crucial because Jim Conley claimed in his affidavit that he helped Leo with Mary's body in the early afternoon. This version of events would have meant Leo committed the murder, employed Jim's assistance, went home for lunch, and went back to work, where he finished the grueling report before he went home for the night.

The defense then asked about the blood spots in the metal room. Darley explained that Lemmie Quinn called his attention to the spots after Barrett had summoned him. Dorsey asked about the hair strands. "They were wound around a lever," Darley answered. "I don't think there were over 6 or 8 at the outside. It was pretty hard to tell the color."[177]

A question about the piece of pay envelope came next. Darley explained,

> There are hundreds of pay envelopes distributed every week in the factory. The rule is that if a person goes outside of the factory and finds an envelope short we do not correct it.... The employees take the money out and scatter the envelopes all over the factory. On the second floor where the metal room is the main place where you would find pay envelopes.[178]

Darley's answer showed that Barrett's piece of envelope could have been anyone's and from any time. If Dorsey's theory that Leo was the killer was correct, why would Leo take the $1.20? That amount wouldn't mean a lot to him, but it would to Conley. By his own admission, Conley had spent the morning buying drinks with the rent money in his pocket. If he drank or gambled the money away, he would be looking to replace the rent.

Some interesting facts came out of Darley's cross-examination. One was Dorsey had served two subpoenas on Darley, who was unaware that Dorsey had no right to subpoena him to make a statement. Again, Dorsey proved the misconduct Lucille described in her letter to the newspapers: he had used intimidation to get Darley's statement. Darley also made the statement that not a day went by at the factory that Leo wasn't nervous. Most of the time, he would wring his hands when he was agitated about something that went wrong. Once again, Darley surprised the court. He told of one afternoon when Leo took a streetcar to the factory, and he had witnessed the car run over a young boy. When he arrived at the factory, Leo was trembling as badly as he was the day he saw Mary's body. He was so affected by the streetcar tragedy that he had to go home.

After being cross-examined again by Dorsey, Darley was excused from the witness stand. His testimony had not helped Dorsey. The defense had gained some ground, but Dorsey didn't seem bothered. He knew his plan to call Darley to the stand could backfire.

Mrs. J. A. White, whose husband, Arthur, was working that Saturday on the fourth floor, described her visit to her husband that Saturday. Her first arrival was at 11:30. The stenographer, Mr. Frank, and two men were on the second floor. After getting permission to speak with her husband, she went to the fourth floor and stayed until 11:50.

Around 12:30, she returned to the pencil factory and found Leo standing in front of his office safe. He gave a slight jump when she spoke to him. He told her to go up to see her husband. Mrs. White departed the building again at 1 p.m., when Leo said he was going home for lunch as soon as he grabbed his hat and coat. He had told her the building would be locked while he was gone and she would be stuck inside. It was when she left the second time that she noticed a Black man sitting in the lobby of the factory near the street door.

"Did you see anyone else?" Dorsey asked.

"Yes, I saw a negro behind some boxes as I came down the steps," Mrs. White answered.

"Where and what time was that?"

"It was the first floor, close to the stairway that goes up to the second floor, and at about 10 minutes to 1."

Mrs. White left the stand after an hour of questioning. Her testimony did place Leo in the office when he said he was, but her absence from 11:50 a.m. until 12:30 p.m. also left time for Miss Stover's testimony to be correct. Conley had admitted to being in the factory, but Mrs. White's testimony corroborated his statement the timeline in his last affidavit. She was excused.

When Dr. Roy Harris, secretary of the State Board of Health, entered the courtroom in the afternoon, it seemed the spectators were holding their collective breath. Most knew he had examined Mary's body when she was exhumed for autopsy, but his findings had not been released to the newspapers. He held a doctor's bag as if it were an extension of his body. He was pale from a three-day illness but showed up for court anyway. He stated Mary's stomach held undigested cabbage from her morning meal. A bottle containing a slight amount of stomach contents was displayed, and small pieces of cabbage were visible. He produced another bottle, taken from a man who was alive an hour after he had eaten cabbage and bread. No cabbage was visible, so Mary must have died thirty minutes to an hour after she ate her meal. Dr. Harris explained that when a person dies, any digestion ends.

When he spoke about the blow to Mary's head, he explained that the wound appeared to be inflicted by a fist and had nothing to do with her death. The cord embedded in her neck caused her death. Dr. Harris admitted he could not tell if Mary had been raped, but he saw what he thought was evidence of violence.

Shortly after this testimony, Dr. Harris fainted and could not be cross-examined. Days later, he returned to the stand, but his powerful testimony remained with the jury. If Mary arrived at the pencil factory around 12:10, she would have been murdered sometime around 12:30 to 12:35 at the latest.

As the afternoon came to an end, spectators filed out of the courtroom. Lucille and Ray told Leo goodbye. He was taken back to the Tower, and the ladies went home. Saturday would be a half-day session, so, like Mary's family, they would return to hang on every word—though the families hoped for very different outcomes.

ᘓ

Though Saturday's half-day of testimony revealed nothing new or important, it was probably one of the most interesting days thus far in the trial. Judge Roan inadvertently held up a newspaper with blazing red headlines in full view of the jury. Arnold was on his feet, asking the judge to send the jury out. Judge Roan assented. The defense left the room and conferred together. Meanwhile, the courtroom was electric with excitement. Lucille's worry was most noticeable. The *Atlanta Constitution* described her as breathing hard and placing her head on the table beside her. When the defense lawyers returned, Luther Rosser made a statement that he would not seek a mistrial, but he hoped Judge Roan would be more careful in the future. He also asked that the jury be instructed to ignore any portion of the paper they may have seen.

Dr. J. W. Hurt, Fulton County medical examiner, took the stand but added little new evidence. He, like Dr. Harris, couldn't say whether Mary had been raped; however, during Arnold's cross-examined, he admitted that he "couldn't tell whether the blood on her underclothes was menstrual blood or not." He continued, "The hymen was not intact, and I was not able to say when this hymen was ruptured. I saw no indication of an injury to the hymen."[179] His testimony planted doubt among the jury that rape was the real motive. The defense was convinced the motive was robbery.

Dr. Hurt did contradict Dr. Harris's testimony about the time of Mary's death when he said cabbage takes several hours to digest and could have been in her stomach longer than was believed.

Helen Ferguson took the stand, and everyone likely assumed she would talk about bringing the awful news of Mary's murder to Fannie and Will. When asked when she last saw Leo, she answered, "I saw Mr.

Frank Friday, April 25th, about 7 o'clock in the evening and asked for Mary Phagan's money. Mr. Frank said, 'I can't let you have it,' and before he said anything else I turned around and walked out. I had gotten Mary's money before, but I didn't get it from Mr. Frank."[180]

When Helen was cross-examined, she admitted she had retrieved Mary's pay from another officer worker and she provided Mary's employee's number. She couldn't remember the number to give to Leo. She also testified that she had never witnessed Leo speak to Mary Phagan. Finishing out the Saturday testimony were Chief Beavers and Officer Lassiter. Court was adjourned until Monday.

The first week of the trial was over. Leo left the courtroom and returned to the Tower. Lucille and Ray returned home. Monday morning would be upon them soon enough.

Saturday evening, police officers took Jim Conley into a concealed courtyard behind the station house and turned a hose on him for a crude shower. William Smith made sure Conley had a fresh haircut and shave. He was fitted in a new suit of clothes, complete with dress shoes. Conley's day on the stand was nearing. At this point, the prosecution had not provided any real proof that Leo murdered Mary Phagan. Jim Conley was the witness they depended on change the course of the trial.

Chapter 23

Jim Conley Takes the Stand

Crowds formed in front of the courthouse by six o'clock Monday morning. The rumor that Jim Conley would take the stand had spread, and the city was on edge, anxious to hear him tell the story of helping Leo move Mary Phagan's body to the basement of the pencil factory. Jim's story, rehearsed over and over while he sat in the Tower, had made him somewhat of a folk hero, an unusual role for a Black man in Atlanta in 1913. In many minds, forty-eight years after the end of the Civil War, Conley represented the South, and Leo Frank represented the North.

Women were particularly drawn to the case, and they lined up in record numbers to get inside. The majority were regular housewives with children of their own. These women were serious about being in the courtroom to hear the trial—many likely identified with Mary's mother. The first week, they had listened quietly and intently to every part of the story. But, that Monday morning as they entered the courtroom, many forgot their decorum and ran for seats, even fighting over them. Some talked the doorkeepers into letting them inside. Some even went as far as to say that their husbands were connected to the trial.

In walked Lucille, both figuratively and literally, in the middle of a war of words that could end in a death sentence. Ray, who must have been feeling the wear of the trial, and Lucille took the side door into the courthouse as they had on previous days to escape the crowds out front. Who would have ever thought a quiet, withdrawn engineer from Brooklyn would draw those crowds.

When the 250 spectators made their way into the courtroom, deputies moved a group of people seated too close to the jury box. The air tingled with anticipation. Finally, there would be testimony that justified the hours they had waited in line.

As he had the week before, Leo sat in front of his mother and Lucille. When the defense lawyers settled at their table, one couldn't help but notice what an odd pair Rosser and Arnold made. Rosser, a broad-chested, stocky man of imposing height, resembled a bulldog in his tenacious ability to badger a witness into telling the truth. In contrast, Arnold's tall, thin frame and studious demeanor, accentuated by wire-rimmed glasses, conveyed an air of intelligence and soft-spoken authority—yet his approach was equally as firm and effective as Rosser's.

At the state's table, seated with several lawyers, Dorsey stood out with his youthful good looks and smile. He was a formidable litigator who kept his cool but spoke out for what he thought was the truth. Still, beneath his composed exterior lay a steely aggression that rivaled Rosser's own. No one could deny that both men believed in what they were fighting for.

The courtroom turned quiet as Judge Roan was seated. Dorsey stood and asked that Jim Conley be brought in to testify. A hushed murmur spread through the courtroom. Lucille and Ray must have taken in a collective breath. The room waited. And waited. Agitated by the delay, Judge Roan ordered deputy sheriff Plennie Minor to bring in the witness. Minor indicated he did not have Conley.

"Mr. Starnes will bring him in," Dorsey said to Roan.[181]

The courtroom was deadly quiet as Jim Conley entered. He was seated in the witness chair and sworn in. The air was thick with expectation.

Dorsey began by asking Conley his name and if he knew Leo Frank. He asked Conley to identify him in the courtroom.

"Right there he is," Jim replied. He pointed directly at Leo. The effect was dramatic. If others thought Leo would shake with nerves, they were disappointed. Instead, he spoke a few words to Lucille, who replied with a weak smile.

Dorsey then questioned Conley about other jobs he performed for Leo. Conley testified that Leo had, on other occasions, paid him to watch the door of the factory while he went to have a "chat" with a woman or girl in his office. Conley claimed on Thanksgiving Day 1912 that a heavy woman went up to speak with Leo while he watched the door. He said she wore a blue dotted dress, tailored gray coat, white shoes, and white stockings. Next, Conley went into graphic detail about what he saw take place between a man named Dalton, two girls (one an employee named Daisy), and Leo Frank.[182] The *Atlanta Constitution* would only print that Conley would stand guard as Frank and Dalton engaged in trysts with various women; Conley had once "surprised Frank and a woman in a compromising attitude" in which "the woman was seated in a chair and Frank was kneeling on the floor."[183] This account was so lurid that the newspapers couldn't print the testimony. Details like these made Jim more believable. The jury leaned forward to catch everything he said.

The *Atlanta Georgian* wrote of observing Lucille and Ray as Jim Conley testified:

> As the charges of degeneracy were being hurled at her husband by the solicitor, young Mrs. Frank hung her head and finally unable to endure the ordeal longer left the courtroom. When she returned, her eyes were red and her cheeks flushed as from weeping...Frank's mother left her place, a look of utter, wearied misery in her eyes, but a determination to be brave in every line of her face.[184]

After this shocking line of questioning, Dorsey moved on to the day Mary was murdered.

That morning, Leo playfully knocked Conley in the chest and told him to sit on a box near the front door of the factory and not to allow Darley to see him. Conley recalled seeing Darley come down the stairs with Mattie Smith, an employee, holding a handkerchief and looking as if she'd been crying. Then Jim Conley described the next girl who came into the factory.

"Who else did you see?"

"Miss Mary Perkins."

"Who?"

"Miss Mary Perkins, I called her, the girl who is dead." He could not remember her last name.

"What else did you hear?"

"I heard footsteps going back towards the metal room, and in a little bit I heard a scream."

Hearing this, Lucille dropped her chin to her chest, and Ray wore an expression of shock and pain.

"What happened next?"

"Miss Monteen Stover came in. In a little bit she went out."

"What did you hear then?"

"Heard footsteps like somebody running on tip toe from Mr. Frank's office towards the metal room."

"What happened after that?"

"I sat down on a box and went to sleep."[185]

Imagine falling asleep after hearing a girl, whom he would later see dead, scream. The casualness of this statement surely settled on the jury and gave the people in the gallery pause. The witness showed more emotion while describing a sex act than he did when telling of Mary's scream.

Dorsey next questioned Conley about what happened when he went up the stairs after Leo called him.

"Mr. Frank was standing at the head of the stairs shivering and shaking."

"Did he have anything in his hand?"

"A cord."

"When Frank called you upstairs that Saturday afternoon, what did he say?"

"He said he had struck a little girl with his fist and she had fallen against something and hurt herself. He told me he wanted me to help him carry her down stairs. He said there was money in it for me."

Dorsey inquired about the removal of Mary's body. Conley stuck to his last affidavit and the story he told over and over to reporters.

Then the solicitor general spoke to the deputy sheriff and asked for Mrs. A. J. White, who had been summoned back to court, to be brought into the room.

The solicitor pointed at her. "Did you see this woman?"

"No, sir."

"Your honor," said Dorsey, "I will put this witness on the stand for a moment."

Rosser objected. "I told you in private we wouldn't consent."

"I thought you said Dr. Harris," returned Dorsey.

"Nobody." Rosser answered.

Dorsey moved on to other questions.

Conley claimed the moving of the body took place at 12:56 p.m. Mrs. White testified earlier that she had left the building at about that time.

ଊ

Rosser began Jim's cross-examination with simple questions such as where he lived and his age. Then he inquired about Conley's ability to spell certain words and to use numbers. The point was to make the jury understand Conley's capabilities, especially since Conley had been dishonest about his reading and number comprehension. Rosser asked about Jim's education, the school he attended, his teacher, and the principal. After asking about Conley's former jobs, Rosser asked about his present position at the pencil factory.

"Jim, when you went to the National Pencil factory, who paid you?"

"Mr. Schiff [assistant superintendent] and sometimes Mr. Frank."

"Give me the dates Mr. Frank paid off."

"I hardly ever drew my money. I had somebody draw mine, usually."

"Why did you do that?"

"Well, I owed money, and I wanted to get it and get away without them getting it all."

"Did you not owe the boys more than you wanted to pay them?"

"No, sir, I just owed 10 or 15 men."

"What were you drawing?"

"$6.48."

"Then the reason you didn't draw your money was that you wanted to get it and get away without paying money?"

"Sometimes."

These questions must have made the jury acknowledge Conley's lies and how he couldn't be trusted to pay what he owed to the men who loaned him money. And he owed a lot of men.

Rosser seemed to want to trip Jim up because the next questions moved to when Conley had watched the door for Leo, returning to Conley's testimony that he had stood guard while Frank (and Dalton) met with women in his office for sex.

"When was the first time you ever watched for Mr. Frank?"

"Sometime last summer."

"What did Mr. Frank say to you?"

"He came out and called me into his office."

"What did he say?"

"Well, he sometimes talked to me about the work."

"When did he first call you in and talk to you about the work? Didn't he call you in during the week sometimes?"

"No, sir. He called me into the office to talk about the work one Saturday night after I went there."

Throughout Conley's time on the witness stand, Leo kept a calm, level stare at the janitor, his former employee, his accuser.

"You say the first time you watched was back there in July? You don't know the name of the man?" This question referred to Conley's graphic statement that the first time he watched the door for Leo, another man and two women entered the factory and went to Leo's office.

"Yes, the man was Dalton."

"You don't know the name of the woman, do you?"

"No, but she lives on West Hunter Street."

Then Rosser requested Conley tell him the name of the second woman with Frank.

"Her name was Daisy Hopkins. She worked on the fourth floor."

"What time was it?"

"3 or 3:20."

Rosser changed the subject and asked Conley about the woman who came on Thanksgiving to meet Leo. What did her clothes look like? What kind of hat did she wear?

"A big black hat with big feathers."

Rosser asked more questions about the alleged meetings with Dalton and the women, one of whom was Daisy Hopkins, and then court was adjourned until two o'clock.

ଊ

Friends talked with Leo during the lunch recess. He dropped his calm demeanor and told them that Conley's story was "The vilest and most amazing pack of lies ever conceived in the perverted brain of a wicked human being."[186] He voiced total confidence in his defense team.

When Jim Conley entered the courtroom again after the lunch recess, the time was 1:55 p.m. Leo sat with his back to the witness stand, speaking with Lucille. Conley seemed calm and collected, staring out at the curious faces that watched him. As Judge Roan walked to the stand, Deputy Sheriff Minor announced all women (except Lucille and Ray) and children—several small ones were in the room—would have to leave for the remainder of the day. The judge had decided the testimony had not been suitable for women, so 150 women, from girls in their teens to women in their eighties, were expelled from the courtroom that afternoon. Their resentment was reflected on their faces as they filed out.[187]

The cross-examination continued.[188]

Rosser began by asking Jim who he saw during the break at the police station. He said his lawyer, William Smith, and Chief Beavers. When Rosser asked Conley what these two men said to him, Hooper, one of the lawyers at the prosecution table, objected. Rosser dropped the question and moved on.

"Well, Jim, what did you do on the Saturday before you watched for Mr. Frank the first time?"

"I don't know."

"What did you do the Saturday after that?"

"I don't know sir, I disremember."

"What about the Saturday after that?" Rosser persisted.

"Well, long about August 1 I watched again."

"Let me see if I get that right—one Saturday you didn't watch and the next Saturday you did, and then you didn't watch any more until Thanksgiving?"

"I don't know exactly. I can't count it like you."

"Well, I got it like you said, didn't I, Jim?"

"The last time I watched was about the last of September."

"Jim, what time was it you watched the second Saturday?"

"I don't remember, sir."

"You don't know what time you left for home?"

"No, sir."

"Jim, we don't want any controversy between us, but tell all about these times you watched."

"I done told you like I remember them."

The questions changed to different events in Jim's recent life, including a two-day stint in prison in 1912. Conley couldn't remember why he had been incarcerated or exactly how many times. He did acknowledge he'd been in jail two or three times during his employment at the pencil factory.

It's important to note that the slightest infraction, such as unemployment or public drunkenness, could result in a Black man going to jail. Rosser revealed Conley's love for drink when he got him to admit that he and a man known as Snowball drank beer in the basement at the pencil factory

Hooper objected to Rosser's rapid-fire questions and pointed out that he wasn't giving Jim enough time to answer. Judge Roan instructed Rosser to be careful with the pace of his questions.

"When did he [Leo] jolly with you the last time?"

"I can't recall."

"Give one little joke you ever heard him crack?'

"I can't recall."

"Give just one?"

"One day he hollered down the elevator and said, 'If you don't hurry up with that elevator I will start a graveyard down in the basement.'"

"What else?"

"Well, he would pinch me."

"Did Mr. Holloway or Mr. Darley see that?"

"Mr. Holloway did."

Rosser posed his questions more slowly now, but Jim often couldn't answer because he couldn't remember. Leo wore a weary expression. Lucille sat beside him with her arm around his shoulder. Ray sat on the other side of him, listening with her eyes closed.

Rosser sat at the table while firing the questions at Conley. He was calmly trying to wear the witness out, but Conley didn't falter.

The afternoon testimony proved tame by comparison to the morning, and while the judge's concerns about further indelicate revelations were understandable, they ultimately proved unfounded for the remainder of the day. There seemed no reason to ban the women from the courtroom.

Rosser began questioning Conley about Dalton, the employee alleged to have been with women in Leo's office while Jim watched the door. Jim described Dalton's appearance: dark-haired, about thirty-five, and about the height of Mr. Arnold. When asked about the first time he had seen Dalton, Conley indicated the man was coming out of the factory basement. After Conley repeatedly answered, "I don't remember," Rosser switched subjects again.

"Do the metal room doors lock?"

"I don't know."

"You know the factory pretty well, don't you?"

"Some parts of it."

"Did you ever sweep the metal room?"

"No, I never swept anything except the fourth floor."

Rosser turned to the part of the building where Quinn's office was. Jim didn't know anything about that part of the building.

"Were you ever back where the ladies toilets were?"

"I put disinfectants back there."

"You said a while ago that you had never been back there?"

"Not since I have been working on the fourth floor. I just sprinkled the floor with disinfectant." So, Conley had slipped up. Rosser was finally wearing him down.

Rosser stood from his chair with papers in his hand: Jim's affidavits.

"Do you know Detective Harry Scott?"[189]

"Yes, sir."

"When you were at the police headquarters you told them that you got up at 9:30 a.m. on the morning of the 25th, didn't you?"

"Yes sir."

"This wasn't so, was it?"

"No."

Rosser held the previous affidavits that Jim made in his hands.

"Yet you looked the in the face and lied, didn't you?"

"Yes, sir."

"You also told them you went to Peters Street?"

"Yes, sir."

"And didn't go?"

"Yes sir. I went to Peters street alright."

"Not long."

"You stayed until 11 o'clock, didn't you?"

"No."

"You told Scott so, didn't you?"

"Don't remember about that."

"Do you remember what you told Harry Scott and John Black?"

"Not all."

"The truth is you lied all the way around?"

"I told some stories. I'll admit."

"Didn't you make three affidavits, neither of which is true?"

"Some of them are true."

"But aren't they all lies?"

"No, there's a lot of truth in all of them."

Assistant prosecutor Hooper objected and pointed out that the affidavits should be shown to the witness as dictated by the law.

Arnold, attorney for the defense, spoke up. "It is easy to see that the negro has been canned and grilled and prepared for this business and would easily recognize the affidavits. This is not what we want to do at present."

"Mr. Arnold I do not think was called upon to explain the history of the affidavits," Hooper, the assistant prosecutor, interjected. "They are here in the court as requested, and the law demands that they be shown the witness...This case should be tried entirely as any other case should be tried."

"We submit that the remarks of Mr. Arnold be considered prejudicious—," Dorsey added; "his remarks that the witness had been canned and prepared in a state satisfactory to the defense. I beg that the judge make a statement to that effect to the jury."

Arnold stood and addressed the judge. "My friend Dorsey, in his usual fussy, snarlish way, has accused me of being prejudicious...We expect to show that the affidavits followed many contradictory statements, and that Conley never admitted anything until confronted with the fact that he could write."

Judge Roan sustained the defense's objection, and the questioning continued. Rosser asked more questions about the timing and if Jim was telling the truth.

"We have no objection to any of this going before the jury," Hooper interrupted, "but this procedure of Rosser's is only an attempt to impeach the witness, and it is in a manner against what is prescribed by law. There is a rule against this method of his, and it is as plain as the nose on your face, your honor."

Mr. Rosser defended his position. "Now, is it to be said that I cannot ask this man what he said on a certain time? I've got a right to do it to test or refresh his memory."

"This rule is universal," Roan pronounced. "This man, Mr. Hooper, is your witness. The defense has ample grounds to test his memory."

"Does your honor hold that this examination is not solely for the purpose of impeachment?" Mr. Hooper spoke in what seemed like an effort to shut down the line of questioning.

"I do not know what will be the ultimate result," said the judge.

The defense won this round and continued questioning Conley about the time he told Black he went to a saloon.

"Didn't you tell Black and Scott that some things you told them were true and some were not?"

"No; they never asked me."

"Didn't you look them straight in the face and lie?"

"No sir. I hung my head whenever I told them a lie and looked them straight in the face when I told them the truth. I thought I'd tell just a little bit of the truth, so Mr. Frank would get scared and would send somebody to come and get me out of trouble."

Conley delivered this line smoothly and effortlessly. Rosser tried to joke by telling Jim they would get to that part of the story later, but he was a smart litigator. He knew the impact Jim's statement would have on the jury, but he regained his footing and began firing questions about Conley's lies at him.

"On May 24, didn't you send for Black?"

"I don't remember, I don't know what date it was; it was when the papers put it in that I was down there suffering," Conley answered. Dorsey objected but the judge overruled, and the questioning continued.

"I sent for Mr. Black and told him I would tell him. I told him I had held back part of it," Conley said.

"You told Black you were going to tell part of the truth and hold back part of it?"

"Yes sir."

"In your verbal statement to Black—the first one—did you say anything about a girl being dead and toting her down into the basement?"

"I don't remember."

"In your second statement, did you say anything about this?"

"Yes, sir—I think I did. I think I remember saying something about it," Conley recalled. Mr. Hooper objected, saying that the defense had the statement in his hands.

"Haven't we a right to show a thing in writing as dictated by the law…?" he asked.

"Suppose the affidavits contradict the statement of the witness?" suggested Judge Roan. "In which case the defense would have grounds for testing the witness' memory. The man says he can't write and did not write it himself. Does the law, in such a case say that his memory may not be tested to oral statement he has made for transcription?"

The defense was allowed to ask the questions. Dorsey stood to read part of a state statute to the judge. Roan turned his head to speak to a spectator while Dorsey read. When the solicitor noticed the judge showed no interest, he threw the book on his table in a fit of irritation.

Rosser continued.

"Now Jim, whenever you are lying or telling the truth please be so kind as to give me some signal. Did you say anything about going into the basement in that second statement?"

"I don't remember."

"You said you were going to keep back some of it—what was it?"

"The best part."

The court prepared to adjourn for the day. Mr. Arnold stood.

"We make a motion that the court take charge of this negro Jim Conley and let the sheriff put him in custody. The law requires such a move, and I ask your honor to do this fair and square. Not to let a soul talk to him, not even the sheriff."

Mr. Hooper agreed that this could be done. The state had no objections.

"Mr. Sheriff, no one is to get to this witness, not even you," Judge Roan ordered.

Conley's attorney, William Smith, spoke up that there was nowhere in the jail to keep others from talking to Conley. He pointed out that Leo received visitors and had special food brought in. Rosser told Smith to feel free to send Conley something if he wanted.

Sheriff Mangum told the judge that they would take special pains to keep Jim away from everyone.

Jim left the courthouse in the sheriff's custody to spend his night isolated from the others, including anyone from the prosecution and his own lawyer. But his lawyer treated him to a steak dinner and a new pair of underwear. He would appear on the stand the next morning to continue testifying.

The day's testimony must have filled Lucille with fear even if she hid it from her family. While Rosser had managed to show Conley was a frequent liar and had a terrible memory, no defense tactic swayed him from his story of how he helped Leo move Mary Phagan's body.

ɷ

Tuesday morning was sunny and breezy, but August in Georgia always promised hot weather. The defense was ready and waiting to prove Conley a liar. Lucille, wearing a dark suit and hat that had a flair of feathers on the front brim, took her regular seat. Mary Phagan's maternal grandmother, Anna Benton, entered the courtroom dressed in a light-colored dress and a dark straw hat with flowers. She wore a look of anger in the photo that a *Constitution* photographer had taken.[190]

Conley calmly took his place on the witness stand again. On Monday, he had testified for five hours. Now he faced Rosser again. The newspapers began to forecast that the trial would last another ten days, possibly two weeks. This would be the longest trial in Atlanta's history if the newspapers were correct.

Rosser picked up where he left off on Monday evening: Jim's many affidavits. Conley answered most of the questions with "I disremember." The defense attempted to prove that Jim lied from one affidavit to another. Rosser pushed Jim to say that Black and Scott tried to get him to change his story, but Conley denied it. Conley admitted that he did get up at six the morning of the murder rather than at nine as he told Black and Scott.

Jim saw no reason to talk about the first trip he took to the factory that morning, saying, "There wasn't nothing doing there then and I didn't see no use mentionin' it."[191]

Rosser showed impatience each time he noted a discrepancy in Jim's several affidavits. This was a long and grueling cross-examination with rapid-fire questions that began with the opening of court and ran until a quarter of eleven, when Conley, Leo, and the jury were allowed to take a five-minute recess. Jim had been under cross-examination, counting the day before, for eight hours.

Upon returning, Rosser asked Jim to describe the burlap that he used to wrap Mary's body for disposal in the basement. When he asked Jim how wide the piece of cloth was, he answered about two feet. Rosser questioned what Conley called two feet, so Jim demonstrated. He put his feet up, toe to heel, in front of Rosser's face and told him this was how he measured two feet; laughter erupted in the courtroom. Once Judge Roan restored calm, he ordered a lunch recess. The defense had not gained any ground. Though they did prove discrepancies, they were unable to shake Jim Conley in the testimony that was so damaging to Leo. Conley held true to his story, never faltering.

When the jury began filing out of the courtroom for lunch, William Smith, Conley's lawyer, stood.

"I do not know by what legal procedure my client is held in jail, as he is not held as a witness," he said. "I should have the right of counsel to talk and consult with him. I met with a good deal of trouble and unpleasantness last night in doing for him what I thought best...."

"I think that it is just and right that Conley should have the rights of attorney," Dorsey agreed.

"Since the solicitor and Lawyer Smith are in such harmonious accord over this witness, I do not think that Smith should be allowed to talk with the witness." Arnold spoke to the judge.

Roan ruled that the attorney should be allowed to speak with Conley.[192]

As the defense lawyers left the building for the lunch recess, they must have discussed the setbacks they had experienced and what this meant for their client, Leo Frank, because when court came to order after lunch, Arnold asked Judge Roan to remove the jury from the courtroom. Judge Roan honored Arnold's request. The twelve men filed out of the room. Arnold made a motion requesting the court to strike portions of Conley's testimony from the day before, specifically, the description of standing guard while Frank met with women in his office and witnessing a sex act he detailed so graphically that the testimony could not be printed in the newspapers. It must have taken the defense a day to realize the extent to which Conley's story would damage their client's credibility.

Arnold argued that portion of the testimony, considered obscene at the time, was irrelevant to the case at hand. But he didn't stop there.

> We also desire to withdraw from the records that part of Conley's statement in which he tells of Frank having told him at the head of the stairway on the second floor of the pencil factory that he was not built like other men, the answer Conley made to Dorsey's question: "What did he mean by that?" and the scene which the witness related.
>
> It is here in the court. I don't want to read it aloud before these ladies present, [Lucille and Ray] so I will show it to your honor. This, I want ruled out. This scene which the negro alleges he witnessed was brought into the case purely to prejudice the court against the defendant.

Frank Hooper spoke for the prosecution.

> On the first motion to rule out evidence pertaining to other cases of Conley's having watched for Frank, it comes too late, and to rule it out would give counsel opportunity to tamper with the courts. They have crossed the witness and brought out both direct and indirect testimony bearing on the particular phase. It's not too late for their objection.
>
> I agree that it should have been ruled out, but should have been ruled out at the proper time. In the motion made to rule out Conley's statement of the scene he declared he witnessed, I think it is a good motion, but I doubt their rights to come in at this late hour and make an appeal to bar testimony which was permitted twenty-four hours ago.

Dorsey addressed the court more firmly. "As an original proposition, this testimony is admissible," he said. "Is it just, as a matter of plain, common sense, to let these men give this negro a grueling examination, and, after they have thrashed it out, to let them expunge his statement? Has it come to that?"

Dorsey pointed out that the defense allowed the testimony on Monday and didn't decide to object to the statements until twenty-four hours later. In that time, they spent hours grilling Conley before asking for the ruling. He reminded Judge Roan that in a recent case, he allowed the prosecution to go back fifteen years to show a dealing with that defendant. The evidence the defense wanted struck was proof that this kind of immoral behavior had been taking place for a while, before Mary Phagan. Dorsey, though, was assuming that Conley was telling the truth. What if he wasn't? What if Jim Conley had been the murderer?

Judge Roan addressed the defense and prosecution. "There is no doubt in my mind but that this evidence, as an original proposition, is inadmissible," he said. "I rule out all except the watching which the negro says he did on the day of the murder. I will reserve my decision, however, until I consider it thoroughly. Also, I will postpone any statement to that effect before the jury."

Dorsey's decision to have Jim Conley testify turned out to be wise. Nothing shook the core story Jim told. If the jury believed him, they would see Leo Mary Phagan's killer and Jim as the accomplice who helped hide the body. The defense's decision not to object when Dorsey questioned Jim about the alleged meetings between Leo Frank and various women a year before the murder had been a mistake. Even if Judge Roan told the jury to disregard this part of the testimony, the damage was done. They wouldn't forget what they heard.

The jury came back into the courtroom, and Rosser began cross-examination again. He brought up the insurance salesman, who stated in his affidavit that Jim confessed to him.

"Did you meet a man named Mincey and he said you had promised to take some insurance with him?" Rosser asked.

"No, sir; because I never saw any such man," said Conley.

"Didn't you tell him that you could not take any insurance—that you were in trouble?"

"No, sir."

"Didn't you say that you had killed a girl and that you didn't want to kill any more people?"

"No, sir."

"Didn't he say that one a day would be 365 a year?"

"No, sir."

"Didn't you, on May 31, make a statement to a *Constitution* reporter that Dorsey had come to you and said it was all right for you to come through—that everything was all right?"

Dorsey objected, saying the reporter's name had to be given. Rosser revised his question.

"On May 31, didn't you talk with Harllee Branch, of *The Journal*, and H. W. Ross of the same paper, and tell them that in your opinion Mary Phagan was murdered in the toilet on the second floor and was later carried to the metal room and that the body was stiff when you reached her?"

"No, sir; I don't remember telling it."

"Didn't you tell them that it took thirty minutes to get the body downstairs and for you to get back to the second floor?"

"No, sir."

"Didn't you tell them that you remembered Lemmie Quinn's visit?"

"No, sir."

"Did you talk with them at all?"

"Yes, sir, a little bit."

Rosser then asked Conley if he knew the meaning of the word "previous." Conley admitted he didn't. Rosser asked about several other words and Conley denied knowing their meaning.

When court adjourned on Tuesday, Conley had testified thirteen hours. Rosser would finish his cross-examination on Wednesday morning.

Out of the thirteen hours, Dorsey had questioned Conley for only two. If this discrepancy didn't signal the defense's determination to take Jim's story apart, what would?

☙

Wednesday morning, Rosser took his position in front of Jim Conley to continue his cross-examination that was much of the same. The gallery must have found the repetition of questions and circling back to the same subjects mind-numbing.

Rosser read from Jim's affidavit the first time he told the story of carrying Mary's body to the basement: "The reason I have not told this before is that Mr. Frank said he would get me out," Rosser read, "but it don't seem that he is going to get out and I have decided to tell the whole truth. I gave him back the $200. He said he would fix it all right Monday."

"This is what you swore, isn't it, Jim?" Rosser pressed Conley.

"Yes, sir. I swore it."

"Jim, didn't Miss Carson ask you on Monday while you were working around her machine when they were going to get you. You answered that you hadn't done nothing?"

"No, sir."

"Didn't she say that Mr. Frank was innocent and the real murderer of little Mary Phagan was the man Mrs. White saw near the steps? You dropped your broom and quit sweeping when she said that?"

"No, sir."

"Didn't you say to Mr. Herbert Schiff on Monday after the murder that you were afraid to go out of the factory and that you would give a million dollars to be a white man?"

"I didn't say just that, but I told him if I was a white man I would go on out."

"He told you to get on out, asking you what you had to be afraid of?"

"Something like that."

Rosser closed his cross-examination with questions about another employee who believed Leo was innocent and said that to Conley.

Dorsey stood and asked Jim Conley if he had seen Mary's pocketbook. He said he saw it on Leo's desk when he was writing the notes Leo dictated to him. The solicitor asked Conley to describe the bag. When Jim said the bag looked like wire, Dorsey asked him what Leo did with it.

Jim response was one of the most damning so far. He said Leo put it in his safe. Dorsey had crushed the defense's idea that Conley had stolen the purse and implied that Leo had disposed of it. Dorsey had finished questioning Jim.

Rosser, barely containing his rage, fired questions at Conley about why he hadn't revealed information about the pocketbook in his interviews with the detectives. Jim indicated that no one had asked him about the purse until then.

At 11:10 Wednesday morning, Jim was allowed to step down from the witness stand. He had spent fifteen hours testifying. Conley was escorted to a room, where he removed his coat and lit a cigarette someone handed him.

Newspaper reporters were in the room. One asked, "How did you like it?"[193]

"I liked it all right." Jim grinned at the reporter.

Jim entertained himself by reading a story in the newspaper about his testimony.

ঙ

At two o'clock Wednesday afternoon, court resumed without the jury. Judge Roan had spent his lunch researching the defense's request to throw out some of the prosecution's star witness's testimony. Both the prosecution and the defense had their say. When he was seated at the bench, Judge Roan spoke: "I have serious doubts as to the admissibility of this testimony as an original proposition. As it has been cross examined you may expunge it from the records but you can't disassociate the original from the cross examination. I am going to allow it to remain in the record. It may be extracted from the record, but it is an impossibility to withdraw it from the jury's minds."

The courtroom erupted with applause. The lawyers, both prosecution and defense, along with the Judge Roan, looked astonished.

"I will ask for a mistrial if such a demonstration as this again arises," Arnold said. "Also, I will ask that the court cleared if it continues. Mistrials can easily be caused by just such actions."

"I am ruling just whatever I deem fit and proper," Judge Roan responded, "whether it pleases or displeases. On the question of the Epps boy's testimony, I rule that it is inadmissible."

"I want your honor to rule positively, now, on this first question," said Rosser. He was speaking about the graphic sex act Conley testified to involving Dalton and Daisy.

"I am going to let it remain," the judge calmly declared.[194] This ruling dashed any hope of removing the testimony from consideration by the jury.

The jury returned, and Dorsey redirected, attempting to repair the little damage Rosser had caused. Conley's crucial testimony was left intact. That was a big win for the state.

Chapter 24

The Trial Moves Forward

Unlike the state's triumph with their star witness, the defense's witness, W. H. Mincey, failed to deliver for the defense, even before he took the stand. When Conley was questioned about the insurance salesman, Rosser couldn't get him to budge.

Wednesday afternoon brought Fannie Coleman back to the stand. She described cooking cabbage at Dr. Harris's request for his experiments, which brought him to the conclusion of Mary's time of death. Fannie had ground and cooked the cabbage to the texture she had cooked the morning Mary died. She did not remain on the stand long.

Outside the Atlanta courtroom, life went on. At one o'clock Wednesday morning, a fast-moving freight train, traveling the Louisville and Nashville track in Marietta, careened off a collapsed bridge and into a deep culvert, killing four men. The photo of the wreckage showed a tangled mess of metal and wood. The accident took place a few miles from Mary's childhood home.

Summer was typically a carefree time of year in Atlanta, and despite what was going on in the courtroom, residents enjoyed afternoon receptions, luncheons, and even an informal dance. The Selig house was somber but not depressing. The family fought to keep their spirits up.

Lucille and her mother-in-law faithfully made their way to court Thursday morning. Soon the prosecution would finish, and the defense would have a chance to vindicate Leo. Both women had faith Leo would be freed.

The state called C. B. Dalton, a railroad carpenter, as the first witness Thursday morning. He was there to corroborate Conley's statements about watching the factory door for Leo.[195]

"Were you ever employed at the National Pencil factory?" Dorsey asked.

"No, sir," Dalton replied.

"Did you ever go there?"

"Yes, sir."

"Do you know Daisy Hopkins?" This was the girl allegedly seen in Leo's office to preform sex acts.

"Yes, sir."

"Did you ever go into Frank's office with her?"

"Yes, sir. I went into his office with her two or three times."

"Were you ever in the basement of the factory?"

"Yes, sir."

"Did Frank know that you were there?"

"I don't know if he knew that I was in the basement. He knew that I was in the building."

"Was there anyone in the office with Frank when you were in there?"

"Some women," Dalton replied. Dorsey ended his questioning, and Rosser cross-examined.

"When was it you saw some ladies in the office with Frank?"

"Some time last fall."

"Do you know who the ladies were—you just know that they were ladies—you don't know if one of the ladies was Frank's stenographer?"

"No, sir," he said. Dalton, when questioned, narrowed the time he saw the women in Leo's office to sometime between September and December 1912—a rather broad timeline.

"Who introduced you to Frank?"

"Miss Daisy Hopkins."

"Did you see Jim Conley there?"

"Yes."

"What was he doing when you saw him?"

"Generally sitting on a board."

"Did you see Frank in the office with ladies any time this year?"

"No, sir," said Dalton. Rosser finished his cross-examination with a few more questions and stepped away.

Dorsey explained that he asked the officers of the pencil factory to show the bank book and cash ledger, so he introduced into the record the amount of cash on hand in the office when Mary was killed. Dorsey told the court, "With this evidence and oral testimony from one or two other witnesses, the state will be ready to rest its case."

Dr. Harris was recalled to finish his testimony, which had been cut short by his sickness earlier in the trial. Then, the state rested its case.

ꝏ

The defense had quite the challenge of exposing Conley's story as false. Leo's life depended on their choices and how they handled the witnesses they called. Arnold admitted to the reporters that the defense wasn't sure which witnesses would be called, outside of the first, Dr. L. W. Childs, a physician and surgeon.

Defense attorney Reuben Arnold placed the specimen of cabbage from Mary's stomach in front of Dr. Childs. Dr. Childs examined it.

"I have seen less changed by the digestive juices than that which had been in a person's stomach for 12 hours," he said.[196] He went on to explain that this class of food, carbohydrates, can remain in the stomach unchanged, with practically no digestive process, for hours. Most of the time, digestion takes place after the cabbage passes into the small intestines. He declared that Dr. Harris's estimated time of death was a guess, at best.

When Arnold asked Dr. Childs about Dr. Harris's testimony that the blow to the head caused Mary to lose consciousness, he said this, too, was only a guess. There was no way to be sure. Dorsey cross-examined Dr. Childs but achieved no real reversal in his damaging testimony.

The defense, at least, made the jury question the state's timeline. Arnold followed his first witness with Harry Scott, the Pinkerton detective, who had been questioned earlier in the trial. This appearance was a surprise to most. Scott stated several times that Conley had told conflicting stories. As the *Constitution* reported, "Conley's story from past records, showed itself to be an unfathomably mess of fabrications."[197]

He didn't give any new testimony, but the defense was able to show where Conley held back or told conflicting stories, which was many times. Scott took up the whole afternoon session on Thursday. Court was adjourned.

ঔ

On Friday, Daisy Hopkins was called to the stand by the defense. She was a small woman and described as having bright eyes. Her dress was striped, made of cotton, and was a "bit too short."[198] Her stockings and shoes were white.

Arnold began questioning Daisy.

"Did you ever work for the National Pencil Company?" he asked.[199]

"Yes. I went to work there about October 1, 1911, and quit June 1, 1912."

"What floor?"

"Second floor."

"Did you know Leo M. Frank?"

"I knew him when I saw him. I saw him pass around the factory."

"Did he ever speak to you?"

"No, never in my life."

"Did you ever go into Frank's office and drink beer and cold drinks with other women?"

"No, I never went into his office and I don't drink."

"Do you know C. B. Dalton?"

"I know him when I see him."

"Did you ever speak to him?"

"I went to his home once to see his sister and spoke to him. That is the only time."

"Did you ever go to the pencil factory with Dalton?"

"No, I never did."

"Did you introduce him to Mr. Frank?"

"No, I did not."

"Did you ever go into the factory and go into the basement with Dalton?"

"No, I don't even know where the basement is. I never have been in it."

This questioning, if the jury chose to believe Daisy, destroyed Jim and Dalton's testimony that women met Leo in his office. Arnold turned the witness over to Dorsey.

"Were you ever married?" Dorsey asked.

"Yes," Daisy replied.

"Where?"

"Redair."

"Who did you marry?"

"E. A. Sills."

"Who married you?"

"Preacher Miles."

"Who is your doctor?"

"Dr. Pound."

"What is he treating you for?"

"Stomach trouble."

"Were you ever in jail?"

"No."

"Do you know this man here, Garner, my deputy?"

"No."

"Did he get you out of jail?"

"No, he was along."

"What were you charged with?"

"Somebody told tales on me."

"Who brought you down here?"

"Mr. Burke."

Arnold redirected.

"Who got you out of jail?"

"My lawyer."

"Did you pay anything?"

"I only paid my lawyer his fee."

"Who was your lawyer?"

"Mr. Bill Smith." Daisy just happened to be William Smith's client too.

In 1913, a woman's reputation was her social currency. If it were tarnished—or even questioned—she could be ruined.

Dorsey destroyed any progress Daisy's testimony made for the defense. While he never directly accused her of misconduct, his questions sowed doubt in the jurors' minds. His questions about her marriage, health, and arrest undermined her credibility with the jurors. Her answer when naming her husband didn't help because it raised the question of why she didn't use her husband's name. When Dorsey asked why she was seeing a doctor, jurors could have interpreted her answer as a euphemism for or lie to hide venereal disease—which is exactly what Dorsey wanted the jurors to think. Finally, the question about Daisy's arrest were blatantly to discredit her. Though Conley had been arrested several times, Dorsey wanted the jurors to believe Jim's testimony, so he downplayed his having been in jail. Also, in the South in the early twentieth century, White jurors' were likely to stereotype Black men and almost expect that Conley would have served time in jail at some point. Southern women, though, were held to a different standard, so Daisy never had a chance on the stand.

W. M. Mathews, motorman on the English Avenue streetcar, took the stand next.

"What was your run on April 26?" asked Arnold.[200]

"English avenue that runs to Bellwood," Mathews replied.

"What time did you pass Lindsay Street?"

"Ten minutes to twelve."

"Was that on schedule?"

"Yes."

"Did a little girl named Mary Phagan get on at Lindsay Street?"

"Yes."

"What is the distance from Lindsay Street to Broad Street?"

"About two miles."

"What time did you get to Marietta and Broad streets?

"At 12:07. We were on time."

"Do you recollect where this little girl got off?"

"At Broad and Hunter streets."

"What time did you reach that point?"

"About two and one-half minutes later. It took that long on account of the crowds." Mathews referred to the crowds who had gathered for the Confederate Memorial Day parade in downtown Atlanta.

"It took that long?"

"Yes, I was not running the car then. I was sitting behind Mary Phagan. There was a little girl on the seat with her."

"Where did she get off?"

"Broad and Hunter streets."

"What time was it then?"

"12:10 as near as I could recollect."

"Where did she go when she got off?"

"She walked to the sidewalk with the girl who was with her."

"Did you see this little girl get on the car?"

"Yes."

"Did a little boy get on the car with her?"

"No."

"Do you know this little boy Epps?"

"Yes."

"Did he get on the car with her?"

"No."

"He didn't sit on the seat with her?"

"No; I didn't see him," Mathews said.

When Arnold finished questioning Mathews, Dorsey took over, cross-examining Mathews about the timing, what kind of dress Mary wore, and about Epps being on the car. Mathews couldn't remember her dress exactly, only that it was a light color, and she wore a hat.

When Dorsey tried to trip him up about Epps being on the car, Mathews stuck to his testimony.

"What time did you hear about her murder?" Dorsey asked.

"Sunday morning," Mathews answered.

"What time did you go down to identify her?"

"About 6:45 in the afternoon."

Challenging Mathews, Dorsey asked, "How did you recognize her?" This question was designed to show Mathews couldn't have recognized Mary because he didn't know the color of her dress. But Mathews surprised him.

"Well, I knew her," Mathews replied. "One day she was late and I waited for her and she said she was mad because she was late. Every time after that I would ask her if she was mad."

W.T. Hollis, the street car conductor for the English Avenue and Copper Street line, was called to the witness stand. Arnold's questioning established that Mary got on the streetcar at Lindsay Street, and Hollis said it took twenty-two and half minutes to get to the city. When Hollis was asked when he saw Mary last, he answered that it was at the morgue.[201] Arnold asked Hollis if he saw George Epps on the car with Mary.

"No; he was not with her when I collected the fare."

"Was the car crowded?"

"There were only three passengers."

Assistant prosecutor Hooper then cross-examined the witness. The most important result of the testimony was that neither the conductor nor the motorman saw Epps on the streetcar that day with Mary. So, the state's timeline was in question.

Arnold then called Albert Kauffman, a civil engineer, to the witness chair to discuss a diagram of the pencil factory drawn by Bert Green, a *Georgian* employee. He had Kauffman review all the basement and elevator shaft dimensions. Kauffman's measurements concurred with the prosecution. The state must have questioned the reasons for this repetition. Then Arnold revealed his motive.

"Is there a long hallway on the first floor?" asked Arnold.

"Yes," Kauffman answered.

"What is it used for?"

"Maybe a storeroom."

"What was in there?" Arnold asked.

"Two toilets," Kauffman responded.

"Is this spot directly over where the body was found?"

"Yes."

"What did you find on the right-hand side, next to the toilet?" Arnold questioned.

"A trap door."

And there it was. If Conley was sitting outside of this hallway/storage room, attacked Mary, pulled her in the room, and killed her, he could have taken her body to the basement through the trap door that was wide enough and directly over where her body was found.

Arnold moved on to Leo's office. This was a point of contention. This time he cut straight to the point.[202]

"Did you observe the door of the safe when it stood open in the outer office?" Arnold asked.

"Yes."

"To what extent did it close off the view to the inner office?"

"Entirely."

"Could you see over the safe door?"

"Yes."

"Could a girl?"

"I don't think so."

The last witness to be called to the stand before the lunch recess was J. G. Adams, a photographer. He displayed photos of the factory and the Selig home for the jury.

"Did you go to the Selig home and take some pictures?" Arnold questioned.[203]

"Yes," answered Adams.

"Did you take a couple of photographs, one from the kitchen door on the outside and one from the hallway looking into the dining room?"

"Only a portion of the window."

"Could you see the mirror from this view?"

"No."

"Did you take one from inside the door?"

"Yes."

Then Arnold turned to the photos of the factory by asking Judge Roan if he could show the pictures. The judge agreed, and he passed the photos to the jurors.

"In every one of these instances, Mr. Adams, did you make as accurate photographs as possible?"

"I did."

Hooper quizzed Mr. Adams, making no real headway and planting very little, if any, doubt, concerning the testimony in the jurors' minds.

☙

When court resumed after the lunch recess, the defense produced a three-dimensional model of the factory with no outer walls so the jurors could see straight inside. The model was constructed by P. H. Willet and John Cox, both pattern makers. There were blocks of wood representing the various machines and furniture in Leo's office and a boiler and trash pile in the basement. The model was placed in front of the jury box; the jurors must have been impressed with the scale and detail. Unlike the state's diagram showing a side view of the four floors and rooms of the pencil factory, the model did not have the dotted lines showing the path the two men allegedly took with Mary's body. Also, the model revealed a first-floor room that extended from the rear elevator shaft to the back wall that was not shown on the state's diagram. For years, a container-maker company, Clark Woodenware, used this room as a workroom, and it had an exterior door. In January 1913, Clark Woodenware relocated, and the room became vacant. This exterior door was directly behind where Jim Conley said he sat on boxes to wait for Leo. This more accurate model helped the jurors visualize the crime as if they were walking the factory themselves.

The defense called N. V. Darley, factory personnel director, back to the stand. The hope was that he would dismantle the prosecution's theories of Mary's death and the removal of her body.

The questioning began with the chute or scuttle door. Arnold asked Darley if a body could fit through it; Darley said it could. Arnold attempted to establish the distances from the metal room to the chute and elevator.

"What kind of a day was April 26?" Arnold asked.[204]

"Cloudy and dark," Darley replied.

"Was the space around the front door darker than usual?"

"Yes."

"What time did you leave the factory Saturday morning, April 26?"

"About 9:40 o'clock."

"If Jim Conley said you left at 11 o'clock, is it true, or not?"

"It is not true."

"Who left the factory with you?"

"Mr. Leo Frank."

"Did you see Jim Conley?"

"No."

Darley went on to reveal that he and Leo had a soda. Leo then went to the Montags' home, and Darley went to Montgomery Theater. Arnold asked if the external door in the first-floor room was kept locked. Darley confirmed they had kept it locked since Clark Woodenware moved out in January; however, two or three days after the murder, the door was discovered broken open. When asked whether Clark Woodenware was provided any way into the basement from the room they leased, Darley said there was a second coal scuttle for them. Here was another way into the basement not revealed by the state.

When it was Dorsey's turn to question Darley, he attempted to get Darley to backtrack, but he had little, if any, luck. This witness helped Leo's case a great deal. When he stepped down from the stand, the jurors should have understood the state had been inaccurate about the factory's layout. These new details could have tarnished the state's hypothesis of how the body was moved.

E. F. Holloway was the last witness to take the stand Friday. Arnold again did the questioning. The *Atlanta Constitution* described Holloway as a character out of one of Dickens's novels. He was about sixty, with cold, gray eyes and thin lips.[205]

Arnold began with questioning about Jim Conley.

"Did you ever see Frank pinch him [Jim] or touch him?"

"Never saw Mr. Frank even touch him."

Arnold asked Holloway if he had missed any Saturdays since starting work at the pencil factory. He answered he couldn't remember any absence.

"Did you ever see any women in Frank's office?"

"None except his wife," Holloway said. He explained that once a month, Lucille came on a Saturday and went home with Leo. He described the salesmen and repairmen who showed up every Saturday. The factory wouldn't have been a good place to meet women on Saturdays because of these visitors.

"If Frank had had any women in his office couldn't you have seen them?"

"Yes."

"Did you ever see Frank bring any women into his office for himself or for Schiff [Herbert Schiff, assistant superintendent]?"

"No."

"Did you know that anybody was practicing immorality in the building?"

"No."

When Dorsey's cross-examination planted doubt about the day watchman's motives. After all, Holloway had made it clear that he didn't believe Leo was guilty. The solicitor accused Holloway of trying to sabotage the state's case by getting Newt Lee's predecessor to claim that Leo had always telephoned after hours. One of the sticking points for Leo was his call made to Newt Lee at work the night of Mary's murder. One of the sticking points for Leo was his check-in call on the night of Mary's murder—the first one made to Newt Lee since he began his job at the pencil factory.

Dorsey went after Holloway on this point, shaking the steady witness's resolve. Then he suggested that Holloway wanted the reward money, so he turned Jim Conley into the police for washing his shirt at the factory. Holloway denied any such intention. Dorsey pointed out that Holloway had made it clear to the police that they should remember he was the one who turned Conley in if he were convicted of the murder. Holloway did admit to stating something like this to officers.

The cross-examination likely caused jurors' to suspect that Holloway, wanting the reward, had motive to dispute anything Jim might have testified to on the stand. This was a loss for the defense.

Court adjourned for the day.

ଓ

On Saturday, court met for a half-day session. The defense called George Epps to the stand. Arnold's questions pertained to the *Georgian* reporter who visited Epps's home to speak with him and his sister, Vera, the Sunday after Mary's murder.

"Do you remember a gentleman, a Mr. Minar, coming to your house and talking to you and your sister?" Arnold asked.[206]

"Yes," Epps replied.

"Didn't he ask you when was the last time either of you had seen Mary Phagan?"

"Yes, he asked my sister, he didn't ask me."

"Weren't you there?"

"No, I wasn't there. I was in the house."

"Weren't you standing by your sister and she said the last time Mary Phagan was seen by her was Thursday before the murder and you stood there and said nothing?"

"No, I didn't hear that. I was in the house but I didn't hear all he said to her."

"Come down," said Arnold, directing Epps to leave the witness stand. But Arnold wasn't finished with Epps's story. He called John Minar, the *Georgian* reporter, to the stand.

"After this girl's body was found did you go out to this boy Epps' home?" Arnold asked.

"I did," Minar replied. Arnold asked what the day and time was, and the reporter responded that it was 27 April at eight.

"Did you ask this boy and his sister when they last saw Mary Phagan?"

"Yes."

"Were they together?"

"Yes."

"Is there any doubt both heard you?"

"No."

"What did they say in reply to your question?"

"The girl said she had seen her Thursday."

"Did the boy say anything?"

"He said he rode to the city with her in the mornings occasionally."

"Did he say anything about riding with her that Saturday?"

"No."

Arnold was able to discredit George Epps with the reporter's testimony. It would be another score for the defense.

Next, Herbert Schiff, the assistant superintendent at the pencil factory, was called to the stand.[207]

Arnold asked about Schiff's duties and his role in creating the financial statement. Schiff collected the data for Leo. Arnold asked whether Leo and Schiff had anything to do with the cash. Schiff explained that the two men had access only to the petty cash.

"Who did the real handling of the finances?"

"The general manager, Mr. Sig Montag."

"Who drew the checks?"

"Mr. Montag."

Arnold asked about Leo's monthly pay and found out he drew $150 at the end of every month. Arnold wanted to show that Leo didn't have access to enough cash to have given Jim Conley the two hundred dollars Conley claimed. Even if Leo had drawn his pay, he would have been fifty dollars shy.

"That financial sheet, what was it for?" Arnold referred to the sheet Leo worked on each Saturday afternoon.

"To show whether the week was a profit or a loss," Schiff explained.

"Why did you make it up on Saturday?"

"Because our report never came in until Friday and the pay roll had to be figured in it."

Arnold asked Schiff about the weekly routine of working on Saturdays. Schiff, Darley, and Leo often worked on the financial sheet together on Saturdays. Often, they left for the day together.

"Did you ever see any women there Saturday afternoons?"

"Never."

"Did Mrs. Frank ever come down there on Saturday afternoons?"

"She would come down some time and go home with Mr. Frank."

Arnold turned the questioning to Thanksgiving Day 1912. The day had been cold and rainy; it had snowed the day before. Schiff, Leo, an office boy, and Jim Conley were there that morning. Conley worked on the fourth floor, stacking boxes, and left around ten o'clock that morning. Both Schiff and Leo left shortly after noon. Leo took the Washington Street car that came before Schiff's Whitehall Street car. Schiff recalled that Leo had a function that night at the Orphans' Home with the B'nai Brith, a charitable organization.

The questions turned to Helen Ferguson, who retrieved her pay on Friday, 25 April, the day before Mary's murder. Schiff remembered Helen requesting her own pay but no one else's. There was a rule that if an employee wanted someone else to pick up their pay, the employee had to give that person a note. Schiff made the point that no one went to Leo for their pay on that Friday.

Arnold's examination of Schiff revealed more about Leo's nervousness when anything went wrong at the factory. Leo would pace, and if an employee got hurt, he was useless to help.

During some point in Dorsey's cross-examination, the courtroom laughed at a remark he made. The judge had to settle the crowd by repeatedly banging his gavel for order. Then, Arnold spoke to the court: "I am going to move that this courtroom be cleared, if there is any more of this disturbance. If we have got to take all of this crowd in, we might as well try the case out in the open."[208]

Judge Roan spoke to the gallery: "Mr. Sheriff, find out who is creating this disturbance and bring them to me. I will see if I can't stop it."

After Dorsey quizzed Schiff on office details, court adjourned until nine o'clock Monday morning. This second week of the trial was much better than the first for the defense. Most believed this trend would continue.

☙

Rain was predicted for Monday morning. Many believed the trial would conclude by the next Saturday. Lucille and Ray faithfully sat in their places in the courtroom. Each day someone from Mary's family sat in the courtroom to listen to the trial. Their placed their trust in Hugh Dorsey to bring the guilty man to justice.

The world outside the courtroom continued. Most citizens were unconcerned with the events in the Atlanta courthouse. In London, police used clubs on suffragettes. The United States Senate debated tax law changes for another week. There was unrest in Venezuela, and the USS *Des Moines*, an armored cruiser, was dispatched to help the thankful Americans stuck there.

Schiff returned to the stand so Dorsey could finish his cross-examination. He got Schiff to admit that if Mary's body had been thrown down the chute in the Clark Woodenware room, it would have landed in a place in the basement where Newt Lee would have seen it sooner.

Under Dorsey's grilling, Schiff admitted that Conley had to be watched all the time since he proved to be untrustworthy.

When the defense redirected, Arnold regained the upper hand when Schiff asserted that finding trustworthy Negroes was difficult. Schiff's statement perpetuated the racial stereotype—common among Southerners of that era—that Black men were shiftless and lazy. This ending testimony proved to be a win for the defense.

Following Schiff's testimony were two doctors to prove the state's witness, Dr. Harris, wrong in his findings about Mary's time of death. Harris had testified that the contents of Mary's stomach put her death within thirty minutes to an hour after she ate her breakfast that morning, and he asserted that the blow to Mary's head knocked her unconscious. Dorsey grilled both doctors, salvaging some of Dr. Harris's testimony.

Then Dr. Willis Westmoreland, a prominent Atlanta physician and surgeon, took the witness chair. Arnold asked the doctor his ethical opinion of a doctor who, in a murder case, would take the organs and stomach from a body to examine in complete secrecy, leaving nothing behind from which doctors for the opposing side might draw their own conclusions.

Dorsey objected.

"We wish to show that Dr. Harris has violated all the ethics of his profession," Arnold rebutted, "as well as the principles of decency and honesty."[209] He was allowed to continue questioning Dr. Westmoreland and asked the doctor to provide details about Harris's professional violations.

"I simply brought charges of scientific dishonesty against him [Dr. Harris]," Dr. Westmoreland explained. "He was found guilty of the charges, but the charges were not thought sufficiently grave to warrant his dismissal from the State Board of Health. I thereupon resigned."

"His testimony on this matter must be a surmise entirely," Westmoreland stated. "His statement in regard to the cabbage is about as wild a guess as I ever heard." The doctor went on to say that Dr. Harris's conclusions were entirely baseless.

Dorsey tried to show that Dr. Westmoreland had a personal grudge against Dr. Harris. Arnold, on redirect, did his best to repair the damage.

As Monday came to a close, Arnold called Joel Hunter to the stand. Hunter was a well-known accountant with clients from all over the country. He insisted, after examining the financial sheet Leo worked on the afternoon of Mary's murder, that it could take no fewer than 172 minutes to complete such a report. Hunter held firm on his assessment during Dorsey cross-examination.

The day closed with mostly wins for the defense.

ര

The first witness of Tuesday, C. E. Pollard, was another accountant. When he looked at the financial sheet Leo worked on that Saturday, Pollard announced that the work was more intricate than Joel Hunter said. This accountant predicted that it would take Leo 209 minutes to complete it accurately. Pollard, even after cross-examination by the prosecution, gave the defense another victory.

Next, the defense called Hattie Hall, the stenographer for Montag Brothers Paper Company. Miss Hall was the perfect example of a successful, professional young woman. She explained that Frank called her, pleading that she come to work that Saturday morning because of his workload. Leo told her his work would keep him in the office until six that evening, but Hattie's first responsibility was to Montag Brothers. She wouldn't have time to help Leo.

At ten, when Leo arrived at Montag Brothers, he again pressed her to work with him that day. Realizing she was ahead of schedule with her own work, she agreed to help him. Sometime between ten thirty and eleven, Hall made the five-minute walk to the pencil factory, where she filled out orders, took dictation for several letters, typed them, and handed them to Leo to sign. She worked for about an hour, so she was ready to leave at noon.

When Arnold inquired if Leo was working on the financial sheet, Hattie Hall answered no. He had been working on the orders and dictating letters to her.

In his cross-examination, Dorsey attempted to get Miss Hall to say she didn't know what Leo was doing in his office, but she stood firm. The solicitor then brought up a weekly pay raise that Hall had received on 1 August. Hattie Hall, in her best professional attitude, said that the pay raise had been planned a long time and was part of her hiring.

Arnold redirected, asking if Hall heard Leo on the phone while she was there. She said Leo had been on the phone with Harry Gottheimer and asked that Gottheimer stop by his office that afternoon. Then she explained that Leo asked her to stay the rest of the afternoon because of the amount of work he had to complete. Her testimony offered proof that he had no plans to meet up with Mary, as Jim Conley claimed.

After Hattie Hall stepped down, the defense called witnesses who addressed the Saturdays well before the day Mary was murdered. These testimonies were intended to show that Leo wouldn't have been meeting women in his office. Coincidentally, all the witnesses came from the county east of Atlanta, where the railroad engineer C. B. Dalton lived; Dalton had corroborated Conley's testimony that Leo met women for sex on Saturdays. Not one of these people had anything positive to say about Dalton. Dorsey declined to cross-examine these witnesses.

The next witness was Alonzo Mann, Leo's office boy. The defense expected that Mann could refute all Conley and Dalton claimed happened on those Saturdays. Alonzo was at the factory every Saturday until noon but hung around the building until four. He testified he had never seen Dalton at the pencil factory, but only fourteen years old, Alonzo was visibly shaken. His voice was soft, and the court stenographer had a hard time hearing his answers. Years later, his testimony would come back to the forefront of the case.

The next witness, Wade Campbell, walked to the witness stand with total confidence, stopping at the defense table to bow to Leo. Campbell was Mrs. Arthur White's brother. Campbell recounted that his sister told him that she saw a Black man sitting at the elevator at noon on Saturday, 26 April. The state had maintained she saw Conley there at one o'clock. Dorsey attempted to get Campbell to waver about the time, but he would not. Each time asked, he repeated his original statement.

After lunch recess, Gordon "Snowball" Bailey, who was the pencil factory's elevator operator and Conley's friend, and Phillip Chambers were called to the stand but did not answer, so Magnolia Kennedy took the stand for the defense. Arnold asked if she knew Helen Ferguson; she said she did.[210]

Arnold then asked Kennedy if she drew her pay on that Friday. She answered she had drawn it at Mr. Schiff's pay window.

"Did you see Helen Ferguson?" Arnold continued.

"I had my hand on her shoulder when got her money," Kennedy replied.

"Was Mr. Frank there?"

"No."

"Did you ask for Mary Phagan's pay?"

"No."

"Did Helen Ferguson ever say anything about Mary's pay?"

"She said at 5 o'clock that Mary was not there."

When Dorsey cross-examined Kennedy, he did not ask about Helen collecting Mary's pay. He asked Magnolia whose hair was in the lathing machine. She answered that it looked like Mary's.

Arnold redirected to ask about the pay.

"You went with Helen Ferguson to get your pay that Friday?"

"Yes."

"Did you see her speak to Mr. Frank?"

"No."

There was a clash between Arnold and Dorsey when Gordon Bailey, who had finally arrived, took the stand next.

"Where did you work in April of this year, Snowball?" Arnold asked.[211]

"At the pencil factory."

"On Friday before Memorial Day did you see Jim Conley talking to Mr. Frank and hear Mr. Frank ask him to come back Saturday?"

"No, sir."

"Did you ever hear Mr. Frank tell Jim to come back?"

"No, sir."

"Did you ever see Mr. Frank bring any women there?"

"No."

"Did you ever see Conley watching at the lower door?"

"No."

"Were you at the factory last Thanksgiving Day?"

"I don't remember."

"Did you ever see Conley reading a newspaper?"

"I saw him looking at the papers down there at the station house."

"You never saw Mr. Frank talking to Conley at any time, did you?"

"No."

Phillip Chambers, the fifteen-year-old former office boy, was called to the stand. He said that he had worked at the pencil factory from 12 December 1912 to 29 March 1913. When asked about Saturdays, he said he worked all day until four thirty, except for eleven to noon, when he sometimes went to the Bell Street plant to get the payroll, and when he took lunch from one thirty to two o'clock. The only woman he ever saw at Leo's office on Saturdays was Lucille. Jim Conley was known occasionally to sweep the pencil factory on Saturday afternoons.

"On any Saturdays or other days, did Mr. Frank ever have any women in his office—did he ever give beer drinking parties?" Arnold inquired.[212]

"No, sir: I never saw any," Chambers replied.

Dorsey then took over the cross-examination.

"Where do you now work?" Dorsey questioned.

"At the pencil factory," Chambers said.

"What did Frank try to get you to [do]."

"I never complained to Mr. Gantt."

"Do you deny that you told Gantt of improper advances and propositions Frank had been making to you?"

"Yes."

"Didn't you tell Gantt that Frank had threatened to fire you if you didn't permit him to do with you what he wanted to do?"

Arnold was on his feet to object. He asked Judge Roan to strike the questions and answers on the grounds of gross prejudice and irrelevance. Roan sustained his objection. Arnold was incensed: "It is the unfairest thing I have ever heard of, brought in this illegal way.... It is beyond indignation to sit here and listen to such stuff. The charge could be brought against you or me or any member of the jury by such innuendos. If it comes up again, I am going to move for a mistrial." Arnold wanted the jurors to seize on the injustice.[213]

"I have already ruled it out," Judge Roan said from the bench.

"Well, we will put up Gantt and let you rule on that," Arnold replied.

What damage did Dorsey's questions do to the defense's case? He had attempted to sway the jury's perception of Frank by reminding them of the prior salacious testimony and implying Frank had engaged in other lurid behavior.

The witness was dismissed, and Minola McKnight, the Seligs' cook, took the stand. The day promised to be anything but boring.

"Where do you work?" Arnold opened his questioning.[214]

"With Mrs. Emil Selig," McKnight replied.

"Were you there on April 26th?"

"Yes."

"At what time?"

"About 6:30 o'clock."

"Did you see him leave?"

"Yes."

"When did you next see him?"

"About 2 o'clock."

"What time did he have dinner?"

"It was ready when he came in."

"What time did he get home?"

"About 1:20 o'clock."

Arnold asked McKnight if her husband, Albert, was at the Selig home during Leo's lunch. She said he wasn't there during dinner or any other time of the day. McKnight testified that Leo left the house to go back to work at two o'clock. If the jurors believed her, they would also have to accept that, at the very least, the state's timeline was wrong. Mrs. McKnight testified that Leo came home that evening around six thirty and ate his supper. Arnold then asked about Minola's arrest on 2 June.

"What did they [the detectives] try to get you to say?"

"One thing that Miss Lucille wouldn't sleep with Mr. Frank because Mr. Frank wouldn't let her."

"What was Albert claiming?"

"That I told him Miss Lucille had come down and said Mr. Frank had come home drunk and had made her sleep on the rug on the floor."

"What did the detectives do?"

"They said they'd put me in jail until I told a better lie."

"Did they make you sign anything?"

"Yes; in order to get out of jail I signed something I didn't know a thing about."

Dorsey then stood to address Minola McKnight. He was facing Lucille's letters in the newspapers calling him out for the arrest and harassment of McKnight. Lucille watched from her chair. There must have been some satisfaction in the moment, but Dorsey didn't seem a bit bothered or nervous. He read the first part of Minola's statement and asked if she made the statement.

"Yes, but some parts of it I didn't," she answered.

He went on to ask about her denials when Albert confronted her about things she allegedly told him.

"They wanted me to tell a lie," she explained.

"What kind of lie?" Dorsey asked. Minola indicated that the detectives wanted her to agree with Conley. She wouldn't because he had lied.

"Didn't Albert put his arm around you and say you were telling a lie, and that he wanted you to tell the truth?"

"Yes; but he was telling the lie," Minola said. Dorsey read the startling affidavit she had made at police headquarters.

"I signed my name to it, but they made me sign it," she protested.

"How did they make you?"

"They said that if I didn't, they'd put me in jail and keep me there."

Dorsey brought up the money that the Seligs allegedly gave her. Minola remained resolute and denied she had received any money.

The last witnesses of the day were Lucille's parents. Emil took the stand first and confirmed that Leo behaved completely normally when he came in for lunch at about twenty minutes after one on the afternoon of 26 April. He observed no scratches or marks of any kind on Leo. He couldn't remember when Leo left to go back to the factory that afternoon, but he did know he returned around six thirty that evening. Emile described that there were a number of ladies visiting that evening to play cards. When asked if Leo played, Emil said that Leo was in the hall, reading some humorous story about the umpire's decision for the Atlanta Crackers game. He went on to say that Lucille and Leo went to bed before the guests left, and he didn't see Leo until late the following morning. Emil said he never heard the phone ringing in the house during the night.

Josephine Selig's testimony was somewhat dramatic, at least for her. Arnold began by explaining he was going to ask her questions about Minola McKnight's affidavit in an effort to get to the truth.

"Is it true that there was talk in your home about the time of the murder of Leo Frank being caught with a girl at the factory," Arnold began, "and that the negro cook asked if it was a Jew girl or a Gentile, and you or Mrs. Frank said it was a Gentile?"[215]

"It is not true: there was no such conversation that I know of," Josephine insisted, near tears.

"Did Mrs. Frank say that he had told her he was in trouble, and that he did not know why he would commit murder, or did she tell you he had asked her for a pistol to kill himself with?"

"No."

"Did you raise the wages of Minola McKnight, your cook, right after the murder?"

"Not a penny."

Dorsey cross-examined her.

"How long after the murder was it before your daughter visited her husband in jail?"

"I don't know," Josephine answered.

"Do you recall the occasion when someone came to your house to get a statement from your cook?"

"No."

"Do you remember that Albert McKnight, the cook's husband, was there on Saturday, April 26?"

"No."

"What time did Frank leave the house that Sunday morning?"

"I don't know."

"What time did he get back that night?"

"I don't remember." Dorsey continued to question Josephine about the timeline, but in most cases, she couldn't remember.

"How long did you say it was after Frank was locked up before his wife went to see him?"

"I don't know. I think it was on Thursday that she first went."

"Did you say that Mrs. Frank did not tell you her husband did not rest well that Saturday night?"

"She did not tell me that."

"She didn't tell you he was drunk?"

"She did not."

"Wasn't it two weeks before your daughter went to see her husband in jail?"

"No."

The solicitor asked more questions about the day of Lucille's first visit to Leo in jail, but Josephine couldn't remember. He moved on to McKnight's weekly pay. Josephine said she paid her cook $3.50 a week. When he asked if she gave McKnight any extra money, she admitted to once having advanced her a week's pay, but the cook paid her back. When asked about the reported five dollars given to McKnight, Josephine said she had given her five dollars but told the cook to go get change so she could be paid.

"When did Mrs. Frank give her a hat?"

"I don't remember."

An argument ensued, and Rosser moved to rule out all references to events that took place before Lucille visited Leo in jail. Roan issued that all references to their married life be ruled out.

Josephine was asked to step down from the witness stand, but before she did, Arnold jumped to his feet. He acknowledged that the circumstances surrounding the murder were terrible and that Josephine probably didn't want to talk about it since she was ill.

"My health is bad and I did not care to hear much of the facts of the crime at the time. I was operated on the next day. Mr. Frank spared my feelings."[216]

Twenty-two witnesses were called to the stand on Tuesday, setting a record for Leo's case and maybe all trials up until that point.

ଓ

Wednesday morning, the defense called another doctor to dispute Dr. Harris's findings about the contents of Mary's stomach and several men who cast doubt on Dalton's testimony of women in Leo's office. Around the middle of the morning, the defense shifted tactics, causing an important crossroads for the case. Arnold called several character witnesses from New York.

Then the defense called Dr. William Owen, a time-motion expert, to the stand. Dr. Owens described using stand-ins at the factory, along with a 107-pound bag of sand, to reenact the time it would take

Conley to remove the body that morning. Owens concluded that it would take at least thirty-six minutes for Jim's scenario to play out. If the timing was as Conley said, disposing of Mary's body would have taken too long, and Leo would not have arrived home when numerous people testified that he did. Hooper's cross-examination did not prove that Jim Conley's timing was correct.

Arnold called Lemmie Quinn to the witness stand and questioned him about his surprise visit to the factory, placing him there only minutes after Mary left Leo's office. This made the prosecution look even worse with the timing. Quinn spoke about Barrett, the employee who discovered the alleged blood spots, stating several times that Barrett wanted the reward money.

Dorsey came after Quinn with all his skill, but he could not shake the man from saying that Leo was hard at work at his desk when Quinn arrived at the factory around 12:20 p.m.

J. Ashley Jones, an insurance representative of the New York Life Insurance Company, took the stand next. A year and a half before the murder, Jones had asked for a report on Frank so he could write an insurance policy. Jones testified that Leo was in good physical and moral condition.

Dorsey cross-examined Jones at about four in the afternoon. It had been a frustrating day for the state. He asked Mr. Jones if he heard that Frank took liberties with little girls in Druid Hills, a neighborhood of Atlanta, and Dorsey gave graphic details.

"No, nor you either—you dog!" Ray, Leo's mother was partially out of her seat.[217] She had taken all she could of this slanderous talk. Deputies rushed to where Ray now stood, staring at Dorsey.

Arnold rose, speaking before she could say another word. "Mrs. Frank," he said, "if you stay in the courtroom I'm afraid you'll have to hear these vile, slanderous lies, and I would suggest that if you have reached the limit of your patience you might retire for a little while."

Herbert Haas, a family friend and one of the defense lawyers, escorted Ray, now crying, out of the courtroom, and put her in a cab to go home.

Ray's reaction did nothing to tame Dorsey, who continued his line of questioning, using the names of so-called victims.

The court adjourned. Toxicity was in the air. The trial had changed.

☙

As court began Thursday morning, the jury was delayed from entering. Dorsey asked the judge to allow neither Lucille nor Ray in court for the duration of the trial. He said the courtroom needed to be kept safe, and the women couldn't handle such testimony, which would continue. Arnold suggested he was being overzealous. Dorsey responded:

> It's a mistaken idea about me being overzealous. I am trying to do my duty. I want to protect myself and the court. You have excluded other women. There is no reason why these should be allowed to remain to offend the dignity of the court. An accused man should not be allowed to bankrupt his wife and mother. Mr. Arnold criticizes my act. The courts have held it is highly improper for a lawyer to express his opinion on the evidence. Mr. Arnold has branded this evidence as lies before I put these good women on the stand.[218]

Dorsey's address to the court sounded vindictive and wholly without empathy for Ray. His statement made it evident he didn't care that the graphic scenarios he described might be spurious. The fact he brought Lucille into this accusation, when she had remained quiet through the testimony, suggested his hard feelings about her letters to the newspapers had not dissipated.

Arnold requested that Jones's testimony be struck down.

Judge Roan addressed Dorsey.

> You are entirely right, Mr. Dorsey, in saying that you are entitled to protection. Other women were put out because the evidence was of such a nature as to be indecent to be heard by them. It is a matter of the discretion of the court to state

> whether these ladies should be allowed to remain. I will say that if there are any more such outbreaks as yesterday I shall be forced to exclude them.[219]

Both Lucille and Ray were present for the argument. They must have felt helpless in the face of Dorsey's scorn, but the prosecutor failed to oust the women from the proceedings.

The jury was called into the courtroom and the morning session began.

Arnold opened the day's testimony intent on confirming Leo's timeline on the day Mary was murdered. The first to take the stand was Miss Helen K. Curran, who was at Jacob's at the corner of Alabama and Whitehall streets. Five minutes after arriving, she noticed Leo standing on the corner. The time was 1:10. According to Jim Conley's story, Leo would have still been in the pencil factory.

Next was Lucille's aunt, Mrs. M. G. Michael, of Athens, Georgia, who was visiting Atlanta on April 26. At two o'clock that afternoon, she was visiting her sister, Mrs. Wolfsheimer, at 287 Washington Street. She saw Leo walking up Washington Street at two o'clock while standing on her sister's porch. Leo walked up to the porch and spoke to her.

During Hooper's cross-examination, Mrs. Michael said Leo was headed toward Washington and Glenn streets. And so it went. Each witness called placed Leo on Washington Street at two o'clock.

How could so many be wrong on the time and Conley be correct? The state failed to shake any of the witnesses' testimony. Arnold had managed to place Leo on a streetcar back to town at two o'clock, which contradicted Albert McKnight's testimony that Leo left much earlier.

Rebecca Carson, a foreman at the pencil factory, took the stand and described a conversation that took place on Monday after the murder. Several of the employees were talking about where they were when Mary was killed. When they got to Jim Conley, he declared that he was so drunk he didn't know where he was or what he did. Carson testified that Conley left the conversation when someone suggested that the murderer was probably the Black man Mrs. White had seen on the first floor.

Sig Montag, president of the National Pencil Company and Leo's boss, was called to the stand. His significant testimony came when he explained that part of the time Jim Conley said he was standing guard for Leo, the Clark Woodenware Company was working in the room on the first floor. He pointed out the room on the model.

Montag also told of Leo talking about seeing Mary at Bloomfield's. When Rosser asked if Leo was nervous, Montag said that he was but no more than Montag himself was. He witnessed no scratches or marks on Leo.

When Montag stepped down, court was adjourned for lunch.

The afternoon brought more character witnesses.

❧

A much larger crowd gathered on Friday morning amid the rumor that the defense would close and Leo would take the stand; however, the only big news on Friday morning was that the defense would not call W. H. Mincey. The insurance salesman would not testify. On more than one occasion, Mincey had said he heard Conley admit to murdering a young girl on the same afternoon as Mary's murder.

Dorsey announced that day that sixteen-year-old Dewey Hewell had returned home from the Home of the Good Shepherd, a home for unwed mothers in Cincinnati, Ohio. Rumors of Daisy had floated through Atlanta; she had returned solely to testify at the trial.

Miss Hewell worked at the pencil factory for four months and quit in March 1913. She testified that while working at the factory, she saw Leo talk to Mary two or three times a day in the metal department. She also claimed to have seen him standing close to Mary, with his hand on her shoulder. Hewell testified that she heard Leo call Mary by name.

The defense spent the morning calling more character witnesses that Dorsey didn't even bother cross-examining.

The afternoon produced more witnesses to impeach Conley's testimony. Arnold then introduced a parade of factory girls as character witnesses for Frank. Mrs. E. H. Carson, a supervisor at the pencil factory, was called to the witness stand late in the afternoon. She had been employed at the factory for three years and admitted to seeing what everyone had called blood spots on the floor in the metal room. When asked when she had last seen Jim Conley, she answered on the Tuesday after the murder, 28 April. "He came to my machine and I said: 'Jim, I see they haven't got you yet,'" she recounted. "Thursday he came again. I told him the same thing. He said that he had done nothing for them to get him about. I said, 'No and poor Mr. Frank hasn't done anything either.' He said: 'No'm, and he's as innocent as you is.'"[220]

Mrs. Carson said that Jim walked away after she told him the police would catch the murderer when they found the Black man Mrs. White saw that Saturday.

Under direct examination by Arnold, Mrs. Carson asserted that she knew all the girls on the fourth floor, where she was a supervisor.

"We intend putting on the stand every girl on the fourth floor to question her whether or not she has ever been in Frank's office and seen other girls there or beer bottles," Arnold said.[221] Arnold intended to show the jury that every girl on the fourth floor would attest to Frank's character and corroborate that he didn't have girls or beer in the office.

Annie Hicks, the maid at the home of Charles Ursenbach (sometimes spelled "Ersenbach" in the papers), Lucille's brother-in-law, testified that Leo called to cancel a baseball game invitation for the afternoon of 26 April. She testified that Frank called at one o'clock, and she took the message. While on the phone with Leo, Annie Hicks heard Leo speak to Lucille. She went on to say Leo stopped by the Ursenbach home on Sunday morning after the murder. Miss Hicks said he was not nervous.

The last witness of the day was Ray Frank, Leo's mother. The courtroom was surprised to hear her name called. The gallery sat straight to listen. Ray raised her hand and took an oath to tell the truth with a strong, confident voice, but her face showed the strain of the trial.

Defense attorney Luther Rosser established that Leo had been born in Texas before his parents moved to New York City, then to Brooklyn, where he grew up. Ray Frank was asked who M. Frank was, and she answered he was her brother-in-law and lived in Atlanta. She went on to say that she had seen him in New York on 27 and 28 April at the Hotel McAlpine.

The prosecution objected when Rosser indicated that he wanted to read a letter to Mrs. Frank. Arnold pointed out that the contents of the letter would help confirm Leo's timeline. Ray was allowed to read it to herself. The letter was from Leo to his uncle, Moses Frank, who received it on the Monday after the murder.

> Atlanta, Ga., April 26, 1913
> Dear Uncle:
>
> I trust that this finds you and dear Tante ["aunt"] well after arriving safely in New York. I hope that you found all the dear ones well in Brooklyn and I await a letter from you telling me how you find things there. Lucile and I are well.
>
> It is too short a time since you left for anything startling to have developed down here. The opera has Atlanta in its grip, but that ends today. I've heard a rumor that opera will not be given again in a hurry here.
>
> To-day was "Yondef" ["holiday"] here, and the thin gray line of veterans, smaller each year, braved the rather chilly weather to do honor to their fallen comrades.
>
> Enclosed you will find last week's report. The shipments still keep up well, tho' the result is not what one would wish. There is nothing new in the factory, etc., to report. Enclosed please find the price list you desired.
>
> The next letter from me, you should get on board ship. After that I will write to the address you gave me in Frankfurt.

With much love to you both, in which Lucille joins me,
I am
Your affectionate nephew,
[Signed] Leo M. Frank.[222]

When Ray Frank finished reading the letter, she confirmed the letter had been written by Leo in his handwriting.

This was the last witness on Friday. Court was adjourned.

Saturday morning the gallery received the excitement they had been seeking. First, Ray Frank was called to the stand for Dorsey's cross-examination. From the first question, Dorsey proved that he intended to make her pay for calling him a "dog" in her outburst. He questioned Ray relentlessly about her husband's investments—twenty thousand dollars' worth. The retired couple lived off the interest but were by no means wealthy. Still, this sum must have seemed a fortune to those twelve men sitting on the jury. He even asked Ray the worth of their home in Brooklyn—ten thousand dollars. Dorsey brought up Moses Frank's wealth.

Rosser redirected, and even though he pointed out that Mr. Frank, Leo's father, worked hard and saved the money they had, the damage had been done to the defense's case.

Another of Leo's many character witnesses, Miss Irene Jackson, took the stand, but her testimony didn't go as planned. Arnold was on alert when he heard Jackson's lukewarm assessment that Leo was of good character "So far as I know."[223]

Dorsey, being keen on Jackson's response, took full advantage of the situation when he cross-examined her. As he questioned this employee, a daughter of county police officer A. W. Jackson, he elicited from her that on several occasions, Leo had opened the door of the girls' dressing room while the girls were changing clothes, looked in, and then closed the door. According to Miss Jackson, the girls had reported the episode to the supervisor, and her sister almost quit because of it.

Miss Jackson had quit her job at the pencil factory the Monday after the murder. She said that Darley had promised the girls that if they stuck by the company and didn't quit because of the murder, they would not "lose anything by it."[224]

The defense attempted to show that the only reason Leo opened the door was because he heard the girls flirting with men out the window that faced Forsyth Street, and he wanted it to stop. This testimony hurt the defense's case even though the next witness, Mrs. Cora Barnes, who worked on the fourth floor, praised Leo and talked about what a good soul he was. Many factory girls were called on Saturday morning to testify to Leo's good character.

One development made public on Saturday was the defense's decision to call 150 women and girls who work at the pencil factory to testify on behalf of Leo's character. Leo was expected to take the stand no later than Tuesday. Many were hoping the jury would get the case by Wednesday.

ଓ

On Monday morning, people clamored to enter the courthouse to get a seat. The trial of Leo Frank for Mary Phagan's murder had entered its third week and turned into the longest in Georgia's history. People wanted to see what sensational testimony Leo would give, but they must have been disappointed because the morning was filled with more character witnesses. Emily Mayfield, one of the workers supposedly changing her clothes in the dressing room when Leo came in, took the stand and denied that Leo ever came into the dressing room. Her answers impeached all of Irene Jackson's testimony. Court was adjourned for lunch.

Leo had prepared for his statement by dictating to Lucille. During the recess, he read over what he would say.

ଓ

When court reconvened around two o'clock, spectators densely packed into the courtroom. Leo Frank was called to testify. The *Atlanta Georgian* called Leo's testimony the most thorough in detail and logic ever related in a Georgia court by a man accused of murder. This was a nice way of saying Leo went into details that didn't lend much to saving him from a conviction.

Lucille smiled at him as he told of their life together. "My married life has been exceptionally happy," he said, "in fact the happiest period of my life."[225]

Leo began at the beginning by telling the jurors where and when he was born. He told in great detail exactly what jobs he held before he came to Atlanta and how he came to be the superintendent of the National Pencil Company. He described his duties in great detail. Then he mapped out Friday, 25 April, beginning with his arrival at the factory at seven that morning. He spent the day doing payroll, and in the evening, Mr. Schiff paid the employees. No one came into Leo's office to request a pay envelope for someone else.

On Friday evening, he arrived home around six thirty, cleaned up, had supper, and then went with Lucille to play auction bridge with friends. They returned home at eleven and went to bed.

On Saturday, 26 April, Leo got up between seven and seven thirty, in no hurry. He had breakfast before catching either the Washington Street car or the Georgia Avenue car. When he arrived at the factory around 8:20 a.m., Mr. Holloway, the day watchman, was in his typical place, and Alonzo Mann, the office boy, was in the office. Leo presented the invoices he worked on Saturday morning to the jurors and described their importance. He went into great detail, likely far more than the jurors wanted to hear.

When he got to the part about Mary coming for her pay, the gallery was silent.

> There were then in the building Arthur White, Harry Denham and Mrs. White. It must have been from ten to fifteen minutes after that this little girl whom I afterwards

> found to be Mary Phagan came in. She asked for her pay. I got my cash box, referred to the number and gave her the envelope. As she went out, she stopped near my outer office door and said: "Has the metal come?" The safe door was open and I could not see her, but I answered "No." The last I heard was the sound of her footsteps going down the hall. But a few moments after she asked me, I had the impression of a voice saying something but it made no impression on me. The little girl had hardly left the office when Lemmie Quinn came in. He said something to me about working on a holiday and went out. A few minutes before 1 o'clock, I called up my wife and told her I was coming to lunch at 1:15.[226]

Leo explained the details of leaving for lunch that had conflicted with Conley's timeline.

Judge Roan called a recess at 4:35 p.m., two and a half hours after Leo began testifying. When court began again, Leo began talking about his nerves that day.

> Now, gentlemen, I have heard a great deal, and so have you, in this trial, about nervousness.... Gentlemen, I was nervous, I was very nervous, I was completely unstrung, I will admit it; imagine, awakened out of my sound sleep and a morning run down in the cool of the morning in an automobile driven at top speed, without any food or breakfast, rushing into a dark passageway, coming into a darkened room, and then suddenly an electric light flashed on, and to see the sight that was presented by the poor little child; why it was a sight that was enough to drive a man to distraction; that was a sight that would have made a stone melt.... Of course I was nervous; any man would be nervous if he was a man.

Before finishing, Leo addressed the insinuation that Lucille did not visit him for two weeks because she believed him guilty. Dorsey had made the accusation more than once.

> Now the truth of the matter is this, that on April 29th, the date I was taken in custody at police headquarters, my wife was there to see me, she was downstairs on the first floor; I was up on the top floor. She was there almost in hysterics, having been brought there by her two brothers-in-law, and her father. Rabbi Marx was with me at the time. I consulted with him as to the advisability of allowing my dear wife to come up to top floor to see me in those surroundings with city detectives, reporters and snapshotters; I thought I would save her that humiliation and that harsh sight, because I expected any day to be turned loose and be returned once more to her side at home. Gentlemen, we did all we could do to restrain her in the first days when I was down at the jail from coming on alone down to the jail, but she was perfectly willing to even be locked up with me and share my incarceration.

Leo, responding to the statements of Dalton, Irene Jackson, and Jim Conley, denied they were telling the truth. In response to the allegations of women coming to his office for beer and sex, he said, "I have no language with which to fitly denounce it."

"Gentlemen, some newspaper men have called me 'the silent man in the Tower,' and I kept my silence and my counsel advisedly, until the proper time and place," Frank continued. "The time is now; the place is here; and I have told you the truth, the whole truth."[227]

Lucille began to cry, and Leo took her in his arms. A few sobs escaped from one juror. After four hours of Leo's testimony, court was dismissed This lengthy testimony and his reserved manner would come back to haunt him.

Chapter 25

Closing Arguments

Early Tuesday morning, Dorsey made known his intention to crush the defense. The state moved on to the rebuttal, and the solicitor asked Judge Roan to dismiss Leo's female relatives because the testimony wouldn't be fit for them. Lucille, in her regular place, was flanked by her mother on one side and her mother-in-law on the other.

When the defense introduced character witnesses, they opened the door for the state to call character witnesses as well. Dorsey had been thrilled when Rosser and Arnold began to call these people to the stand; his mission was to take apart the defense's case piece by piece.

Dorsey's attempt to show that Minola McKnight in no way was coerced into signing her statement backfired when George Gordon, Minola's lawyer, said that Dorsey refused to sign an order to release McKnight. Gordon recalled that Dorsey claimed he didn't have Minola arrested and he wouldn't do anything that would get him in bad with detectives.

The prosecutor then attempted to repair the damage done to Dr. Harris's testimony about the time of death. Dr. S. C. Benedict, president of the state board of health, took the stand. The defense and state haggled over the state board of health minutes, and each of Dorsey's questions was ruled out. Dr. Benedict failed to help the state rehabilitate Dr. Harris's testimony.

Four witnesses were called to attack Daisy Hopkins's character, followed by ten witnesses who corroborated Dalton's credibility—and thus lent credibility to his stories about women in Leo's office. One of these many witnesses was Willie Turner, a farmer who had worked at the pencil factory in March before Mary was murdered in April. Turner stated he witnessed Frank speaking with Mary in the metal room around noon on a day in mid-March. No one else was in the room that Turner could see. When asked if he heard anything, Turner replied, "She told Mr. Frank she had to go back to work." When pushed for more, Turner revealed he heard Leo say to Mary that he was "superintendent of the factory and that he wanted to talk to her."[228] When Rosser pressed Turner during cross-examination to describe Mary, Turner was vague, describing her with light hair. Mary had auburn hair. In a win for the defense, Turner also couldn't name or describe any of the other girls watching.

Several streetcar workers called to the stand said the English Avenue car Mary rode that morning was ahead of schedule. Their testimony was intended to impeach the conductor's statement for the defense. Soon after, Dorsey rested his case.

The defense was allowed their own rebuttal, but the likelihood of repairing the damage wasn't great. They called a handful of witnesses who made little difference. Leo was allowed to take the stand again to add to his previous statement. He also addressed statements made by Willie Turner and the previous girls on the stand, including Dewey Hewell, the girl brought from the home for unwed mothers in Ohio who testified that Leo spoke to Mary frequently and that she had seen Leo touch her shoulder. Leo was adamant that Turner's accusation that Mary was backing away from him in the metal room was totally false. He added that testimony by Hewell and others—that he had talked to Mary—could have been true, but he didn't recall doing so. He said he often spoke to employees about their work, but he didn't know them or their names.

Two witnesses had testified that they saw Leo enter the girls' dressing room with Rebecca Carson several times; when on the stand, Rebecca had denied ever being in the dressing room with Leo; Leo also denied it. As far as he knew, he said, Rebecca Carson was a young lady of upstanding character.

The defense rested their case. All that was left of the longest trial in Georgia history were the closing arguments. Court was adjourned.

On Thursday morning, 21 August, the *Atlanta Constitution* wrote, "Saturday should write *finis* to the most famous case in the annals of Georgia crime, and Leo M. Frank should know his fate."[229] The Mary Phagan murder trial remains widely known even 112 years later, with ongoing debate over Frank's involvement. The controversy surrounding this case is as intense, if not more so, than it was in 1913. The closing arguments and verdict only fueled further questions and debate. This historical moment was far from resolved on that fair, cloudy August morning. The high temperature reached eighty-seven degrees, considerably cooler than the beginning of the trial at the start of August.

Mr. Hooper, the assistant solicitor, was the first to speak in closing arguments. He acknowledged the prosecution's burden of proof; they must provide enough to these twelve men so they had no doubt of Leo M. Frank's guilt. Not one member of the prosecution team would harm Leo, according to Hooper, and Leo shouldn't be treated differently because of his wealth. Justice was available to all classes of defendants, Hooper argued, describing the arm of the law as strong enough to reach the highest places to drag down the guilty and pull up the lowest from the gutter.

He reminded the jury that the defendant shouldn't be convicted simply to provide the state with closure—though he suggested this case was the most important in Georgia history. Hooper walked the jury through different aspects of the case, including how Leo convinced Conley to come to the factory and help him move Mary's body. At one point, Hooper compared Leo to Dr. Jekyll and Mr. Hyde, drawing attention to the ease with which people who saw only one side of Leo might think him moral and virtuous when inside lurked a monster.

Hooper closed with asking why Mincey, the insurance salesman who allegedly said Jim confessed to him, didn't testify. The man who could have cleared up the confusion of what happened that morning.

"Where is Mincey?" Hooper demanded. "He is the man who could clear it and so, besides the shirt. He is the man around whom it appeared that the whole fight would center. If he could convince you that Jim Conley confessed the murder to him that would let Leo Frank out!"[230]

The jury left the room for a few minutes while a placard about the size of an ordinary sign, which had bullet points of the main testimony.

The jury returned and Hooper read to them the law that defined reasonable doubt.

"Simply use your common sense in the jury box," said he. "I thank you."

And Hooper was finished.

Arnold would speak first for the defense. When he began his argument at noon, the model of the pencil factory was brought in. Arnold began in a calm, intimate voice, as if he were speaking to a group of friends. He acknowledged the jurors exhaustion from such a long trial and how the men had been held at the hotel at night. Almost a month had passed since they had been with their families.

"The members of the jury are in a sense set apart on a mountain, where, far removed from the passion and heat of the plain, calmness rules them and they can judge a case on its merits."[231]

Arnold sparked an argument with Hooper by quoting something he said in his speech about the jurors being no different from the men on the street. Hooper interrupted with clarification. So the sparing between the defense and state continued, blending into the closing arguments. Arnold went over the case, bit by bit, circling around to Hooper again. "The trouble with Hooper is that he sees a bear in every bush," Arnold explained. "He sees a plot in this because Frank told Jim Conley to come back Saturday morning. The office that day was filled with persons throughout the day. How could he know when Mary Phagan was coming or how many persons would be in the place when she arrived?"

Arnold went on to take apart each avenue the state had traveled, his argument stretching late into the afternoon. He brought up one of the state's witnesses, Kenley, who claimed on the stand that he saw Leo speaking with Mary. At this point, Arnold raised the issue of anti-

Semitism. "That fellow Kenley is a fair example.... His mouth is set like a catfish. He is the type of lying blowhards that constitutes the so-called public sentiment...he is the man who said, 'Hang this Jew for the murder of that poor little girl whether he is innocent or guilty.' I had rather be in Leo Frank's shoes to-day than Kenley's."[232]

Arnold, some hours later, concluded his argument.

> But, above all, gentlemen, let's follow the law in this matter. In circumstantial cases you can't convict a man as long as there's any other possible theory for the crime of which he is accused, and you can't find Frank guilty if there's a chance that Conley is the murderer.
>
> The state has nothing on which to base their case but Conley, and we've shown Conley a lie. Write your verdict of not guilty and your consciences will give your approval.[233]

Court adjourned unto the next morning at nine.

ଊ

On Friday morning, after the spectators were seated, with the streets still crowded outside, Luther Rosser stood to give his closing remarks in his last attempt to save Leo M. Frank's life. Burly Luther—known for his booming voice—began his attack on the prosecution's case softly. The fatigue of the case showed in his face, but he was far from beaten. He pointed out flaws in Dalton's story.

> Well, if you believe Dalton's story and let's presume it true now. If you believe he went into that scuttle hole there at the factory with Daisy.
>
> Dalton took that woman into the factory, into a dirty, nasty, fetid hole where the slime oozed and where no decent dog or cat would go and there, he satisfied his passion. That's what he told us.[234]

Rosser continued to reveal what he thought were obvious holes in the state's case. He brought up that when Sig Montag told Leo to hire a detective, Leo hired the Pinkertons. Then he made this point about Leo:

> Here is a Jewish boy from the north. He is unacquainted with the south. He came here alone and without friends and he stood alone. This murder happened in his place of business. He told the Pinkertons to find the man, trusting to them entirely, no matter where what they found might strike. He is defenseless and helpless. He knows his innocence and is willing to find the murderer.

Rosser then doubled down on Conley's story.

> Did you hear the way Conley told his story? Have you ever heard an actor, who knew his Shakespearean plays, his "Merchant of Venice" or his "Hamlet." He can wake up at any time of the night and say those lines, but he can't say any lines of a play he's never learned.
>
> So it was with Conley…

Rosser spoke his last words to the jury.

> Gentlemen, I want only the straight truth here, and I've yet to believe that the truth has to be watered and cultivated by these detectives and by seven visits of the solicitor general. I don't believe any man, no matter what his race ought to be tried under such testimony. If I was raising sheep and feared for my lambs, I might hang a yellow dog on it. I might do it in the daytime, but when things got quiet at night and I got to thinking I'd be ashamed of myself.
>
> You have been overly kind to me, gentlemen…old Sol Russell used to describe… "Well, I've lectured off and on for forty years, and the benches always stuck it out, but they was screwed to the floor." You gentlemen have been practically in

> that fix, but I feel nevertheless, that you have been peculiarly kind, and I thank you.

Rosser ended his five-hour closing argument.

ର

The solicitor general began the final argument in Leo M. Frank's case at three thirty on Friday afternoon, guaranteeing he would run over into the Saturday morning session. Later, historians would question whether this was intentional. Dorsey began his argument by thanking Judge Roan for the courtesies he had given the state. He then turned his complete focus on the jurors, twelve men who had spent three weeks away from their families: "It is important to society, to each and every one of you and of us, and I do not feel like slurring over any point of it. Although it would be convenient for you, I know you would not have me do it, and would not respect me if I did."[235]

Dorsey went on to speak about the case and the defense lawyers.

> The case is extraordinary because of the larned counsel pitted against me Arnold and Rosser and Herbert Haas. It is extraordinary because of the defendant, it is extraordinary because of the manner in which it has been argued and the means and methods pursued by the defense.
>
> They have had two of the ablest lawyers in the country on this case, and I know, too, that Herbert Haas is an able lawyer.
>
> They have had Rosser, the rider of the winds and the stirrer of the storm, and Arnold (and I can say it because I love him), as mild a man as ever cut a throat or scuttled a ship.

Then Dorsey dropped his mild manner and became the ruthless prosecutor jurors had come to know. "They have abused me," he said, "they have abused the detective department, they have heaped so much calumny on me that the mother of the defendant was constrained to arise in their presence and denounce me as a dog."

Here Dorsey unleashed some of the resentment and emotions he had barely contained during the trial: "I don't want your approval. I don't seek it: I don't want you to put the stamp of your approval on me.... Gentlemen, do you think that these detectives and I were controlled by prejudice in this case? Would we, the sworn officers of the law, have sought to hang this man on account of his race and passed over the negro Jim Conley?"

Dorsey went on to argue whether prejudice played a role in the case.

> Those gentlemen over there were disappointed when we did not pitch our case along that line, but not a word emanated from this side, showing any prejudice on our part, showing any feeling against Jew or Gentile.
>
> We would not have dared to come into this presence and ask the conviction of a man because he was a Gentile, a Jew or a negro. Oh, no two men ever had any greater pleasure shown on their faces than did Mr. Arnold and Mr. Rosser when they stated to question Kenley and began to get before the court something about prejudice against the Jews. They seized with avidity the suggestion that Frank was a Jew.

And so, the afternoon rolled by. The prosecution continued to attacked the defense's points and how those points were made. Dorsey moved through his grievances with the defense's witnesses step by step, his speech stretching into the evening hours. As he drew to a close on this portion of the argument, the solicitor addressed many of the character witnesses.

"You tell me of the testimony of the good people down on Washington Street and at the orphans' home and Dr. Marx!" he exclaimed. "Do they know his character like the little girls who have worked at the pencil factory, but are no longer connected with the pencil company and under its influence?"

As Dorsey continued to berate Arnold and criticize his tactics, the judge asked Dorsey if he was drawing near the end of his argument.

"Your honor, my time is unlimited, and as yet I have not touched the case," he replied.

Judge Roan adjourned court. Dorsey would be back at it on Saturday morning. The tide was turning in Hugh Dorsey's favor. Usually, the spectators from the courtroom went home after court ended, but on this evening, they waited in the street and on the sidewalks at the request of William Smith, Jim Conley's lawyer. At six o'clock, Dorsey appeared on the courthouse steps. The crowd erupted with cheers and applause.

☙

Crowds began gathering in front of the courthouse before daybreak, hoping for a chance to nab one of the 250 seats in the courtroom. People wanted to see the solicitor general finish his closing argument. Over a thousand people were in line that morning.

Leo entered the courtroom, his demeanor calm, but inside he must have been playing out scenarios in his mind. He took his seat between Lucille and Ray and chatted with Lucille for a few minutes before court began its session. Her hand was on his shoulder—his touchstone for what would come.

Dorsey began his speech that morning with biblical references. "Many a man is a white sepulcher on the outside and rotten within," he said. "But suppose he has a good character. David had a good character until he put Uriah in the forefront of battle that he might be killed that he could get his wife. Judas Iscariot had a good character among those Twelve Men until he accepted those thirty pieces of silver."[236]

He continued his assault on the defense by dismantling some of Leo's alibi. Dorsey displayed the defense's timeline chart. "'One p.m.—Frank leaves the factory,'" he read. "It looks mighty nice on the chart. Turn that chart to the wall, Mr. Sheriff. Let it stay turned to the wall. That statement is refuted by the defendant himself when he didn't realize the importance of this time proposition."[237]

The solicitor pointed out that Leo's statement at police headquarters on 28 April said he started home to lunch at 1:10. This made his alibi questionable. His innocence hinged on the timeline of when he left for lunch and how long he was gone. Dorsey pointed out that Leo had sworn on the stand a few days before that he left the factory at 1 p.m. If Leo did leave at 1:10, the whole timeline was thrown off, and the testimony of the Curran girl (who said she saw him at Alabama and Whitehall Street at exactly 1:10 p.m. as she stood on the street corner) was cast into question. Dorsey again pointed out Leo's timeline inconsistencies were only minutes, but they proved that the timeline was not solid.

The worst came when Dorsey described Leo's alleged murder of Mary in vivid detail. He was so descriptive that Fannie Coleman screamed, and Ollie, Mary's sister, wrapped her arms around her mother. Both women were seated at the prosecution table. Did Dorsey pause to consider their pain? No. He rushed headlong with details of Mary being gagged. Lucille and Ray sobbed, but still, Dorsey kept going, in a feverish determination.

The solicitor went on for hours and finally requested they adjourn until Monday—when he would take up his argument again.

ଓ

Dorsey spent Sunday, 24 August, quietly readying himself for the final part of his closing speech. Luther Rosser spent Saturday and Sunday night in Warm Springs, Georgia, with his wife, where he was besieged with fans. Leo had a typical Sunday in jail seeing his many visitors. Lucille and Ray came in the afternoon and met Leo in the jailer's dining room on the first floor, where he always visited with Lucille. There he read newspapers for the progress on the trial.

On Monday morning, one of the biggest crowds gathered in front of the courthouse and cheered as Dorsey entered. Like Lucille and others, Dorsey could have entered by another door, but he chose to give the people what they wanted. He wasn't at all averse to the spotlight.

Judge Roan warned the spectators to be mindful of their behavior so as not to interfere with the proceedings.

Dorsey opened by reminding jurors what he was talking about on Saturday before court adjourned. Then he moved to the subject of Lucille not visiting Leo on the day he was arrested or for the next two weeks.

> He [Leo] stated that she [Lucille] was there with his father-in-law and his two brothers-in-law. He said Rabbi David Marx was with him and that he consulted Dr. Marx on the advisability of having her to come up to the top floor and see him surrounded by policemen, reporters, and snapshotters. He doesn't prove by a living soul that this statement is true. You must rely on his own lips for its value.[238]

Arnold objected, outraged that Dorsey brought Lucille into his speech.

"Let me see the evidence on which you are speaking, Mr. Dorsey," Judge Roan instructed.[239]

"Frank said that his wife would not come to see him because she was afraid of the snapshotters and reporters and that she did not want to go through this line of newspapermen every time she came to see him," Dorsey replied. "I tell you gentlemen, there never lived a true wife who would not have gone through a line of snapshotters and reporters in spite of the contrary advice of a rabbi or anyone else."[240]

The prosecutor continued through yet more points within the defense's case, wreaking havoc on the defense as he went. Finally, after his three-day closing argument, he addressed the jury and the court: "Your honor, I have done my duty," he concluded. "And I redirect, may it please your honor, that under the law that you give in charge and under the honest opinion of the jury of the evidence produced, there can be but one verdict, and that is: we the jury find the defendant, Leo M. Frank, guilty!"[241]

Outside, the bells of the Church of the Immaculate Conception began to ring the noon hour. With each of the twelve rings, Dorsey yelled "*Guilty!*" The jury would soon retire and be instructed to deliberate.

Arnold did petition for a mistrial, as was expected. Judge Roan denied him, and that was that. Judge Roan then charged the jury.

Chapter 26

The Verdict

A late August evening in Atlanta can be produce one of the prettiest skies of the year. The shadows stretch long, announcing fall is on the horizon and the oppressive heat will fade. And so it was on that Monday, 25 August 1913. Judge Roan, fearing for Leo's and his lawyers' lives if he were acquitted, removed them from the courtroom before the verdict was read. The spectators had also been removed, and only a handful of people remained, silent. The prosecutor and his team, along with Will and Fannie Coleman, sat at the state's table. A few reporters waited, as did Luther Rosser's son, who remained at the defense table with some of Leo's close friends.

Leo was taken back to his cell in the Tower, where Lucille waited with him. Ray went to the Seligs' home to wait. No one expected to hear from the jury immediately.

The jury was sequestered on the two floors above the courtroom, but a group of reporters went across the street to the sixth floor of the nearly finished new courthouse, where they could observe the jurors. Once again, the twelve men existed in a fishbowl, but this time, the reporters could only guess what they were doing or saying. The jury deliberated for an hour and forty-five minutes and reached a verdict after two ballots. The time was 3:39 p.m.

The jury filed into the courtroom, their drawn expressions telling those in the courtroom all they needed to know. At 4:56 p.m., Judge Roan asked the jury foreman to read the verdict.

Guilty.

Newspaper reporters hurried to the telephones, and the crowd of five thousand people outside learned the verdict. A loud cheer went out. The trial was truly over.

Judge Roan spoke: "Gentlemen, I am now taking leave of you. You have been here for a month, and it has been a hard and trying time for all of us. Gentlemen, I want to thank you for your faithful service and consideration of all details in this most arduous case." The judge's voice broke. "Gentlemen," he continued, "I hope you find your families well."[242]

William Coleman shook hands with each juror. Hugh Dorsey left the courtroom.

Outside, people crowded the street from Whitehall to Central Avenue, on to Hunter Street and from Alabama to Mitchell on Pryor streets. Men, women, girls, and boys, leaned on buildings, crowded windows, and sat in the doorways. A loud hum came from the spectators while mounted policemen yelled orders. When the word *Guilty!* was shouted, chaos ensued with a shout that reached the sky. Men threw hats in the air, and women wept.

Solicitor General Dorsey stood in the doorway of the courthouse, and the crowd cheered him with a roar of voices combined. Three men placed Dorsey on their shoulders, passing him across the street to his office. He raised his hat, and newspapers say tears ran down his cheeks. When the solicitor was seated in his office, exhausted, a *Constitution* reporter asked for a statement.

"I feel sorry for his wife and mother," he replied. This was all he said, but this comment revealed that even the inexorable Dorsey had empathy, however short-lived.

Among those present in the courtroom for the verdict was Dr. David Marx. When asked for a comment, he said, "I am stunned. I cannot believe it. I know he is innocent—I know he is incapable of such a crime. My faith in Leo Frank has not diminished one bit."

Southern Bell reported that Monday night, within the hour of the verdict, more people used the telephone than in all the company's history.

ᘓ

While the jury read the verdict, Leo sat with Lucille. Both were smiling and talking about the future. Downstairs in Sheriff Mangum's office, a group of Leo's closest friends, along with Dr. Marx, tried to decide how to break the news to Leo and Lucille. Dr. Rosenberg, the family physician, was asked to hurry to the jail. A great crowd had gathered in front of the Tower, but it was an orderly group of mostly Black men and women who had gathered at the same spot each morning and night to watch him go and come from court.

It was decided that Dr. Rosenberg would tell Leo and Lucille. Shortly after 5:50, the men began their trip to Leo's cell. Both smiled as their friends entered the cell.

If Leo guessed the news they brought, he didn't let on. "I'm glad you came up," Leo said to the doctor.

"Leo, the jury has found you guilty," Dr. Rosenberg said. Lucille moved closer to Leo in the terrible silence. The *Constitution* described her as having a wild-eyed stare.

"My God! Even the jury was influenced by mob law!" Leo exclaimed.[243]

Lucille wrapped her arms around Leo's neck and sobbed. Leo managed to smile and stroked her hair, pleading with her to be brave. Somehow, neither Lucille nor Leo had believed he would be found guilty. Leo asked Dr. Rosenberg and Dr. Marx to help Lucille home. She sobbed as they guided her out of the building, one on each side. Newspaper reporters hurled questions at her. She continued to cry as she was placed in a car and taken home.

Leo made a simple statement to the reporters: "I am as innocent today as I was one year ago."[244]

At six fifteen, the Seligs' car pulled up to the jail, and the chauffeur carried Leo's supper up to his cell, where he ate with relish and thanked the driver for his trouble. While Leo ate his supper, a *Constitution* reporter visited Jim Conley. When the reporter asked what he thought of the verdict, he answered, "Me, boss, Lawd, I's got nuthin ter say."[245] He said nothing else.

Then the reporter went to Newt Lee, who was still in jail, waiting to be released. "I'se sorry. I sho' is sorry," he lamented when he heard of the verdict. He wouldn't comment further and was anxious to know if now Dorsey would let him go.

Will Coleman, Mary's stepfather, made a statement to the press.

> I want to say that I am entirely satisfied with the manner in which the trial has been conducted, and also with the verdict returned.... I would not, for any consideration, like to see an innocent man pay the death penalty, but I feel sure that anyone in the world who has kept up with the trial in all its phases and with every scrap of evidence submitted, would have found Frank guilty as these honorable gentlemen have done. I am deeply grateful to them and to Judge Roan.

ꝏ

Early Tuesday morning, Leo was abruptly taken from his cell in the Tower to Judge Roan's courtroom for sentencing. This decision was made so quietly and quickly that Lucille wasn't notified until it was too late for her to attend.

Judge Roan asked Leo why the sentence of death should not be pronounced upon him.

"Your honor, I say now, as I have always said," Leo replied, "that I am innocent, further than that my case is in the hands of counsel."[246] He looked Judge Roan squarely in the eyes.

Judge Roan sentenced him to death by hanging on 11 October. Leo's lawyers made a motion to seek a new trial. Judge Roan set the hearing date for the new trial on 4 October.

Newt Lee was released from custody, where he had been since the day after the murder.

Jim Conley would be indicted as an accessory to murder, for which the maximum punishment was three years. Conley's sentence was expected to be less since he had turned state's evidence.

Neither Dorsey nor Hooper was present to see Leo sentenced to death.

As deputy sheriffs John H. Owen, George Brodnax, and T. A. Burdette led Leo from the Thrower building back to the Tower, Lucille arrived. She gave him a smile and followed him to the jail, where she hugged him and kissed him over and over. Lucille's biggest battle was yet to come. She had to stand firm and find the strength to help save her husband's life.

Chapter 27

Shadows of Normal

Normal no longer existed for Atlanta and those involved in the Mary Phagan murder case. Before this event, life was more innocent—not that the city hadn't known murder and violence—but citizens didn't think much about their daughters going to work in factories or the city being unsafe. But the brutal murder changed the city, and even Leo's conviction didn't quell the fears that if a young girl had been murdered once, then it could happen again. Those involved in the case had a much harder time adjusting to the outcome.

For Fannie Coleman and her family, the long nightmare was not over. The newspapers, while calmer in their reporting, kept Leo in the headlines. Each time Fannie picked up a newspaper, more news about the case or the convicted murderer was splashed throughout. And how would life ever be "normal" for a mother who's lost her youngest child? How would she move forward? Before the beginning of the trial, the family had moved to a new home at 704 Ashby Street, so perhaps the new location shielded them from attention.

Just before the trial, Fannie's mother, Anna Benton, had come to stay with the family. She had intended to be a support to Fannie, but on just the second day of the trial, Anna was struck by what the *Constitution* called "grief and incessant worry" from what she witnessed at the trial. She was confined to bed, never leaving it again.[247] Mary, often called Anna's favorite grandchild, had spent her first eight years in her grandmother's home in Marietta, and the two were very close. Anna, unable to leave her bed, hadn't attended Mary's funeral, but she often asked about the progress of the trial.

Midway through the trial, Anna dreamed Mary came to her. Standing in the room with Anna, Mary was very much alive and happy. The next morning, she told the dream to Fannie, describing how Mary looked.

"My mother's eyes were bright when she waked Sunday morning," Fannie said, "and until I learned the cruel cause of their brightness, I was sure that she was better." Late that night, Anna died.[248] Many believe she died of a broken heart. Her children were present at her bedside, and she was awake and knew them all until the end came.

In the pain and chaos of losing her daughter and enduring the trial and publicity, Fannie had lost her mother. In comments to a reporter, she said, "After my mother was confined to her bed, her one hope was that she would live until the end of the trial...."[249] "She is with Mary now, though," Fannie said to another reporter, "and I am sure must be far happier than if she were still here."[250]

Anna, dead at seventy-three, was buried in the Benton family plot at Sardis Cemetery on Paper Mill Road in Marietta, straight across town as the crow flies from her beloved granddaughter.

Fannie continued to attend the trial with Will. On occasion, one or more of Mary's siblings were there. Listening to the testimony must have been an emotional maelstrom, and the verdict had to have brought great relief. Fannie and her family had put all their faith in the justice system. Like most of the citizens in Atlanta, they believed in the power of the criminal justice system.

ଔ

Leo accepted that he would be in the Tower indefinitely. If Judge Roan turned down the request for a new trial, Rosser and Arnold planned to appeal to Georgia's Supreme Court. Leo didn't anticipate being executed any time soon. Being pragmatic, he began this new, and hopefully temporary, life with improvements to his cell. The floors were washed and oiled, the windows cleaned. A new bed arrived on 27 August, accompanied by two chairs and a table. The cell looked more like a living room than a place for a convicted killer.

Shortly after noon the same day, Lucille visited for the first time since the verdict. Ray came to visit him for a while in the afternoon. Lucille remained until nightfall.

Leo told friends that he was preparing a statement for publication that addressed Dorsey's closing speech. He branded the remarks as unjust and underhanded.

"It was full of holes as a sieve and if I could have hand just one hour in which to reply to his argument," Leo said, "I could have convinced the jury that I was an innocent man and that the solicitor was misrepresenting facts."[251]

Instead of feeling sorry for himself, Leo began a health routine. He slept eight hours a night and woke at seven each morning. Once out of bed, he did deep breathing exercises at the wire-covered window to allow the fresh air to fill his lungs. For twenty to thirty minutes he worked out with dumbbells that officials allowed him. The jailers commented that he did his exercises with gusto. Afterward, he showered in a bath adjacent to the cell. Then, in his robe, he read newspapers at the table.

Emil, his father-in-law, was his first visitor every day. He brought a breakfast of cantaloupe, coffee, and rolls most mornings. Leo ate and talked with Emil, catching up on what was happening in the Selig household.

Each morning, Sig Montag, the head of the pencil factory, and Herbert Schiff, assistant superintendent, came to the Tower for an hour to discuss business and seek Leo's advice. The reality was that Leo ran the factory from his jail cell.

Friends visited daily and remained until a little after noon. Leo used this time to work on his case. Nothing about this prisoner showed signs of losing his faith in winning a new trial.

The dinner meal arrived around one thirty. When he finished eating, he stretched out on his new bed and rested.

Lucille, looking her prettiest, arrived each day, except Sundays, around four o'clock and sat outside his cell to talk with him through the bars. The deputies did not disturb the couple. At six thirty, Leo's supper arrived, and the two would talk. Once Leo finished supper, they gave each other a farewell kiss, and Leo was left alone to go through the many newspapers and magazines his friends brought. From eight to nine-thirty, visitors came to talk. On some days, Leo had as many as eighty visitors. Most of the time, one of these visitors was the rabbi Dr. David Marx, a true advocate.

After the friends left and before bed at eleven thirty, Leo worked on his case with the determination of a soldier in battle. And so, his days went, a routine intact and comforting to this analytical-minded man. Nothing about Leo resembled a man guilty of murder and sentenced to hang.

Chapter 28

The Fight for a New Trial

Hugh Dorsey understood the fight was not over, but he was confident Leo would hang. This was not the time to be sloppy. He left Atlanta for Valdosta, Georgia, to prepare his argument that the new trial shouldn't be granted.

Reuben Arnold left for a long-planned vacation, and Luther Z. Rosser set to work, putting together the motion from his offices at the Grant building in Atlanta. He was quiet about his strategy, but it was known he had two major points. First, the uproar of cheering for Hugh Dorsey was heard by the jury and could have intimidated them; and second, Rosser and Arnold contended that Judge Roan had gravely erred by allowing Jim Conley's sexually explicit testimony to remain on the record. Rosser refused all interviews but did admit that if the motion for a new trial was denied, the lawyers would take the case to the Georgia Supreme Court.

Most disturbing about this trial's aftermath was the bitterness between many Christians in the city and the Jewish community. A darkness had formed that was not there before the trial. While Dr. Marx was at the Tower the evening of the verdict, his wife, Eleanor Marx, drove to the gates and pleaded to see Leo, but Marx told her she couldn't; he wanted to protect her from the reporters swarming the Tower. She sobbed to Marx to take her away from Atlanta. Her father was Abraham Rosenfeld, one of the original founders of the Temple, so she didn't make this statement lightly. Eleanor would have known Lucille and her family well. Lucille's grandfather Jonas Cohen was an original founder as well.

Though Hugh Dorsey reiterated that Leo's religion had nothing to do with the verdict, the Jewish community must have felt otherwise.

He subscribed to the belief that verdict could only have been caused by anti-Semitism. Until the verdict, he believed that Georgia was free of such prejudice. After the trial, Marx took a train to New York City. Marx was going to speak to well-known and powerful Jewish leaders about what was happening to Leo. One of the leaders on his list was Adolph S. Ochs, publisher of the *New York Times*. Ochs was Southern Jew raised in Knoxville, Tennessee. He was the founder of the *Chattanooga Times*, which he still owned. He saw himself as a non-Jewish Jew and hated and avoided Jewish issues.[252]

Marx also wanted to see the president of the American Jewish Committee, Louis Marshall. He was known for championing causes that fought anti-Semitism but avoided involving the organization in single incidents. While Marx wanted to make a stand and let the country know what was happening in Atlanta, Ochs and Marshall, who sympathized with Leo Frank's case, felt it would be better to help from behind the scenes.

Lucille, unlike Leo, took a few days to get her balance while she lived in the shadow of a hangman's noose. To say she enjoyed her afternoons with Leo at the Tower may be a stretch, but she found it steadying to help Leo with assembling the evidence for his new trial. She understood it was useful and gave them purpose together. Together, they went through each piece of evidence of the four-week trial.

One of the forces that drove Lucille to help—other than saving Leo's life—was finding a way to introduce proof that she didn't avoid visiting him in jail because she believed he was guilty. Because she was not allowed to testify for or against Leo, the misinformation Dorsey used in his argument couldn't be disproved.

Leo's cheerful belief that justice would prevail helped her decide to help him prove his innocence.

Ray joined in these conferences quite a few times, but when word came that Rudolph, Leo's father, was ill, she left for Brooklyn. Rudolph was not well before the murder, but when his son was convicted, he took a turn for the worse. Ray planned to return to Atlanta in time for the hearing for the new trial on 4 October.

Lucille and Leo understood the fight to save his life would be a long one. But Lucille used her precious time with Leo wisely, whether they were searching through testimony or talking about life taking place outside the Tower. She was his eyes and ears. This was what she could do to make a difference.

While Lucille visited with Leo, Dorsey worked in Valdosta, and Rosser plugged away at his trial motion in his law offices, Clara Belle Griffin, a young girl who worked at the pencil factory, went missing. Griffin had left for work on Monday morning and didn't return home. The girl's parents were frantic, thinking what happened to Mary Phagan happened to their daughter. Police rushed to the pencil factory to search; then word came that she was at Grady Memorial Hospital. Griffin said she felt faint at work and went to be checked out. She was too sick to return home or notify her parents. Her brother found her at the hospital on Tuesday when he went on his own search.

ଓ

On 1 October, the defense for Leo M. Frank filed the motion for a new trial. It cited 115 counts of prosecutorial or judicial error. Dorsey took the motion and went to work, but with a 4 October hearing date, he had only three days to prepare. Judge Roan was slated to retire, but he would not do so until he saw the finish of this case.

One of the key points the motion included was the conduct of the crowds that attended the trial. The defense believed their outbursts of applause intimidated the jury.

As the *Atlanta Georgian* reported, "'Threats to clear the room were made by the trial judge,' the motion states, 'but they were absolutely disregarded, and the threats were not enforced, despite the objection of the counsel for the defense.'"[253]

There were two other important counts: First, two jurors had been identified as biased before they were placed; and second, the judge had allowed Jim Conley's sexually charged testimony. One of the jurors accused of bias, Marcus Johenning, denied the charge to the *Atlanta Georgian*. "I served on that jury because I did not want to try to lie out of doing so even though I would gladly have escaped the work," he said. "And now, to accuse me of having told a falsehood to secure the month's service is rank injustice." A.H. Henslee, the second juror charged with bias, had moved to Barnesville, Georgia, but strongly denied the charges.

Dorsey began going through the motion as soon as he received it, but there was too much to cover in three days, so the hearing was postponed.

ঌ

When the hearing finally happened on 22 October, the attorneys' anger from the trial sparked like a hot ember in dry grass. The sparring between the state and the defense was intense. At one point, Rosser yelled at Dorsey, "You'd hang this man on the dotting of an 'i' or the crossing of a 't.'"[254] To which the solicitor general answered, "You're making a mountain out of a mole hill."[255]

These arguments went on for days, but by Friday, 31 October, Dorsey, Hooper, Arnold, Rosser, members of the Selig family, and a small army of reporters gathered in Judge Roan's chambers. The tension hung heavily in the air.

> Gentlemen, I have given this question long consideration," the judge began. "It has given me more concern than any other case I ever was in. And I want to say here that, although I heard the evidence and the arguments during those thirty days, I do not know this morning whether Leo Frank is innocent or guilty."
>
> "But I was not the one to be convinced. It appears that the jury was convinced, and I must approve their verdict and overrule the motion."[256]

Dorsey objected to the judge's voicing his uncertainty.

"Well, that's exactly the way I feel about it, gentlemen," Judge Roan replied; "you can do with it what you wish."[257]

Rosser missed only half a beat before he was on his feet to insist that Judge Roan preface his ruling with his remarks. Dorsey sternly objected, but Judge Roan did place his remarks on Leo's innocence before his official ruling.

The defense would appeal to the Georgia Supreme Court.

Meanwhile, at the Tower, Leo and Lucille, along with her parents and family friends, received the news that Judge Roan had denied the new trial. Lucille wept on Leo's shoulder, and he attempted to calm her. Their hopes had been high, and the decision was a devastating blow.

"My belief remains unshaken that justice will ultimately be done and the truth be known," Leo responded, "—the truth that will prove my entire innocence."[258] Friends said the comment was true to his character.

Lucile remained with Leo after her parents and friends left at eleven o'clock. She didn't speak much. What words were there? Leo refused to see newspapermen. Somewhere in the Tower sat Jim Conley, now indicted and awaiting trial. He, too, refused to speak to the papers.

The final fight for Leo's life was beginning.

Chapter 29

The Final Fight

Leo saw Judge Roan's thoughts about his innocence as vindication. Had somehow the jury heard Judge Roan's opinion before they deliberated, he might have been acquitted.

The Georgia Supreme Court would not be influenced by the lower court's ruling. These men would decide the merits of granting Leo a new trial by reviewing the lengthy appeal.

Roan's comments only deepened the concerns of Atlanta citizens, who believed the murderer was behind bars and their daughters were safe. Many trusted Judge Roan and wondered for themselves if Leo Frank was innocent. The *Sunday American* stated the following:

> Mary Phagan was murdered—diabolically and an indictment says Leo Frank murdered her.
>
> Did he? The judge who tried him—who heard EVERY WORD of the evidence, and EVERY WORD of the argument in doubt about it.
>
> That is a solemn and intruding thought!
>
> No fair-minded and just man will brush it lightly aside.
>
> You who stand in the streets and say, "Frank is a pervert!"
>
> How do you know it? Did YOU hear the evidence?[259]

☙

On 8 November, the American Jewish Committee, led by Louis Marshall, met for their monthly meeting in New York. On their agenda was Leo M. Frank's case and whether they support him vocally—or anonymously, as was their habit. Leo's case was becoming expensive, and Moses Frank, his uncle, had thus far paid for his defense. Albert D. Lasker, an advertising magnate from Chicago, donated one thousand dollars, roughly equivalent to more than thirty-one thousand dollars today. His father and a friend matched his donation, giving Leo three thousand dollars toward the case that would go before the Georgia Supreme Court.

Their financial support was critical, but others were less ready to offer help.

Adolph Ochs, returning to New York from Europe, heard the pleas for him to take on this story. Ochs committed the *New York Times* to Frank's innocence, but he wasn't ready to commit headlines. He didn't yet want to take the risk, but if the need did arise, the *Times* stood ready.

ᘓ

On 15 December, Arnold, Rosser, Dorsey, and Georgia's attorney general Thomas Felder appeared before the state Supreme Court to use their allotted two hours to argue why Leo should—or should not—have a new trial. When they finished two days later, the justices studied the arguments over Christmas and into the new year.

On 17 February, the judges issued a 142-page decision that denied the appeal by a four-to-two vote.

The defense team had three options. The first would be a motion for a re-hearing. The second was an extraordinary motion for a new trial (on the grounds of new evidence) before the superior court where Leo was originally arraigned. The third was an appeal to the United States Supreme Court on the grounds that Frank was deprived of his constitutional rights in the first trial.

Rosser and Arnold were at a loss as to what to do, but they swore they would not give up.

In the Tower, Leo was calm. He spoke to a jail worker from his cell: "The truth will finally [come] out," he said. "It can't be pinned down forever.... I will be cleared. It will take time, but time will do it."[260]

Lucille was at her sister's house when a *Constitution* reporter called her.

"Certainly the decision came as a surprise," she told him, her voice full of sadness. "We are only waiting for the truth to claim its own. My husband is in good health and he is bearing up well. I am too nervous and unstrung to talk much. Later, maybe, I will talk more and have many things to say. But not tonight."[261]

The day after the Georgia Supreme Court handed down their decision, Leo issued a statement. One section must have made readers take notice: "I can truthfully say that there rests not bitterness or recrimination in my heart against those who, with the authority of the law behind them, have enmeshed me, an innocent man, in the meshes of the law's machinery," he wrote. "I only know that they all have made a great mistake."[262]

It would have been understandable if Leo and Lucille had been bitter. Was this a speech from a guilty man? What did Solicitor Dorsey think when he read the statement?

Things were looking worse than they had the previous August. But Leo would not give up. This would not be the couple's last fight.

Chapter 30

Blue Sky after the Storm

Lucille and Leo continued their routines, but they began to receive letters after the verdict in August. At first, letters came from family, friends, and business associates, but strangers soon began writing as well. While most were addressed to Leo, some were addressed to Lucille. Reading the letters helped her; the idea that people cared uplifted and strengthened her. An excellent stenographer, she began helping Leo with his notes on the trial and hearings. Often it was Leo's optimism that pushed Lucille forward. The couple was closer than they had ever been. No matter how dark the days, they looked for the best in each moment together.

On 20 February, an important story broke. As the *Atlanta Georgian* reported, Friday "provided the defense with a weapon with which to continue the battle for Frank's life through the medium of an extraordinary motion for a new trial on the grounds of newly-discovered evidence."[263]

Dr. Harris made public that the hair found on the lathe in the metal room where Mary worked was not hers—and that he had notified the prosecution. The *Atlanta Journal* broke the story first, reporting that Harris "reported this fact to the solicitor and the latter told him there would be no necessity of going any further with the hair theory."[264]

Hugh Dorsey did his best to downplay the released story. "Whether they were or were not," he said, "I never considered the matter as of great importance to the State's case."[265]

Rosser and Arnold, as expected, reacted strongly to the news, accusing Dorsey of misconduct.

Unsurprisingly, Luther Rosser had an opinion about this news. He told the *Atlanta Georgian*,

> The story that the State and its chief medical expert knew during the trial of Leo M. Frank that the hair found in the pencil factory was not the hair of Mary Phagan amazes us beyond words...Unless we are much mistaken in the fairness of the people of Fulton county, the admitted facts about this hair will awaken great wonder as to what other things were concealed and misrepresented in the same way.[266]

The controversy over the strands of hair wasn't the only news related to the case. On Saturday, 21 February, Barrett, the former pencil factory employee who found the hairs on the lathe, filed a petition to receive the thousand-dollar reward offered by the city. He claimed the state built its case around the hairs and couldn't have gained a conviction without them.

Meanwhile, Rabbi Marx and Herbert Haas's work to garner support for Leo was paying off through money raised from prominent Jewish businessmen. That support might have translated into the next significant development: famed detective William J. Burns arrived to investigate all aspects of the case (his assistant had been involved briefly in the early days of the case). Burns announced that he had not been hired by the defense and that he hadn't accepted employment, but it was well known that on his arrival in Atlanta on 20 February he held a long conference with the friends of Leo Frank.

Leo, with help from Lucille, had been studying and conducting his own investigation of the evidence. In his statement, released shortly after the Georgia Supreme Court's decision, he still hopes to persuade the public of his innocence and Conley's guilt:

> The one fact that lifts the case from the realm of mystery and makes it an ordinary murder is that two notes were found by the body. Unquestionably, the person that wrote those two notes killed Mary Phagan. There can be no question of that. The two notes are evidence that can not be changed or

> twisted on the witness stand. They always will proclaim that the hand that wrote them tied the cord around poor little Mary Phagan's neck.[267]

More sensational news involving the case hit the newspapers on Sunday. Albert McKnight admitted that he did not see Leo on the day of the murder, and he was coached on what to testify. McKnight's affidavit that he gave late on 21 February stated that there was a frame-up of evidence that formed a long, strong chain to convict Frank. He stated that a White man worked with him on concocting evidence to make Leo look guilty. McKnight admitted to the *Sunday American* that his testimony was entirely false.

McKnight disappeared after doing this interview. Roy L. Craven, his employer, said that he and others would continue to hunt for McKnight until they found him. Then, the group would force him to tell them to their faces about his false testimony. Is there any wonder McKnight was missing? Craven went on to accuse Leo's friends of having spirited him away.

Leo and Lucille received wonderful news in the form of a headline on 21 February: "Split Court Denies New Trial to Frank." The headline was one of many like it, but the source was not: The front page of the *New York Times*. Adolph S. Ochs had committed to Leo's story; his plight was going to reach the rest of the country, and Leo and Lucille finally had a significant show of support from outside the South—good news indeed.

On Monday, 23 February, Jim Conley came before Judge Ben Hill to stand trial on two charges: accessory after the fact and attempting to dispose of the body. Despite Conley's repeated claims about his role in the crime, William Smith, Conley's lawyer, said that his client would not plead guilty.

The same day, the defense declared that they had prepared the appeal, and it would cite fifty or more times where the court either overlooked points of the argument or refused to consider important points. Rosser and Arnold admitted that they didn't have much faith in being granted a new hearing, but the appeal would make way for the motion for a new trial before Judge Ben Hill of the superior court. The defense was counting on this strategy to work.

A blizzard to the west of Atlanta was predicted to move in on that Monday night, with temperatures dipping into the twenties. This change of weather didn't dampen the happy feelings that both Lucille and Leo had after a few days of encouragement.

On Tuesday, 24 February, Conley was found guilty of aiding Leo and sentenced to one year. Since Lucille and Leo believed that Conley was the real murderer, this sentence must have stung.

Nina Formby was the next state witness to recant her testimony, in which she said Leo had been a regular customer at her establishment and had called the day of Mary's murder seeking a room to rent. In her new affidavit, Formby swore that Leo never called her or came to business. Formby now swore that two detectives from Chief Lanford's office told her, "We know that man is guilty, and you know he is guilty, and we have got to get him, and we are going to get him."[268]

But the landmark retraction came from George Epps, who had been fourteen when he testified. Epps said that his testimony was entirely false—and that Detective Black had made it up for him. He said that Black suggested large blocks of his testimony and then forced him to say it on the stand. Epps, at the time of the second affidavit, was in a reformatory in Milledgeville. He insisted that he told Black the testimony was a lie, but the detective reassured him that everything would be all right. Black also told Epps that he would give him money to get out of town after his testimony. George Epps's statement included the following: "I am glad of the chance to tell the truth and relieve my mind and conscience and clear myself of the perjured testimony given at both hearings."[269]

The news of Epps's affidavit was much needed since the papers reported on the same page an article about Solicitor Dorsey asking for Leo to be resentenced. The defense expected that the sentence would be the same as the first one made by Judge Roan.

On 4 March, William J. Burns once again arrived in Atlanta and went into conference with Milton Klein and Dr. B. Wildauer, whom many believed engaged Burns's service. In truth, these men were the front for Leo's largest benefactor, Albert D. Lasker, the Chicago advertising magnate who had first given a thousand dollars. Lasker stepped off the train in Atlanta's Terminal Station, but no one noticed him or suspected a connection to Burns or Leo Frank. And this was exactly how he wanted it.

Burns announced, "I am on the Frank case to the finish."[270]

The next day, the headlines shouted of a panic-inducing earthquake that shook all of Atlanta around three o'clock. People began calling the newspapers to see what was going on. The same day, a headline announced that Leo's sentencing date would be kept secret so as not to attract crowds. Some superstitious people might have seen an earthquake on the same day a sentencing date was set as a bad omen. Leo was anything but superstitious.

Leo and Lucille felt that luck had swung in their favor.

☙

Leo was taken from his cell on Saturday morning, 7 March, at 10:55 and transported to the Thrower Building to hear his sentence once again. Judge Hill sat at the bench when Leo entered the courtroom at eleven. Arnold and Herbert Haas were there to represent Leo. Dorsey was there for the state.

The defense said they had no intention to ask for clemency. Judge Hill instructed Leo to stand.[271] Leo stood.

"Is there any reason why sentence should not be pronounced upon the prisoner at this time?" the judge asked.[272] He looked at the defense. "Mr. Arnold, have you anything to say?"

"No, but I believe Mr. Frank wishes to say a few words."

Leo began to speak, pointing out that he understood Judge Hill had nothing to do with the results of his case or the decisions that were made. Then he went on to address the judge.

> But I wish to say in your presence and in the presence of the Supreme Being whose eye now is upon us that I am innocent of the murder of little Mary Phagan, and I have no knowledge

> of how it occurred… What a spectacle it will be, your honor! The State will be guilty of murder in the event that the sentence which has been before pronounced upon me is carried out.[273]

Leo continued eloquently. When he was finished, he addressed the judge: "Your honor, I am now ready for sentence to be pronounced upon me."[274]

Judge Hill hesitated, adjusting his glasses, and moved on to pronounce Leo to die by hanging on 17 April. Though all expected this outcome, it seemed cruel for Leo to go through it again. But those there that day heard Leo's statement. Never again would he be viewed as the prisoner who didn't have much to say.

ᘓ

The defense released more affidavits of state witnesses retracting their testimony. Helen Ferguson was one of them. She stood strong on her testimony that Leo wouldn't allow her to get Mary's pay on that Friday, but she added a damaging story. On Saturday, a week before Mary's murder, Jim Conley accosted Helen in the factory lobby. He was quite drunk, according to Miss Ferguson. She saw his whiskey bottle in his back pants pocket. With a strange look, he stared at her. She moved back, but he advanced. Helen jumped up the stairs as fast as she could to get away from him.

The *New York Times*'s headline read, in part, "Witness at Atlanta Accuses Negro; Says Conley Molested Her in the Very Spot Where a Week Later Mary Phagan Was Murdered."[275]

On the heels of the sentencing, the defense released another affidavit. This time, it was not from anyone formally involved in the case. Ethel Harris Miller and Maier Lefkoff—both known in the Jewish community—volunteered that they saw Leo at 1:10 p.m. the afternoon of the murder as the two walked down Whitehall Street. Leo bowed and spoke to Mrs. Miller, tipping his hat. This statement proved that Leo was not in the factory when Jim Conley claimed they were moving Mary's body.

Albert Lasker provided the funds to hire attorney Henry Alexander for the defense team. Alexander wrote a booklet with clear photographs of the documents that pertained to the murder case. He revealed that not only did the notes written by Jim incriminate him but the paper he had used also proved his guilt. The pencil factory stationery had belonged to an employee long gone from the job, and the notepads had been thrown in the basement garbage. So, Leo would not have had access to them in his office the day Conley said Leo made him write them.

Alexander presented his evidence to the newspapers, and they ran with it. The *Atlanta Journal* became convinced of Leo's innocence. On 10 March, they announced in their headlines that Leo should get a new trial and detailed their reasons in an editorial that stirred people to send in letters declaring that Leo deserved a new trial. One of these letters came from Eugene Muse Mitchell, father to a thirteen-year-old girl named Margaret Mitchell.

But Detective Burns's popularity had turned into celebrity. Reporters followed him wherever he went, and he even told stories over meals. "There is certainly no mystery that can not be cleared up," he said, "and facts will speak for themselves when made public. I am confident that Mr. Dorsey is open to conviction [of whoever was guilty] if it should develop that a grievous mistake has been made."[276]

There was an attempt to keep Burns from questioning Conley, but most believed Detective Burns would get his way. This man did seem to be a bright light shining on Leo's case.

While Burns was away up North investigating evidence, he left two of his best men to keep the local work going. But it was the defense that kept the case in the headlines. They released more retractions, and the best one came from C. B. Dalton, the witness who corroborated Conley's tale about Leo meeting women in his office. The new statement he made said the police invented the story of office parties where he and Leo shared women. So once again, a key witness of the state reversed their testimony. This was astounding news for Leo.

Chapter 31

Another Storm on the Horizon

Here entered the *Jeffersonian*, a newspaper owned and published by Thomas E. Watson. In his early years, Watson was a liberal but time would change alter his politics. He was elected to the Georgia General Assembly in 1882 and the US House of Representatives in 1890. He would serve as a senator for a short time before his death in 1920. In 1896 the Populist Party nominated him as their presidential candidate, and he gain him national recognition. He was one of the top trial lawyers in Georgia.

In the beginning, he was known as a voice for the disenfranchised. He supported taxes for public education and stood up for the needs of poor farmers and sharecroppers, Black and White. Somewhere along the way, his views changed, and he became a raging White supremacist and spouted anti-Catholic rhetoric.

It was at this point in his psychological evolution when he began to stir up people against Leo Frank. He is probably one of the most complex characters in this story. He never met Lucille in person, as far as we know, but he addressed her at least once in his running commentary about Leo and the case.

After the *Atlanta Journal* declared that Leo Frank deserved a new trial—and other newspapers followed—the *Jeffersonian* published its unvarnished opinion: "The Frank Case: When and Where Shall Rich Criminals Be Tried?" The article, which ran on 19 March, asked, "Does a Jew expect extraordinary favors and immunities because of his race?"[277]

With this article, Watson emerged as one of Leo's most lethal enemies.

At the same time, Dorsey found his footing after the recent setbacks. He wouldn't be defeated. Pulling together his resources, he began to work on his plan to keep Leo from winning a new trial.

☙

Tom Watson's commentary in the *Jeffersonian* came to Leo and Lucille's attention, but they kept up their hopes that this new trial request would work. The new evidence and witness retractions were overwhelming, and most of the newspapers rallied for a new trial. But Lucille and Leo had their own perspective: they still believed in Georgia's justice system. They couldn't fathom disliking a person or wishing them ill based on prejudice, whether against wealth, race, religion, or geography—such as having been raised in the North. This was a naive outlook, but Lucille was born and raised in Atlanta as a Jew. Neither her family nor ancestors ever felt anything but part of the city. Leo never experienced discrimination living in Brooklyn.

The couple, even though they understood that Dorsey and the police department were not to be trusted, more than likely had no real intuition about what was in the air. Maybe their parents did. We know their support system of important Jewish businessmen understood. This group of men publicly stood behind Leo's innocence—but not behind blaming anti-Semitism and anti-Northern bias for his conviction because doing so would make them and other Jews targets. They must have recognized this type of discrimination, this feeling that they couldn't say what they believed without retaliation.

As the tide changed, tragedy and grief hit the Selig family. Emil, for several months, had been in bad health but not bedridden. The illness had subsided, and he was feeling much better. On 29 March 1914, illness seized him again. Emil Selig died in daughter Rosalind's apartment in the early hours of 30 March. The body was removed to Greenberg & Bond's, where funeral services were held the following morning. Emil was sixty-five and had lived longer in America than he had in his birth country of Germany. The family took his death hard, especially Lucille and Josephine. Emil was buried in Oakland Cemetery.

Her father's death was a staggering blow to Lucille, especially in the middle of fighting for her husband's life.

ɞ

Throughout April, Tom Watson blasted Detective William Burns. He resented that Burns was from out of town and made this known in the paper. To make matter's worse, Watson's following was growing, and these followers thought his word was the gospel. Copies of the *Jeffersonian* sold out and left readers wanting.

On 1 May, Burns and one of his associates rode in a chauffeur-driven car to Cedartown, northwest of Marietta. When Burns's car reached Marietta Square, close to the courthouse, the three men exited the automobile. Robert E. L. Howell, a prominent citizen who felt strongly about Mary Phagan's murder, recognized Burns and asked if he was the detective working on the Phagan case. Burns answered yes. A crowd gathered around the two men. Howell removed his coat and struck Burns. As the group grew, it quickly became a mob. Burns and his associate were forced to flee in different directions. Quite some time passed before the three men were reunited and left Marietta.

In Atlanta, the hearing for Leo's new trial was in session.

Dorsey was ready to prevent a new trial no matter what he had to do. He, too, had new affidavits. The way the witnesses' testimony changed was much like a volley ball game with the ball being lobbed back and forth between the teams.

On 7 May, the *Jeffersonian*'s headline read, "William Jackass Burns, at Another Angle: Some Tarnished Lawyers; Some Bought Newspapers; and the Murder of a Little Georgia Girl."[278]

The article read,

> It is a bad state of affairs, when the idea gets abroad that the law is too weak to punish a man who has plenty of money.... Yet, our common sense tells us that none but the guilty would object to being asked fair questions.... The extreme tenderness of the law, the firm impartiality of the judge, the ease

> with which shrewd lawyers for the defense could confuse witnesses, the power of eloquence in touching the feelings of the jury…there was hardly a term of court at which I did not see guilty men escape.[279]

And so began Watson's sustained attack on Leo Frank. He wanted nothing more than to whip those followers into a frenzy of anger and violence.

☙

The new hearing went into lengthy discussions. Dorsey accused the defense of providing fake affidavits and tore apart the defense's new evidence, making Burns look bad by discrediting his investigation piece by piece. As a result of Dorsey's many attacks on the defense, Judge Hill informed Dorsey there was no need for him to hear the state's argument, and he pronounced that the defense's request for the extraordinary motion was denied.

Each time Leo received this kind of news, it became easier for him to not be surprised. Again, Lucille was by his side, and this time, Leo gave a *Georgian* reporter a short statement: "I had expected that action."[280]

The defense team vowed to appeal to the US Supreme Court.

Soon after Leo again lost his bid for a new trial, Minola McKnight, the Seligs' former cook, was attacked by a man she would not identify to the police. He left her with a five-inch cut across her face. The former cook, who defended herself and her boss by calling the state "liars," was not speaking any longer.

Chapter 32

Peace Is the Opposite of Struggle

Come July 1914, almost a year after Leo's trial, things became quiet. The newspapers found other, more interesting stories to write about. Even Tom Watson moved on to other subjects. What came now was a lengthy waiting game for the appeal to the Supreme Court. Lucille sat outside Leo's cell bars every evening. Leo and Lucille read the many letters that arrived. Leo played a regular bridge game through the mail with Florence Irwin, the bridge writer for the *New York Times*. Life was far from perfect, but it was a brief peace for Lucille and Leo.

William Smith, attorney for Conley, was battling his own internal war. Smith had witnessed the conversation between Dorsey and Dr. Harris about the hair found in the metal room at the pencil factory. What bothered Smith was the fact that Dorsey didn't push Dr. Harris to tell the truth about the hair when he testified. But this wasn't the only issue that gave him pause. Always, Smith had believed Jim Conley's account of what happened the day Mary Phagan was murdered, but as time passed, something happened that remained with him. It made him realize he might need to rethink his decision to believe his client. Early in the investigation, Jim wanted to send Lorena Jones a message asking her to visit him in jail. Conley wouldn't allow Smith to take her a message and didn't want to talk about what the message contained. Something told Smith that Jim was hiding something serious, but he had no proof. In early June 1913, more than a month before the trial, Smith visited Chief Lanford and told him about Jim's request. Lanford thought he would trap Conley by placing a police officer in the crawl space under his cell. When Lorena was escorted to the cell, Jim became auspicious and discovered he was being watched. Of course, Conley never knew his own lawyer was involved with the trap. But William Smith never shook the feeling that Jim was hiding something. Though he was not ready to go to the defense's side, he decided to do some sleuthing on his own. He enlisted his wife and reviewed everything Jim Conley had said.

He began studying just how literate Jim was. Smith and his wife reviewed all Jim had written during the trial, comparing that writing to letters he had written before the murder. Smith understood that Jim Conley had lied about how well he could read and write. The more he examined the situation, the more he saw how masterfully Conley had duped everyone.

Smith still had one more area to investigate. The state always maintained that Jim couldn't have been the author of the murder notes because he never used the verb "did" correctly. Often, he would use "done" instead. Smith went through all of Conley's testimony and saw that he used "did" correctly most of the time.

Smith realized that believing Jim had been a dire mistake. He was convinced that Conley, not Leo, was the murderer. Now, what would he do with the information? It wasn't as easy as telling someone what he had found, and Leo would be released. He assembled what he saw as strong proof and made an appointment with Beavers and Lanford and later with Dorsey. By this point, it was the middle of September. Each meeting was a failure. No one wanted to see the case they worked on so hard was flawed beyond repair.

While William Smith tried to keep his movements on the case a secret, a *Constitution* reporter called him, asking if he now believed Leo was innocent. Smith admitted he now saw things differently. The reporter wrote, "Smith states that with the proper co-operation of officials, Frank will be freed, and that the mystery of Mary Phagan's murder will be solved."[281]

"I have come definitely to the conclusion—or, at least," Smith told the reporter, "this is my personal judgment after much study—that Leo M. Frank is innocent."

Newspaper headlines went crazy. All of Atlanta was up in arms. Jim Conley was serving a year at the Bellwood Prison Camp. Jim made it clear that he would speak with the solicitor and explain Smith hadn't acted like himself the last few weeks. Then he asserted his innocence in the murder and repeated that Leo Frank was the killer.

Smith had given Tom Watson a second opportunity to air his vitriol. In his 8 October issue of the *Jeffersonian*, he wrote that everyone knew they would open Leo's case again and that the only question was "Who would the defense use this time?"

William Smith would fight Tom Watson for a long while. Now that Smith understood his error in believing Jim, he knew he and Hugh Dorsey bore the responsibility for Leo Frank's conviction. He would fight to see justice served, to right his mistake.

Chapter 33

Is This All There Is?

On 14 October, the *Georgian* ran a headline: "Leo Frank Loses." The Supreme Court of Georgia had unanimously upheld Judge Hill's ruling on the extraordinary motion. Leo's supporters remained positive, encouraging him to do so too. The Tye-Peeples motion on the constitutional issue of Frank not being present for his sentencing was still pending a ruling from the Supreme Court. A month later Leo lost his last fight in the Georgia State Supreme Court, which said the defense had signed off on the arrangement and failed to challenge it in a timely manner.

"I had put great faith in the plea of my lawyers and had looked for a favorable decision by the Supreme Court," Leo lamented. "That is all I have to say."[282]

The news must have devastated Lucille, but no newspaper mentions her reaction to the loss. Perhaps she had no more to say to the press.

On 20 November, Leo received another blow. The Supreme Court refused to certify a writ of error that would facilitate a US Supreme Court ruling on the Tye-Peeples motion. But still, there were several ways to reach the nation's highest court. There was hope.

Six days later, the defense sent their application for review by another Supreme Court justice, Oliver Wendell Holmes Jr., a well-known Civil War veteran who fought for the Union. While he gave encouraging words, he did not issue the writ. Holmes did communicate his concerns about what had happened in Atlanta, so the loss was slightly less bitter. A Supreme Court justice of the United States acknowledged that Leo did not have what he viewed as a fair trial due to the hostile atmosphere.

So, on 30 November, Louis Marshall stepped out in public and assumed control of Frank's defense and went before the US Supreme Court once again with the writ of error, but what made the difference was Marshall wasn't giving it to one judge as before, but to all the Supreme Court justices.

The national attention that Leo received brought Watson out again.

> Why is it that, when the Governor of Georgia goes to New York to borrow money for the state, he should be asked to talk of the Frank case?
>
> John Slaton has been in New York for the purpose of arranging a big loan to refund the old loan, and the rich Jews of the North have apparently made a dead set at him.
>
> If the Governor does not resent this, the people do—and they consider it an outrage.
>
> Is the State of Georgia to be held up, in the money market?
>
> Must the Governor give some sign in favor of the condemned Sodomist and murderer, before he can borrow money to refund the bonds?[283]

On 7 December, more bad news came Leo's way. The US Supreme Court rejected the request for a writ of error. Leo reacted in his typical calm manner. Surely, he had become used to this kind of news. But Lucille and Leo were aware there were ways to save Leo from the gallows. C. P. Connolly had written an in-depth article for *Collier's Weekly*, a popular magazine in the North. The article would be in the two December issues. This exposure was just what the defense needed. Connolly addressed the prejudice in the South. Again, Watson expressed his anger toward those supporting Leo.

Judge Hill set a new execution date for 22 January 1915. Leo could be dead in less than a month. Louis Marshall directed the Atlanta lawyers to file a petition for a writ of habeas corpus before Judge

William T. Newman of the US District Court of the Northern District of Georgia. This petition drew on both Louis Marshall's expertise and on the Fourteenth Amendment, which protected newly freed slaves from state interference with their rights as citizens. The amendment was written in such a way that it encompassed all people to receive equal protection of the laws.

Newspapers in Atlanta and across the country adopted a pro-Leo Frank stance. The word was spreading. Dorsey attacked Marshall's strategy, but he was no longer dealing with Rosser and Arnold. Now Henry Alexander, Louis Marshall's hand-picked lawyer, issued a response challenging Dorsey. He pointed out it was unfair to warp facts in order to charge Leo with seeking favor. There would be a last effort at the nation's capital to save an innocent prisoner sentenced to hang.

On Christmas, Louis Marshall went to see US Supreme Court Associate Justice Joseph R. Lamar at his home. He went alone; Alexander was in Atlanta preparing an application for clemency, should Marshall fail.

Christmas was on a Friday, so there would be a wait through the weekend to see whether Marshall succeeded. Lucille and Leo's parents visited with him over the holiday weekend.

Monday, 28 December, brought the best newspaper headline in the Leo Frank case. The *Georgian*'s spread read: "Frank Wins Appeal to Supreme Court."

Lucille, Ray, and Rudolph were in the Tower with Leo when the word came. This time there were happy tears. Finally, Leo had a chance. This was not a complete win, but the ruling would give him a fair chance. Friends and more family began to show up at the Tower.

Lucille admitted a *Georgian* reporter, who wanted to let Leo know the decision.

"We've heard it already," she cried with a little laugh. "Our lawyers have told us the good news. It looks as if it were only the bad news the newspapers tell us first."[284]

Leo was smiling and trembled with happiness when he spoke to his well-wishers.

The newspapers predicted the trial would be held in thirty to sixty days, but Alexander said he had no idea when the case would be heard. Dorsey had his work cut out for him.

☙

The case was *Frank v. Mangum* because, under the law, it was the Fulton County sheriff, Wheeler Mangum, who deprived Leo Frank of his constitutional protections. Louis Marshall argued this case before the Supreme Court. Warren Grice, Georgia's attorney general, argued the state's case. Now, all that could be done was to wait for the nine-member panel to decide.

Weeks went by, but Leo's case was alive and well in the newspapers across the country. Tom Watson, on more than one occasion, fired back with articles addressing the *New York Times,* which he called outsiders.

On 19 April, the US Supreme Court upheld Judge William Newman's denial with a seven-to-two vote.

Leo's characteristic calm finally cracked. He smoked a cigarette and paced his cell. When Lucille got there, she was composed and approached the cell. She reached through the bars and pulled Leo to her, kissing him on the cheek.

Chapter 34

Is There No Way to Save This Innocent Man?

In December 1914, as Leo's defense battled to win an appeal, Judge L. S. Roan battled for his life, and like the defense, he faced huge challenges that would prove impossible to overcome. In December, Roan was at the Berkshire Hills Sanatorium in North Adams, Massachusetts, where he was receiving treatments for the cancer that was killing him. He dictated the following letter to a nurse:

> After considering your communication asking that I recommend executive clemency for Leo M. Frank. I wish to say that at the proper time I shall ask the Prison Commission to recommend and the Governor to commute to life imprisonment. This I shall not do until the defendant's appeal shall have been filed and the Governor and Prison Commission shall have had opportunity to study the record in the case.
>
> It is possible that I showed undue deference to the opinion of the jury when I allowed their verdict to stand. They said by their verdict that they found the truth. I was still in a state of uncertainty, and so expressed myself. My search for the truth, though diligent and earnest, had not been so successful. In the exercise of judicial discretion, restricted and limited, according to my interpretation of the decisions of the reviewing courts, I allowed the jury's verdict to remain undisturbed. I had no way of knowing it was erroneous.
>
> After many months of deliberation, I am still uncertain about Frank's guilt. The state of uncertainty is largely due to the character of negro Jim Conley's testimony, by which the verdict was evidently reached. Therefore, I consider this a

> case in which the chief magistrate of the State should exert every effort in ascertaining the truth. The execution of any person, whose guilt has not been satisfactorily proven to the constituted authorities is too horrible to contemplate. I do not believe that a person should meet the extreme penalty of the law until the court, the jury, the Governor shall all have been satisfied of that person's guilt. I shall enlarge up these views directly to the Governor and the Prison Commission.
>
> However, if for any cause I am prevented from doing this you are at liberty to use this letter at the hearing.[285]

Roan died die before Leo lost his case before the US Supreme Court. In May 1915, William M. Howard, speaking for Leo's counsel, announced that the letter from Roan, along with more letters, would be used to apply for clemency. He waved the letter in front of the reporters. "This is the most precious document in the entire case," Howard said. "It is in reality a voice from the tombs, and is a lease of life for Leo Frank."[286]

The lawyers went to the Tower to talk with Leo. Here, they were stopped in their tracks. Frank refused the request for clemency because he was innocent and didn't want mercy for something he didn't do.

Henry Alexander and the other lawyers pointed out to Leo that a commutation was far from an admission of guilt, and if he won this, he won more time to prove his innocence. On this point, Leo agreed, and the lawyers wrote a petition. Leo gave it his signature.

The petition was submitted on 22 April 1915. They had to wait to see what would happen with the Prison Commission and Governor Slaton.

On 10 May, Leo faced Judge Hill in the new Fulton County Courthouse. Lucille sat at a table in the front of the full gallery. Leo again addressed the judge concerning his innocence. A new execution date was set for 22 June. With this, Lucille covered her eyes with a handkerchief and bit her bottom lip. How many times could a wife hear a death sentence pronounced on her husband? On the street in front of the Tower, Leo smoked a cigarette and spoke with his parents, who had just arrived and planned to stay as long as it took. Leo had hope. The commutation was his last straw.

People across the country were discussing the Leo Frank case. The defense had succeeded in making his plight known. Geraldine Farrar, who was performing in the annual Atlanta opera season, paid a visit to the Tower with an armful of flowers. She was delighted to know that Leo had proposed to Lucille after the couple attended an opera in Atlanta and heard her sing.

"His faith and spirit are wonderful," Farrar said. "I have never seen a man with such a personality. One might hear everything that could possibly be considered a detriment to his case, but to sit and talk with him would convince even the most callous of his innocence."

Miss Farrar enjoyed speaking with Lucille and described her visit to a reporter. "There is poignant pathos in the grief of his wife," she said. She continued,

> She was present when I talked with him [Leo], and her hand went through the bars to rest in his all the while we chatted. Deep down in her heart there is sorrow untold, but when he take hone of her fingers and glances into her eyes, a smile brightens her face that is supremely eloquent.
>
> The torture this poor woman has withstood would have driven any ordinary soul to distraction. She loves him intensely. I can see that plainly.[287]

When Miss Farrar left the jail, she went straight to send a 130-word telegram declaring Leo's innocence to a New York newspaper.

The Prison Commission announced that they would take up the commutation petition at a special 31 May session. Again, circumstances were looking up for Leo.

ঔ

In May, newspapers began running full-page articles with a large photo of Lucille asking that people around the country gather signatures on petitions to free Leo. They were asked to send them to Governor Slaton.

"I beg the American people to save my husband's life, because he is innocent," Lucille pleaded. "Every bit of evidence produced at the trial, and that which has developed since the trial, show completely that my husband is not guilty. In the end, I know his name will be cleared."[288]

Within a week, four hundred thousand people had provided their signatures. A letter-writing initiative began. The letters came from ordinary citizens, senators, and even governors, eight of whom sent messages. All the letters and notes were sent to Governor Slaton. Many of Georgia's companies fought for Leo by letting Slaton know their thoughts. Tom Watson opined on how embarrassing it was that John Slaton was a member of the law firm representing Leo. Watson threatened what would happen if the governor or the Prison Commission commuted Leo's sentence. One of those items went as follows:

> (3.) That if the Prison Commission or the Governor undertake to undo—in whole or in part—what has been legally done by the courts that were established for that purpose, *there will almost inevitably be the bloodiest riot ever known in the history of the South.*
>
> Consequently, the Prison Commission and the Governor, in such a contingency, would be directly responsible in morals for whatever lives were lost.[289]

ꕥ

On 31 May, the Prison Commission met to hear the argument for Leo's commutation. Letters from Roan's brother, Paul Donehoo, the coroner, and Lucille pleading for his life were read. It was Lucille's that made a lasting impression.

> Our marriage has been exceedingly happy and has never been marred by the slightest cloud...When my husband was first arrested on this charge and was detained at police headquarters, I hurried to Decatur Street, accompanied by my father and brother-in-law. I was not allowed to go up to my husband and remained in the office of the probation officer, from whence my friends prevailed upon me to return home. Being assured that my husband would be released at any moment, I remained at home, but as soon as if became apparent that he would be detained indefinitely I went to him immediately and have been going to him every day since.[290]

The final submission was William Smith's study of the murder notes. When Chairman Davison asked if anyone wanted to speak from the opposition, no one stood up. Dorsey had skipped the meeting and vowed to speak personally with Governor Slaton. The chairman closed the hearing.

ᘓ

A meeting in Marietta was held to object to the commutation of Leo Frank's death sentence. Almost one thousand people attended. By the end of the meeting, it was decided a delegation would travel to the Prison Commission the next day to deliver their thoughts. The group of fourteen well-known Cobb County citizens went to the hearing room in the capitol. The fourteen men included John Tucker Dorsey, a cousin to Hugh Dorsey; E. P. Dobbs; Bolan Glover Brumby; Gordon Gann; Josiah Carter Jr., editor of the *Marietta Journal*; former Cobb County sheriff William J. Frey; Elmer Phagan, Mary's uncle; and Herbert Clay, solicitor general of the Blue Ridge Circuit and son of Senator Alexander Stephens Clay, who had served in office from 1896 to 1910.

Herbert Clay began. All the men gave reasons Leo Frank's sentence should not be commuted. When they finished the hearing ended.

☙

Eight days later, on 9 June, the Prison Commission, by a two-to-one vote, declined Leo's petition for commutation of his death sentence. Lucille and Rabbi Marx arrived shortly after Leo found out. They were followed by other in-laws. All were crying. How could this have happened when so many had come to Leo's defense?

☙

On 12 June, Governor Slaton entered his office to oversee the last hearing for Leo M. Frank. He must have known that being in a hornet's nest would have been safer for him, both personally and politically. No matter his decision, many would be upset with him.

When Slaton adjourned for the weekend, a large crowd gathered on the Washington Street steps of the capitol demonstrated in favor of Leo being hanged as planned. A popular musician of some fame, Fiddlin' John Carson, sang "The Ballad of Mary Phagan," his new composition. He played it over and over.

When Slaton had heard from Howard and Dorsey over days of arguments, the hearing was finished. All that was left was Slaton's deliberation. He left the capitol that night with his executive secretary and several boxes of transcripts, legal briefs, and other documents to pore over. With the execution set for six days away, the pressure on him couldn't have been more intense. The two men left for a quiet place to study the case. From early Thursday morning until Saturday around lunch, Slaton and a colleague immersed themselves in the files. They did venture out once to the pencil factory, where they tested the elevator. William Smith had two private interviews with Governor Slaton.

☙

On Saturday near noon, in the library of his home on Peachtree Road, Slaton had decided the fate of Leo M. Frank. The rest of the weekend was spent writing a report on his decision.

Sunday was a typical day in the jail for Leo. There had been no word on Slaton's decision, and he retired that night at nine thirty. At eleven thirty, a deputy came to his cell and told him to dress. Leo's last entry in the diary he kept while in the Tower read, "Sunday night @ 11 was told to prepare to leave for state farm. Left Tower @ 11:45."[291]

The Prison Commission had called Sheriff Mangum. Slaton had commuted Leo's death sentence to life in prison. For safety reasons, he would be moved to the state prison in Milledgeville overnight. They would catch the 12:01 train to Macon. Leo had to leave his things behind. He dressed in six minutes, and they left for the Terminal Station.

They arrived in Macon at 2:44 a.m. They went by car the rest of the way to Milledgeville. Upon arrival, Leo stated, "I had begun to think I wouldn't get to see this place."[292]

ɞ

Monday morning, folks in Atlanta found out that Leo's sentence had been commuted. The headlines splashed the news. A group of five thousand gathered at city hall. Officers attempted to contain the crowd, but rage was in the air. At Five Points, a group of four thousand decided they should call on John Slaton at his mansion on Peachtree and Paces Ferry. The crowd started out on foot. The Fulton County Police were ahead of the mob and had barricaded the property with barbed wire and officers. When the governor found out the size of the mob, he declared martial law. The state militia's Fifth Regiment was mobilized. The mob reached the mansion only a few minutes after the troops arrived, complete with bayonets on their rifles. Shortly after, the mob was contained.

In Marietta, an effigy of the governor was raised at the courthouse with a sign that read: "John M. Slaton, King of the Jews and Traitor Governor of Georgia."[293] Troops were sent to the rear of the property because two hundred citizens of Marietta were approaching from the north.

Watson didn't hesitate to incite violence. "Hereafter, let no man reproach the South with Lynch law," he wrote, "let him remember the unendurable provocation; and let him say where Lynch law is not better than no law at all.[294]"

The next day 150 people from Marietta, known as the Knights of Mary Phagan, met at Mary's grave and promised to avenge Mary's death.

John Slaton made it to the inauguration ceremony of the incoming governor, Nat Harris. Mr. Slaton and his wife, Sallie Grant, left Atlanta. After nights of clashes with mobs and troops at the mansion, the couple left for New York on a train.

John M. Slaton must have truly believed that Leo was innocent, and he must have known commuting Leo's death sentence would end his political career. These were his choices despite the consequences, and they reveal his character even today. John Slaton shines.

Chapter 35

State Prison Farm

Early on the morning of 21 June, a *Georgian* reporter knocked on the Seligs' door. Josephine and Lucille now lived at 301 Washington Street. Josephine answered the door and explained that Lucille was ill and lying down, that she had no statement to make or plans. How could she have plans? She was thrilled Leo had been spared, but now he was gone, spirited away in the night without even a goodbye or a moment to celebrate. There is no information on how she learned his sentence had been commuted or that he had been taken from Atlanta. Was it a phone call in the night?

Lucille had to adjust to not seeing Leo every day as she could when he was in the Tower. They wrote each other several letters a day. Lucille must have felt as much a prisoner as Leo, especially in the first days after he left. Leaving her home would have been dangerous. The mobs were threatening, but reporters also waited to pounce on her. The ordeal had taken a toll on her.

Leo spent the first few days after arriving at the prison seeing doctors. He had caught a bad cold, but the doctors realized the stress of all that had happened contributed to his condition. Though the newspapers proclaimed that Leo would be working in the expansive fields surrounding the prison as most of the prisoners did, he was assigned to inside duties with other prisoners with health issues.

His letters were full of praise for Warden J. E. Smith and J. M. Burke, prison superintendent. Moses Frank, Leo's uncle, had a good friend, Roy Alford, who had married into one of Milledgeville's best families. Alford not only provided Leo with towels, washcloths, soap, and a razor, but introduced him to some of the local leading citizens. They supported his cause. Many brought him gifts of fruits, including local peaches. The New York Public Library sent him books. He even received phonograph records that he played on a Victrola in the warden's office. Slowly, Leo began to heal. He spent part of the day writing letters. Strangers wrote to him often, and he answered. He sent many heartfelt messages to those who made it possible for him to continue living. But the most exciting event was the documentary film that Hal Reid was making. The filmmaker arrived with a crew and a camera at the prison. Reid had filmed in Atlanta at Slaton's home and, of course, had captured the unrest caused by Leo's second lease on life.

Leo was ready once again to prove his innocence. Reid set up in the warden's office. He got shots of Leo alone and with Warden Smith.

He shot for a day and rushed back to New York, developed the film, and hosted a screening for Ray Frank, who loved what she saw and agreed to pose for Reid. Next came Lucille, who had retreated to Athens to stay with her uncle and aunt. She was battling depression—this was certain—and needed a change of scenery, hoping it would make a difference. But one doesn't heal overnight from two years of trauma.

"I'm so lonesome, with no place to go, but home," she wrote.[295]

Leo acknowledged what she had been through, encouraging her to rest and get back to herself.

ᘓ

Lucille's journey back to Athens was a trip designed to find the happy girl she had been after accepting Leo's marriage proposal. Now, she was a shell of the woman she had been before the nightmare began. The days were long and lazy, just what Lucille needed. She remained in bed late and ate breakfast alone. She took her time to write letters. Without the pressure of another battle, she listened to music and napped or played bridge with her aunt and friends. She roamed downtown to the family department store, where she didn't have to worry about a reporter following her. After supper, she gave herself the pleasure of reading a book, and sometimes the family held seances; they enjoyed the occult.

Still, none of this truly healed her. The world turned threatening with trouble around each corner when she least expected it. One of her biggest fears was saying something that would be misconstrued and then used to harm Leo.

When Lucille found out the film crew was coming to Athens to film her, she panicked. In one of her letters, she told Leo she was fat and ugly. Like many people, she ate when stress was too heavy on her shoulders. Most people never saw the stress she felt; she was outwardly calm and collected. No one understood the extent of her turmoil. When Reid was there, most of the morning was spent with her in front of the camera. Filming went well, but as soon as the crew left, she picked apart her performance, wondering if she did anything that could make people think she was too happy. Reid let Lucille know how happy he was with the film and her performance, and it was a performance. This calmed her.

☙

Lucille arrived around 14 July to visit with Leo. She was staying on the grounds in Superintendent Burke's home as a guest. Each afternoon, she spent several hours talking to Leo. While they touched on their problems, they mostly gossiped and talked like any married couple would. On Saturday, 17 July, she again visited Leo. Their time together had been a balm for her soul. Her depression and anxiety eased a little. There were actual spans of time when they were together that Lucille forgot about the murder, trial, and verdict.

Around six o'clock, Lucille returned to the big white house on the edge of the prison grounds. Leo went to eat and retired to his cot at the front of the large barracks. The lights dimmed at nine. At the door stood a trustee who kept watch all night.

That night, just a little after eleven, William Creen, a convicted murderer in a cot four beds away from Leo's, asked for permission to speak to the trustee. He carried a folded newspaper in his hand and made his way to the door. Just as he passed Leo, Creen jumped on

Leo's chest and drew a butcher knife from the folded newspaper. He pulled the blade across Leo's throat in an uneven sweep.

Leo's scream brought everyone out of their slumber. Blood was squirting from his neck. The trustee and several inmates wrestled Creen to the floor. Two inmates, doctors J. W. McNaughton and L. M. Harris, ran to Leo. There was a seven-and-a-half-inch wound from beneath Leo's left ear to the other side of his Adam's apple. The two doctors carried Leo to the prison hospital not far away, and McNaughton examined the injury when they arrived. Leo's jugular vein was severed. The prisoner doctor was called, but he was fifteen minutes away, so McNaughton tied off the vein with sutures to slow the flow of blood. When Dr. Guy Compton arrived, he understood McNaughton had saved Leo's life, but he had lost a lot of blood. He started Leo on a saline drip and then operated. It took two hours, with the help of McNaughton and Harris, to close the opening and dress the wound. Leo, conscious throughout the surgery, asked if he would die. He indicated that if death was the case, he was ready—nothing stood between him and God.

When Lucille regained her composure after hearing the news, she called Leo's doctor, Dr. Howard Rosenberg, in Atlanta.

It isn't known whether Leo or Dr. McNaughton understood the connection they had. Reuben Arnold represented both men in their murder trials. Arnold was still working on McNaughton's trial when he took on Leo's. Had McNaughton not been there in the barracks that night, Leo would have died.

Sunday morning, William Creen was chained by his feet to a post in the barracks. He was thought of as "not quite right," and most didn't want to tangle with him. He told the *Atlanta Journal* he wished he had been stronger. Lucille would remain in Milledgeville, staying with Roy Alford and family. Within three days, Leo was strong enough to move into the prison hospital. He would live. Lucille arrived each morning to attend to his needs. She helped feed and bathe him and sorted his mail, deciding what was most important.

On the advice of Herbert Haas, Lucille became Leo's ambassador, doing everything in her power to win the friendship and kindness of those who were in charge at the prison. She also looked after Leo's finances. The last thing that needed to happen was for the public to become aware that men like Albert Lasker were helping cover Leo's bills. She paid for medical care and such out of her account, which she could replenish whenever a check came from Lasker.

And so, Lucille would spend the rest of Leo's life with him at the prison.

In Marietta, the group of men who went to see the Prison Commission had tired of trying to navigate Georgia's justice system. They decided to take matters into their own hands.

Chapter 36

Mary's Hometown

Homes began to spring up near the Cherokee town of Kennesaw, and the community of Marietta would begin by 1824. The Cherokee villages, Sweet Water Town, Kennesaw Town, and Buffalo Fish Town surrounded what would become Marietta. The Cherokee Nation resisted removal, taking their case to the US Supreme Court. In the landmark case *Worcester v. Georgia* (1832), the Supreme Court ruled in favor of the Cherokee, asserting that the state of Georgia had no jurisdiction over Cherokee lands. Despite the ruling, Andrew Jackson famously said, "John Marshall has made his decision; now let him enforce it."[296]

In 1835, a faction of Cherokee leaders signed the Treaty of New Echota, releasing their lands to the government in exchange for territory in present-day Oklahoma. This treaty was not representative of the majority of Cherokee people, but Jackson and the federal government used it as a pretext for removal.

Fast forward to the late 1830s and the heart-wrenching echoes of the Trail of Tears, when the Cherokee completely lost their battle with the federal government and were forced to walk to Oklahoma. The trail conditions were harsh, and thousands died of exposure, inadequate provisions, and disease. Georgia carved the Cherokees' land into ten counties.

James Anderson sketched the first city plat for Marietta in 1833, and by 19 December 1834, the Georgia legislature sanctioned Marietta as a town, entrusting its fate to five commissioners elected annually. An 1837 edition of the *Georgia Gazette* painted a whimsical origin for Marietta, attributing its name to the graceful Marietta Cobb, wife of Senator Thomas Willis Cobb.[297]

Visualize Marietta's center pulsating with life and a bustling courthouse, reminiscent of the era's quintessential town square. The approval by the state assembly of the Western and Atlantic Railroad construction ignited a feverish boom. Three taverns sprouted, becoming focal points in the town's ever-expanding tapestry. In 1838, the roadbed and trestles were built, but Colonel Stephen Long stepped down from his post, halting the work. Imagine the abandoned roadbed transforming into a racetrack with the echoing of thunderous horses' hooves—a sport that captivated the people of Marietta. A resurgence of railroad construction under Charles Fenton Mercer Garnett brought the project back to life. Garnett chose a new area that would become Marthasville and then Atlanta as home base. Finally, in 1845, the Western and Atlantic was up and running from Atlanta to Adairsville, and five years later, the line ran to Chattanooga.

John Glover arrived in 1848, breathing economic vitality into Marietta with a bank and a tanyard run with enslaved labor. The city was officially incorporated in 1852, electing Glover as its inaugural mayor. His influence set the stage for Marietta's flourishing growth.

Marietta welcomed a stagecoach stop, the Howard House, and a distinguished hotel—the Kennesaw House. Near the base of Kennesaw Mountain, Dr. Cox pioneered a "water cure," luring visitors seeking respite from Georgia's insect-infected coast. By 1861, Dr. Cox laid the foundation for a substantial tourist industry, combining health care and leisure.

In 1851, the Georgia Military Institute was built about a mile from Marietta's square. When the school opened, there were seven students. By the end of the year, the institute had grown to twenty-eight. Then tragedy hit Marietta in the form of three separate fires. The first happened in 1854 and destroyed the Howard House. Mayor Glover offered his warehouse that had not burned to the owner of the Howard House. The owner took the generous gift and named it the Fletcher House, renovating the building into a hotel. Two more fires destroyed a good part of Marietta, but by 1861, the small town had recovered and began to prosper again. On 11 April 1861, twenty-one men checked into the Fletcher House, and two more stayed in the nearby Kennesaw House. Early on the thirteenth, these twenty-three men gathered at the Marietta Train Station. James Andrews was among them. The group boarded the train bound for Chattanooga, Tennessee. When the train reached Big Shanty, the men commandeered the train and traveled fifty miles before being forced to stop just north of Ringgold, Georgia, less than twenty miles south of their target, Chattanooga. This incident would become known as "The Great Locomotive Chase."

As the Civil War pushed South, with the Union winning, citizens became worried for good reasons. General Sherman marched into town in 1864, a dark chapter for Marietta. When he moved on, General Hugh Kilpatrick, Sherman's "Merchant of Terror," set Marietta on fire and left it to burn.[298] Yet Marietta would survive.

By the turn of the century, Marietta had rebounded, boasting a robust public school system, including separate high schools for White and Black students. Businesses thrived, rising from the ashes of the devastation of war.

Alexander Stephens Clay came to Marietta after he was admitted to the bar in 1877 and set up a law practice on the square. He served on the city council from 1880 to 1881. As he finished his term as councilman, one of his six children, Eugene Herbert Clay, was born. This son would take up the baton of politics like his father, who went on to serve in the Georgia House of Representatives before he became a senator. He would be holding this office when he died in 1910.

Enter prominent families—the Clays, the Brumbys, and Glovers—whose roots intertwined with the city's very soul, shaping its political landscape and steering it toward the momentous events of summer 1915. Marietta's journey, a phoenix rising in the making had only just begun.

ঔ

Tom Watson continued to attack Slaton in his paper but had added what he called the "rich Jews" to his onslaught. He attacked anything and anyone that was remotely connected to Jews. He incited those in Marietta already given to a mob mentality over Leo Frank's escape from death. Tom Watson's hateful rhetoric became the voice in these men's ears.

Soon after Leo was taken to the prison under the cover of night and Slaton left for New York, a group of Marietta businessmen entered a building on or just off Marietta Square. The place was kept secret, but the rumor floated around that it was the law office of Herbert Clay, solicitor for the Blue Ridge Circuit. This building still exists today with the original wooden floors. The names of those who attended this meeting are not clear, but the most important were the planners, the men who were leaders in this movement and elsewhere: Eugen Herbert Clay, John Tucker Dorsey, Fred Morris, Bolan Glover Brumby, former governor Joseph M. Brown, and Judge Newton Augustus Morris. These are the very men who would listen to Tom Watson, agree with him, and answer his call to action. Their plan would rob Leo of his life and Lucille of her one true love.

When Slaton left Georgia, the Prison Commission announced that the Leo Frank case was a thing of the past. Moving forward was best for everyone. They warned potential vigilantes that no one had the right to take the law into their own hands. But these highly esteemed officials of Marietta were not seen as vigilantes, and they didn't see themselves that way. What they wanted to do was correct the terrible error in justice they felt Slaton had committed. They saw this as their duty, their job for the people they represented.

But putting Leo Frank to death would be a challenge. None of these men could risk being identified as architects of the plan. Milledgeville was about 130 miles from Marietta. Part of that path went straight through Atlanta, where many of Leo's supporters lived.

Herbert Clay, thirty-four, was loved by Cobb County as much as his father, Senator Alexander Stephens Clay had been. Marietta cherished Herbert, and he might as well have been local royalty. At twenty-nine, he became the mayor of Marietta. His wife, Marjorie Lockwood, was a Montgomery, Alabama, Southern belle with all the beauty that came with the title. But most knew him better for the scandals in his personal life. Naturally, he had invited scandal since boyhood and would most likely continue throughout his life. It was rumored all those involved in what the group was planning owed Herbert Clay personal favors.

John Tucker Dorsey was another unlikely up-and-comer. Those who knew him well called him "John Tuck." At thirty-seven, he was a star in politics and in law, yet "John Tuck" had hidden brutality. He was a killer who, in 1905, bludgeoned a man to death in Gainesville—fifty miles northeast of Marietta—during a drunken fight. Dorsey was convicted twice of manslaughter—one verdict was overturned due to error. He served on the Cobb County chain gang for a short time, and his ankles were scarred from the shackles that had dug into his flesh. Now, he was one of Marietta's premier trial lawyers. At the time of the meeting, he was a new legislator who had just been appointed chairman of the House Penitentiary Committee. He was in the perfect position to wield power over Warden Smith and all those under him at the state prison.

Fred Morris was an Eagle Scout compared to the first two men. He was thirty-nine and in his first term in the legislature. He jumped in to organize a troop when the Boy Scout movement began.

Bolan Glover Brumby, thirty-nine, came from a family of Confederate soldiers, among them his own father James Remley Brumby. James came home from the war to begin the furniture manufacturing company that produced their best-known piece, the Brumby rocker. His cousin, Richard Brumby Russell, would soon take a seat on the Georgia Supreme Court.

The most honored and loved among this group was former governor Joseph Brown. Even as governor, he had always spoken his opinions regardless of others' judgment. The rumor was that he served as the group's link to Tom Watson.

Judge Newt Morris saw the group's plan as an opportunity, plain and simple. Morris, at forty-six, was seen as one of the most intimidating public figures in Marietta. He always came out on top.

These men, who had to keep their involvement secret, knew they had to select capable leaders to organize a group of loyal men to carry out their plan. They chose the leaders first: George Daniell, Gordon Gann, and Newton Mayes Morris (Judge Newt's double first cousin, known as Black Newt). These men could take control and execute the plan from beginning to end.

George Daniell owned a jewelry shop on the Marietta Square. Gordon Gann was a lawyer and saw Judge Newt as his mentor. Black Newt ran a Cobb County convict camp better known as a chain gang. He was responsible for paving the roads. Black Newt would be the leader of the mission to Milledgeville.

Then, the men chose the remaining participants. They knew that the chosen men could not be lawless or of bad reputation. They believed twenty-five men would be needed, and that was what they chose, including the three leaders. These men, their minds twisted to believe in what Watson preached, joined the conspiracy with full knowledge of what was expected and what could happen if things went wrong.

The men assumed their roles. Jim Brumby serviced the cars. L. B. Roberson, freight agent for Western and Atlantic Railroad, loaned his Stutz Bearcat. Mayor E. P. Dobbs lent a car. William Frey, former sheriff of Cobb County, tied the noose. Yellow Jacket Brown cut the phone wires to and out of Milledgeville. An array of others lent their expertise however they saw fit.

Chapter 37

The Last Footprint

When the apple table was kicked out from under Leo's feet at Frey's Gin, the time was 7:05 a.m. The leader who pronounced the "court's" sentence was Judge Newt Morris. William Frey, the former sheriff and owner of the land, was the first witness on the scene. He brought a friend from Augusta. The next was the editor of the *Marietta Journal*, Josiah Carter, and Gus Benson, retailer. Frey claimed that he was picking peaches in his yard and that when the convoy passed by, he knew something was up. He went in his house, ate breakfast, and cleaned up before going to his gin. When he walked into the grove, he spied Leo's body hanging from the tree.

Frey arrived thirty minutes after the lynching. Leo's body was still warm because his death by suffocation death wasn't instant. Blood had oozed down the front of his shirt when his throat wound reopened.

The newspapers announced that Leo had been kidnapped from prison. Marietta citizens and those just outside began their trek to the site. The roads were full as people traveled from further and further away as word spread. By eight thirty, more than a thousand people had gathered, and more arrived with each passing minute. Most people just gazed at his body. Children were there to witness the man hanging from the smallish tree. The crowd grew to more than three thousand, all to see a former pencil factory superintendent they were sure committed murder. What would you call what happened to Leo? It certainly wasn't justice.

When one witness decided to attack Leo's body, Judge Newt Morris climbed on a tree stump and begged the crowd to leave Leo's body alone. They had avenged Mary's death. All was finished.

One spectator, Robert E. Lee Howell, wanted to desecrate Leo's body—and tried to—but the undertaker's men fought to get Leo in the back of the wagon. Judge Newt Morris and John Wood, the attorney from Canton, saw themselves—and their involvement in the lynching—as moral. They saw the desecration of Leo's body as immoral, so they intercepted the wagon, placed Leo's body in the back seat of their Model T, and rushed to Atlanta.

John Woods stopped the Model T long enough in Smyrna for a phone call to Greenberg & Bond Funeral Home. They agreed to send a hearse that they would meet at the corner of Marietta and Ashby. Leo was returning to Atlanta.

Word spread that Leo's body was at the funeral home and threatening crowds formed. Captain L. S. Dobbs, who was a sergeant two years before when he arrived at the pencil factory after Newt Lee's call, ordered forty mounted officers to escort Leo's remains to the funeral home's chapel. By dark, more than fifteen thousand people had viewed Leo's body.

ꕥ

On Wednesday night after Leo's lynching, a *Georgian* reporter, O. B. Keeler, placed Leo Frank's wedding ring under his pillow so as not to lose it before the next day. This was the ring Leo requested be given to Lucille. At eight o'clock Wednesday night, a knock came on Keeler's door. There stood a man he had never seen, holding something white. The man gave Keeler a note and handed him an envelope, then turned and walked away. Inside was the wedding ring. The note read, as best the reporter could remember, "Frank's dying request was that his wedding ring be given to his wife. Will you see that this request is carried out?"[299]

The band was heavy gold. An inscription inside read, "Idem L. S. To L. M. F., Nov. 30 1910."[300] Keeler set out on Thursday to deliver the band. At 11:20 a.m., he placed the ring in the hand of Sarah Marcus, Lucille's sister.

Lucille would wear her band and keep Leo's until the day she died.

☙

Lucille missed receiving the wedding band because, on Thursday morning, she was on a Southern Railway 36 at Pennsylvania Station, bringing Leo's body back home to Queens. The station crawled with plainclothes detectives and uniformed officers. Cities all over the country, but especially in New York, showed an outpouring of grief.

A few people were allowed onto the platform when the train pulled in. A few newspapermen stood around Rudolph Frank and Marian Stern, Leo's sister, with her husband. They waited for Leo to come home for the last time.

Lucille took over the arrangements before she left Milledgeville. Her strength had held until she got off the train and saw Leo's father and sister. "It's over," she sobbed.[301]

Lucille stood in Pennsylvania Station, a place that would mark the last footprint Leo would make on this earth. She had brought him home.

☙

Early Friday morning, Leo was laid to rest at Mount Carmel Cemetery in Queens. Only invited family and friends attended.

In Lucille's pocket planner, she had written, "My darling is buried. What has life for me now."[302]

Some things never end, never stop hurting. Lucille would carry this pain, loss, and trauma for the rest of her life.

Chapter 38

Life After

Lucille returned to her Georgia Avenue home in September. She was in constant pain with headaches and nausea. These illnesses seemed to stem from her loss and trauma. Friends and family made many suggestions: take walks each day, listen to classical music, don't eat chocolate. The walks would put her on public display, a fish in a fishbowl, with everyone watching "Leo's widow." Classical music would only take her back to Leo and listening to the Victrola at the prison. Instead, Lucille attempted to contact Leo through psychic mediums. His wedding band comforted her, and she always kept it with her or close to her.

When Lucille returned home, stacks of mail awaited her. One of those letters came from an inmate at the prison the night the mob came for Leo. He explained to Lucille what took place from his point of view and described his futile efforts to help: "I exerted and exhausted every available energy and effort to prevail upon the Night Watchman in charge, Mr. Hester that the seven automobiles were within a half a mile of the building to send Mr. Frank out the back way, under guard, as he would then be protected."[303] He went on to tell her a former Marietta sheriff was among those who took Leo. He asked her to please keep the letter confidential.

Lucille's final public words on Leo's death came through a letter to the editor of the *Augusta Chronicle*:

> I am a Georgia girl, born and reared in this State and educated in her schools. I am a Jewess; some will throw that into my face, I know, but I have no apologies to make for my religion. I am also a Georgian, an American, and I do not apologize for that either. I sat beside Gentiles in school, they were my playmates, and I loved them.... I only pray that those

who destroyed his life will realize the truth before they meet their God—they perhaps are not entirely to blame, fed as they were on lies unspeakable.[304]

By spring 1916, Lucille left for Memphis, Tennessee, to manage a women's wear shop for Charles Ursenbach, her brother-in-law. She remained there for six years, living in a boardinghouse. By the time she returned to Atlanta, Lucille was thirty-three. She took a job, once again offered to her by Charles, at the glove counter at J. P. Allen Department Store. Lucille waited on the wives and children of the men who were responsible for Leo's death. Judge Newt Morris's daughter was a regular customer and remembered Lucille's charm and kindness.

Lucille was always well dressed, but most of the time in black. Living in the fashionable Druid Hills, she slowly reclaimed her life. She played bridge every weekend with women around her age. She read literature and history and loved listening to radio broadcasts of the New York Metropolitan Opera on Saturday afternoons. On the outside, she was poised, graceful, and collected, but that gentility hid the damage of her trauma. In truth, she was more out of sorts than when the lynching first occurred. Her nephew was later reported to say that she was always looking to argue and was antagonistic. She refused to speak about the lynching because she became so angry. It seemed she stuffed all that trauma in a box and closed the lid.

When Lucille's sister, Rosalind, died, Charles Ursenbach, now a very wealthy man, moved Lucille and himself into two apartments in a building owned by the Selig family. The Seligs were establishing a name for themselves in real estate and continue to be real estate developers today. When the building was sold, Lucille and Charles relocated to the Briarcliff Hotel on Ponce de Leon Avenue in Atlanta. Lucille no longer worked, and, thanks to Charles's generosity, she purchased a LaSalle sedan. Lucille hired a chauffeur to take her to bridge games and run errands.

Lucille lived the rest of her life with unacknowledged trauma, and depression relentlessly followed her. In the 1950s, mental health treatment was primitive, and discussing it was taboo. Central State Hospital was known throughout Georgia simply as "Milledgeville," and it was common to say that someone might "end up in Milledgeville" if they exhibited the slightest mental slip. Once hospitalized, they might remain there for a long time. Lucille's reluctance to seek psychiatric care was understandable.

When Charles Ursenbach died, the trust he left for Lucille and her remaining sister, Sarah, allowed them to live comfortably. Sarah was now a widow with two grown sons. The sisters moved to apartments in the Howel House, also owned by the Seligs. Lucille purchased the first TV in her extended family, a purchase her great-nephew, Charles "Chuck" Marcus, attributed to her love of watching *Meet the Press* on Sundays. He was thirteen in 1957 and recalls that Lucille was quiet and sweet and loved violets. Around this time, Lucille was diagnosed with hardening of the arteries, and on 23 April 1957, she died of heart disease.

Her great-nephew first learned about Leo's lynching as his parents prepared for Lucille's memorial service. Newspapers reported on her death, and the family requested police presence. The fear lingered.

Lucille's true desire was to have her ashes scattered over Leo's grave, but with his grave in New York, she knew such a request would be challenging. She settled on a public park, likely Grant Park, to avoid unwanted attention. However, Atlanta's ordinance prohibited scattering ashes, so Lucille's ashes remained in a box at the funeral home until 1963, when the funeral home called the nephews to request they retrieve the ashes.

When the nephews cleaned out Lucille's home, they found old letters and Leo's wedding ring. This is the saddest part of Lucille's story. Her life, in many ways, stopped when he was lynched. She never remarried or even dated another man.

One morning at dawn, the nephews went to Oakland Cemetery and dug a hole between Emil's and Josephine's headstones. As the city woke up, the two men buried Lucille's ashes where she belonged, among the old Jewish families that helped build Atlanta, the progressive Gate City.

Today Oakland Cemetery is surrounded by a bustling part of midtown, a trendy area with the young and old alike. Tall skyscrapers catch the sunlight and reflect it back toward the horizon above the tall old oaks. If one is still and quiet, one might hear the whispers of history in the breeze. Lucille's final resting place is there among those who believed in Leo and surrounded the couple with love and support. I have to believe her soul is at peace. No one woman deserved peace more than she did.

Epilogue

Years after Lucille's death, Alonzo Mann—Leo's office boy at the time of Mary's murder—came forward to tell his lifelong secret. On the day of Mary's murder, shortly after noon, as he opened the door to the pencil factory, he saw Jim Conley with a limp girl in his arms. When Conley saw Mann, he threatened to kill the office boy. Alonzo fled. When he told his mother what had happened, she advised him not to say anything about what he saw because they didn't want to get involved. The truth was that both Mann and his parents were terrified of what might happen to him.

At the age of eighty-two, Mann testified in front of the Georgia Board of Pardons and Paroles for an application for a posthumous pardon for Leo Frank. As sensational as Mann's testimony was, it provided no real proof, except that Conley lied about using the elevator and carried Mary down the steps instead. The first application for pardon was denied. Again, the lawyers filed a second application, this time asking the state to admit culpability in his death. The board granted that Leo Frank was denied his constitutional rights by not protecting him while he was incarcerated at the prison.

It's one hundred and ten years after Leo's lynching, and we will never really know what happened to Mary Phagan on 26 April 1913. I did not write this book to express my opinion on Leo's guilt or innocence; I wrote it to tell the story of Lucille, a woman I find brave and strong. Few of us at her age, or any age for that matter, could stand as strong when faced with such an onslaught.

What I learned from writing this book is that no history is simply black and white. There are many gray areas in the story of Leo M. Frank's trial. I am still pondering the answers to the questions that drove me through this writing. But one thing is clear: Lucille Selig Frank believed her husband was incapable of committing this crime. She believed him innocent.

And most of all, she was a victim of the outcome. For the rest of her life, she carried those two years in her head and in her heart, going over them, wondering if, somehow, she could have changed the outcome and saved his life, their lives.

Acknowledgments

There are too many people who generously gave their expertise on the subject of Mary Phagan's murder and the aftermath to possibly list here. Please know your contribution was deeply appreciated. I hold so much gratitude toward Mike Weinroth for contacting Bookmiser and reaching out to me. If he had not made this effort, I would not have gained a lot of knowledge, opportunities, and a friend or two or three along the way. Chuck Marcus, I lack the words to articulate my gratitude for the gifts you bestowed upon me. You brought Lucille alive with your stories and possessions. Holding the simple gold band in my hand was a full circle moment. I am indebted to you for this experience. I consider you a dear friend. Thank you, Dave Schechter, for taking an interest in my book and writing the articles. In many ways, your kindness opened doors. I want to take a moment here to acknowledge the rich heritage of The Breman Museum and how much they helped with the writing of this book. Leslie Gordon, the executive director of The Breman Museum, showed boundless support when she shared a photo of a beautiful young Lucille for the cover of this book. This meant more than you will ever know. Thanks to the generosity of Steve Oney, I had the courage to keep myself in the writing chair. My knowledge doesn't hold a candle to yours, but you always made me feel competent whenever we talked. I owe many thanks to Mercer University Press for their support and faith in my writing of books. Both Marc Jolley and Marsha Luttrell have often made me feel like I was the only author MUP has.

I want to give a nod to my husband, Jack, and my whole family, who have championed my writing habit. To Ella and Daniel, who spent many Saturday nights discussing this book with me. I know you must have grown tired of the subject. Jack, your artistic ability came out in true form for this book. Thank you for your efforts. I love you. To Rarri, my eighth-grade granddaughter, who is studying the Leo Frank Trial as of this writing. May you take away what my granny, your second great grandmother, shared with me: History repeats itself, and it is our job to keep the stories alive so that others won't find it easy to become complacent.

Bibliography

Books

Allen, Frederick. *Atlanta Rising*. Atlanta, GA: Longstreet Press, 1996.

Blackmon, Douglas A. *Slavery by Another Name*. New York: Anchor Books, 2008.

Burns, Rebecca. *Rage in the Gate City: The Story of the 1906 Atlanta Race Riot*. Athens: University of Georgia Press, 2006.

Chernow, Ron. *The Warburgs: The Twentieth-Century Odyssey of a Remarkable Jewish Family*. New York: Vintage, 2012.

Clemmons, Jeff. *Rich's: A Southern Institution*. Charleston, SC: The History Press, 2012.

Davis, Helen, and Ren Davis. *Atlanta's Oakland Cemetery*. Athens: University of Georgia Press, 2012.

Davis, Marni. *Jews and Booze: Becoming American in the Age of Prohibition*. New York: New York University Press, 2014.

Dinnerstein, Leonard. *The Leo Frank Case*. New York: Citadel Press, 1964.

Dorsey, Hugh. *Argument of Hugh M. Dorsey, Solicitor General of Atlanta Judicial Circuit, at the Trial of Leo M. Frank, Charged with the Murder of Mary Phagan*. Atlanta: Johnson-Dallis Company, 1914. Copy available in the Georgia Room, Switzer Library, Marietta, GA.

Evans, Eli N. *The Provincials: A Personal History of Jews in the South*. Chapel Hill: University of North Carolina Press, 1973

Golden, Harry. *A Little Girl Is Dead*. New York: World Publishing, 1965.

Greene, Melissa Faye. *The Temple Bombing*. New York: Addison Wesley, 1996.

Jordan, Bruce L. *Murder in the Peach State: Infamous Murders of Georgia's Past*. New York: Midtown Publishing, 2019.

Katz, Jeremy. *The Jewish Community of Atlanta*. Mount Pleasant, SC: Arcadia Publishing, 2021.
Oney, Steve. *And the Dead Shall Rise*. New York: Pantheon, 2003.
Rawlings, William. *A Killing on Ring Jaw Bluff: The Great Recession and the Death of Small Town Georgia*. Macon: Mercer University Press, 2013.
———. *The Second Coming of the Invisible Empire*. Macon: Mercer University Press, 2016.
Rothschild, Janice Blumberg. *One Voice: Rabbi Jacob M. Rothschild and the Troubled South*. Macon: Mercer University Press, 1985.
———. *What's Next: Southern Dreams, Jewish Deeds and the Challenges of Looking Back While Moving Forward*. Savage, MD: Bartleby Press, 2022.
Samuels, Charles, and Louise Samuels. *Night Fell on Georgia*. New York: Dell Publishing, 1956.
Wilkerson, Isabel. *The Warmth of Other Suns*. New York: Vintage, 2010.

Newspapers

Atlanta Constitution
Atlanta Georgian (and *Sunday American*)
Atlanta Journal
Augusta Chronicle
Jeffersonian
Marietta Journal
New York American
New York Journal
New York Sun
New York Times
Washington Post

1913 Newspaper Collections

Atlanta Georgian. 1913. Georgia Historic Newspapers. Digital Library of Georgia. University Libraries, University of Georgia. William

Randolph Hearst began publishing Sunday editions of the *Atlanta Georgian* as the *Sunday American* on 6 April 1913. <https://gahistoricnewspapers.galileo.usg.edu/lccn/sn89053729/issues/1913/>.

Atlanta Semi-Weekly Journal. 1913. Georgia Historic Newspapers. Digital Library of Georgia. University Libraries, University of Georgia. <https://gahistoricnewspapers.galileo.usg.edu/lccn/sn86090947/issues/1913/>.

Jeffersonian (Atlanta). 1913. Georgia Historic Newspapers. Digital Library of Georgia. University Libraries, University of Georgia. <https://gahistoricnewspapers.galileo.usg.edu/lccn/sn82014546/issues/1913/>.

Trial Documents

Leo M. Frank Plaintiff in Error vs. State of Georgia Defendant in Error. In Error from Fulton Court at the July Term 1913. Brief of the Evidence. 2 parts. Part 1. < <archive.org/details/01-part-one-boe-1-leo-m-frank-plaintiff-in-error-brief-of-evidence-i/01-Part-One-BOE-1-leo-m-frank-plaintiff-in-error-brief-of-evidence-i>; Part 2. <archive.org/details/01-part-one-boe-1-leo-m-frank-plaintiff-in-error-brief-of-evidence-i/02-Part-Two-BOE-2-leo-m-frank-plaintiff-in-error-brief-of-evidence-149>. Cited as *Brief of the Evidence.*

Pinkerton Report: Leo Frank Case. 3 May 1913. Interviews of relevant members of the Leo Frank murder trial by Pinkerton detectives. Transcript. From the Leo M. Frank Collection, MS-237, box 1, folder 1. American Jewish Archives, Cincinnati, Ohio. <https://archive.org/details/pinkerton-report-frank-case/pinkerton-report-frank-case-transcribed/>. Cited as *Pinkerton Reports.*

Archives, Libraries, and Digital Collections

Leo Frank Collection. Atlanta History Center, Kenan Research Center, Atlanta, GA.

Leo Frank Trial Collection. Brandeis University, Waltham, MA. <https://guides.library.brandeis.edu/blogs/system/newly-available-online-the-leo-frank-trial-collection>.

Leo Frank Diary. (1915). Ida Pearle and Joesph Cuba Community Archives, William Breman Jewish Heritage Museum, Atlanta, GA.

Notes

[1] Only the mob was allowed in the grove when the lynching took place. To protect those who kidnapped and killed Leo that morning, people were allowed in only after the deed was done.

[2] Steve Oney, "What Jon Ossoff means for the South and its buried Jewish past," *Washington Post,* 18 January 2021 (washingtonpost.com/opinions/2021/01/18/what-jon-ossoff-means-south-its-buried-jewish-past/).

[3] Lucille's last public statement on the lynching, *Augusta Chronicle,* 1 October 1915 (quotes below are also from this statement).

[4] Leo's last statement, *Atlanta Georgian,* 17 August 1915.

[5] Letter from Rachel "Ray" Frank to Leo Frank, 16 August 1915, Atlanta History Center. Rachel Frank was commonly known as "Ray," and her headstone in Mt. Carmel Cemetery in Queens, New York, reads "Ray Frank." At the time of her son's trial, the papers often referred to her as "Mrs. Rae."

[6] The mastermind of the plot was Herbert Clay, Marietta's mayor from 1910 to 1911. He was solicitor general for the Blue Ridge Circuit and served on the state Democratic Committee. If you stand in front of his grave, you can see Mary Phagan's grave a few yards away. Newton Morris was a superior court judge of the Blue Ridge Circuit. John Tucker Dorsey, Marietta's premier trial lawyer and distant cousin of Hugh Dorsey, was solicitor general for Fulton County. Fred Morris was in the Georgia General Assembly at the time of the lynching and was believed to be part of this group. The only person who planned the lynching and helped picked the mob who *wasn't* a part of Georgia's judicial system was Bolan Glover Brumby, who owned the Marietta Chair Company (Oney, *And the Dead Shall Rise,* 513).

[7] "Leo M. Frank," film reviews, *Variety* 39/9 (30 July 1915): 19–20 (archive.org/details/variety39-1915-07/page/n141/mode/2up).

[8] "This Day in Athens [27 July 1882]," Athens-Clarke County Library Heritage Room blog, 27 July 2010 (accheritage.blogspot.com/2010/07/27-july-1882-michael-brothers-open-for.html).

[9] "Vigilante," *Merriam Webster* (unabridged.merriam-webster.com/collegiate/vigilante).

[10] Steve Oney, *And the Dead Shall Rise* (New York: Pantheon Books, 2003) 562.

[11] *New York Tribune,* 18 August 1915; *Atlanta Georgian,* 17 August 1915 (first edition), 2, and (night edition), 3; Oney, *And the Dead Shall Rise,* 562.

[12] *Atlanta Georgian,* 17 Augusta 1915 (night edition), 3.

[13] *Atlanta Journal*, 17 August 1915, 2.

[14] Oney, *And the Dead Shall Rise*, 562.

[15] *Atlanta Georgian*, 17 August 1915 (extra edition), 1.

[16] *Augusta Chronicle*, 23 August 1915. See also Oney, *And the Dead Shall Rise*, 563.

[17] Milton County merged with Fulton County on 1 January 1932.

[18] "Frank Brave as He Faces Death," *New York Times*, 19 August 1917, 3. This article places Judge Morris in Marietta and implicates him in the crime.

[19] Oney, *And the Dead Shall Rise*, 562.

[20] *Augusta Chronicle*, 23 August 1915. See also Oney, *And the Dead Shall Rise*, 564.

[21] Ibid.

[22] "Frank Brave as He Faces Death," *New York Times*, 19 August 1915, 3.

[23] "Frank Ring Returned to Family," *Atlanta Georgian*, 19 August 1915, 1, 2.

[24] "Frank Refused to Confess on Demand of Lynchers," *New York Evening World*, 18 August 1915, 1.

[25] *New York Times*, 18 August 1915.

[26] American Name Society, "How Atlanta Got Its Name" (americannamesociety.org/how-atlanta-got-its-name/).

[27] Lance Russell, "Why the Gate City?" SaportaReport.com, 1 April 2024 (saportareport.com/why-the-gate-city/media/stories-of-atlanta/lancerussell/).

[28] The Breman (@thebremanmuseum), "This is none other than Caroline Haas…," Instagram photo, 15 April 2021.

[29] Despite representing only 1 percent of Atlanta's population, these twenty-six people owned more than 10 percent of Atlanta's retail businesses. See Mark K. Bauman, "Jewish Community of Atlanta," *New Georgia Encyclopedia*, last modified 11 October 2016 (georgiaencyclopedia.org/articles/history-archaeology/jewish-community-of-atlanta/).

[30] Hasia R. Diner, "Civil War in the United States," *Jewish Women's Archive*, 23 June 2021 (jwa.org/encyclopedia/article/civil-war-in-united-states).

[31] "History," The Temple (the-temple.org/history).

[32] The Central Presbyterian Church, built in 1860, is the only sign in the modern area that this was once a regal neighborhood.

[33] "Debating," *Pratt Institute Monthly* 10/8 (June 1902): 231 (hdl.handle.net/2027/uc1.b2874501).

[34] "H. Morse Stephens Debate Club" (photo), *Senior Class Book: Compiled by the Class of 1906* (Ithaca: Cornell University, 1906), 281 (hdl.handle.net/2027/coo.31924050396039).

[35] "National Meter Company," Novelty Theater (noveltytheater.net/buildings/national-meter-company); "Crown Water Meter," National Museum of American History, Behring Center (americanhistory.si.edu/collections/object/nmah_1411376).

[36] Leo Frank to Lucille Selig, 10 June 1909, Leo Frank Trial Collection, series 2 (Leo Frank Correspondence), box 2, folder 1, Robert D. Farber University Archives and Special Collections, Brandeis University Library, Waltham, MA.

[37] Ibid., folder 2.

[38] Ibid., folder 3.

[39] Ibid., folder 4.

[40] "Edison Invents Aero," *Washington Post,* 1 December 1910, 3.

[41] Oney, *And the Dead Shall Rise,* 85.

[42] See Exodus 2; Phyllis Trible, "Miriam: Bible," *Shalvi/Hyman Encyclopedia of Jewish Women,* Jewish Women's Archive (jwa.org/encyclopedia/article/miriam-bible).

[43] "Phagan Descendents" (freepages.rootsweb.com/~morganandrelatedfamilies/genealogy/families/phagan.htm). Philip Phagan's will was signed on 5 October 1796, one year before he died.

[44] History sheet found on Ancestry.com dated 1979.

[45] Mary Phagan to Myrtle Barmore, 30 December 1912, Benton Family/Leo Frank Papers, box 1, folder 4, Atlanta History Center.

[46] Leonard Dinnerstein, *The Leo Frank Case* (New York: Citadel Press, 1964), 7.

[47] Testimony of George Epps, *Leo M. Frank Plaintiff in Error vs. State of Georgia Defendant in Error. In Error from Fulton Court at the July Term 1913. Brief of the Evidence* [hereafter cited as *Brief of the Evidence*], Part 1, 1 (archive.org/details/01-part-one-boe-1-leo-m-frank-plaintiff-in-error-brief-of-evidence-i).

[48] *Pinkerton Report: Leo Frank Case,* 3 May 1913, 1 (archive.org/details/pinkerton-report-frank-case/pinkerton-report-frank-case-transcribed/). From the Leo M. Frank Collection, MS-237, box 1, folder 1, American Jewish Archives, Cincinnati, Ohio. Hereafter cited as *Pinkerton Report.*

[49] Testimony of Newt Lee, *Brief of the Evidence,* Part 1, 2–3.

[50] Ibid.

[51] Ibid.

[52] "Watchman Lee Tells Story on the Stand," *Atlanta Georgian,* 30 April 1913 (night extra),4.

[53] Testimony of L. S. Dobbs, *Brief of the Evidence,* Part 1, 7.

[54] "State's Exhibit Y," *Leo M. Frank Plaintiff in Error vs. State of Georgia Defendant in Error. In Error from Fulton Court at the July Term 1913. Brief of the*

Evidence [hereafter cited as *Brief of the Evidence*], Part 2, between pages 252 and 253 (https://archive.org/details/01-part-one-boe-1-leo-m-frank-plaintiff-in-error-brief-of-evidence-i/02-Part-Two-BOE-2-leo-m-frank-plaintiff-in-error-brief-of-evidence-149).

55 "Newt Lee Tells His Story during Morning Session," *Atlanta Constitution*, 1 May 1913, 3.

56 "State's Exhibit Y," *Brief of the Evidence*, Part 2, between pages 252 and 253.

57 *Atlanta Journal*, 30 April 1913. See also Oney, *And the Dead Shall Rise*, 21.

58 "Testimony at Leo Frank's Trial," *Atlanta Constitution*, 3 August 1913.

59 "Police Think Watchman Can Clear Mystery," *Atlanta Journal*, 28 April 1913, 3.

60 "Slain Girl Modest and Quiet, He Says," *Atlanta Georgian*, 28 April 1913, home edition, 1.

61 "J. M. Gant Is Arrested," *Atlanta Journal*, 28 April 1913, 1.

62 "John M. Gantt Accused," *Atlanta Georgian*, 28 April 1913, home edition, 1.

63 Testimony of Leo Frank, *Brief of the Evidence*, Part 2, 209.

64 Ibid.

65 Ibid., 210

66 Ibid.

67 Ibid., 214.

68 *Atlanta Georgian*, 29 April 1913 (night extra),2.

69 Ibid.

70 Testimony of Leo Frank, *Brief of the Evidence*, Part 2, 215.

71 "Locked Up Doors," *Atlanta Constitution*, 30 April 1913, 2.

72 *Atlanta Georgian*, 29 April 1913 (night extra), 2.

73 Testimony of Leo Frank, *Brief of the Evidence*, Part 2, 215.

74 *Atlanta Georgian*, 29 April 1913 (5th extra).

75 Ibid. (6th extra).

76 *Atlanta Georgian*, 29 April 1913 (night extra), 2.

77 Testimony of Leo Frank, *Brief of the Evidence*, Part 2, 219.

78 Ibid., 216.

79 Interview with Ollie Mae Phagan, *Atlanta Georgian*, 29 April 1913 (7th extra), 4.

80 *Pinkerton Report*, 2.

81 "Neighbors of Slain Girl Cry for Vengeance," *Atlanta Georgian*, 28 April 1913 (home edition), 4.

82 Ibid.

[83] "Mrs. Coleman Prostrated by Child's Death," *Atlanta Georgian*, 28 April 1913 (home edition), 3.

[84] Ibid.

[85] Ibid.

[86] Ibid.

[87] Ibid.

[88] Ibid.

[89] "Stepfather of Dead Girl Outspoken Against Negro Watchman, Newt Lee," *Atlanta Georgian*, 29 April 1913 (7th extra), 2.

[90] Ibid.

[91] *Pinkerton Report*, 2.

[92] "'I Feel as Though I Could Die' Sobs Mary Phagan's Sister," *Atlanta Georgian*, 29 April 1913 (7th extra), 4.

[93] "While Hundreds Sob Body of Mary Phagan Lowered into Grave," *Atlanta Constitution*, 30 April 1913, 2.

[94] "Pastor Prays for Justice at Girl's Funeral," *Atlanta Georgian*, 29 April 1913 (7th extra), 2.

[95] "While Hundreds Sob," *Atlanta Constitution*, 30 April 1913, 2.

[96] Ibid.

[97] Ibid.

[98] Ibid.

[99] "State Enters Phagan Case; Frank and Lee are Taken to Tower," *Atlanta Georgian*, 1 May 1913.

[100] "Frank Tried to Flirt with Murdered Girl Says Her Boy Chum," *Atlanta Constitution*, 30 April 1913, 1, 2.

[101] "Watchmen Newt Lee on Stand Tells His Own Story of the Mary Phagan Mystery," *Atlanta Georgian*, 30 April 1913 (night extra), 2.

[102] "State Enters Phagan Case; Frank and Lee Are Taken to Tower," *Atlanta Georgian*, 1 May 1913 (final), 1.

[103] *Pinkerton Report*, 4–5.

[104] Ibid.

[105] "Girl Will Swear Office of Frank Deserted Between 12:05 and 12:10," *Atlanta Constitution*, 10 May 1913.

[106] *Atlanta Constitution*, 17 May 1913, 1.

[107] *Atlanta Georgian*, 10 May 1913 (extra edition), 1.

[108] "Good Men on Staff," *Atlanta Constitution*, 11 May 1913, 2.

[109] "Tobie Is Studying Mary Phagan's Life," *Atlanta Constitution*, 21 May 1913, 1.

[110] Testimony of James Conley, *Brief of the Evidence*.

[111] "Detective Harry Scott's Hunch—Thrilling Story," *Atlanta Constitution*, 13 July 1913, 7.

[112] Ibid.

[113] "Defendant's Exhibit 37: Statement of James Conley of May 24, 1913," *Brief of the Evidence*, Part 2, 282–83.

[114] "Suspicion Turned to Conley; Accused by Factory Foreman," *Atlanta Georgian*, 28 May 1913 (extra), 1.

[115] "Defendant's Exhibit 38, Statement of Jim Conley, May 28, 1913," *Brief of the Evidence*, Part 2, 283.

[116] "Defendant's Exhibit 39: Conley's Statement of May 29, 1913," *Brief of the Evidence*, Part 2, 289–91.

[117] "Hang Guilty Man, Says Frank," *Atlanta Georgian*, 30 May 1913 (extra night edition), 1.

[118] "Negro's Part in Factory Crime Re-Enacted," *Atlanta Georgian*, 30 May 1913 (home edition), 2.

[119] Ibid.

[120] Ibid.

[121] "Mary Phagan's Murder Was Work of a Negro Declares Leo M. Frank," *Atlanta Constitution*, 31 May 1913, 1.

[122] "It's up to Frank," *Atlanta Constitution*, 31 May 1913, 2.

[123] Oney, *And the Dead Shall Rise*, 145.

[124] "Plan to Confront Conley and Frank for New Admission," *Atlanta Georgian*, 31 May 1913 (night edition), 1.

[125] "Tornado Hits Ponce Park; Panic Threatens as Wind Wrecks Signs, Rocks Stand," *Atlanta Georgian*, 1 June 1913 (sporting section). 1.

[126] "Conley Is Removed from Fulton Tower at His Own Request," *Atlanta Constitution*, 1 June 1913, 1.

[127] Ibid.

[128] Ibid.

[129] *Atlanta Constitution*, 4 June 1913, 2.

[130] "Says She Heard Frank's Wife Tell Mother Frank Had Threatened Suicide," *Atlanta Georgian*, 4 June 1913 (home edition), 1–2.

[131] "Cook Repudiates Entire Affidavit Police Possess," *Atlanta Georgian*, 5 June 1913 (night edition).

[132] Ibid.

[133] Ibid.

[134] *Atlanta Constitution*, 5 June 1913; see also "'My Husband Is Innocent,' Declares Mrs. Leo M. Frank in First Public Statement," *Atlanta Journal*, 5 June 1913, 2.

[135] "Dorsey Replies to the Charges of Mrs. L. Frank," *Atlanta Constitution*, 6 June 1913, 1.

[136] Ibid.

[137] "Mrs. Frank Writes about Phagan Case," *Atlanta Constitution*, 8 June 1913, 3.

[138] "Lanford Silent on Rosser's Card," *Atlanta Constitution*, 11 June 1913, 3.

[139] "Conley Released Then Rearrested," *Atlanta Constitution*, 14 June 1913, 2.

[140] Ibid.

[141] "Dorsey Aide Says Frank Is Fast in Net," *Atlanta Georgian* (afternoon edition), 16 June 1913, 1.

[142] "Arnold to Aid Frank," *Atlanta Georgian* (*Sunday American* edition), 22 June 1913, 2.

[143] "Detective Chief Tells Grand Jury of 'Third Degree,'" *Atlanta Constitution*, 15 June 1913, 4.

[144] *Pinkerton Report*, 27.

[145] "New Evidence in Phagan Case Found," *Atlanta Georgian* (final box score edition), 9 July 1913, 2.

[146] Ibid.

[147] "Seek Negro Who Says He Was Eye-Witness to Phagan Murder," *Atlanta Georgian* (*Sunday American* edition), 13 July 1913, 1.

[148] "Negro Made Boast of Killing a Girl, Agent Declares," *Atlanta Georgian*, 10 July 1913 (final edition), 1.

[149] "Grand Jury Meets to Indict Conley," *Atlanta Constitution*, 19 July 1913, 2.

[150] Ibid.

[151] "Dorsey Fights Movement to Indict Conley," *Atlanta Georgian*, 20 July 1913 (*Sunday American* edition), 5A. William Randolph Hearst began publishing Sunday editions of the *Atlanta Georgian* as the *Sunday American* on 6 April 1913.

[152] "Scott Believes Conley Innocent, Asserts Lanford," *Atlanta Constitution*, 19 July 1913.

[153] "Counsel of Frank Says that Dorsey Has Sought to Hide Facts," *Atlanta Georgian/Sunday American*, 20 July 1913, 1A–2A.

[154] [An Old Police Reporter], "Mincey Story Declared Vital to Both Sides in Frank Case," *Atlanta Georgian/Sunday American*, 20 July 1913, 2A.

[155] "Protest of Solicitor Dorsey Wins," *Atlanta Georgian*, 22 July 1913, 1–2.

[156] "Date of Frank Trial Depends on Weather," *Atlanta Constitution*, 21 July 1913, 1.

[157] Oney, *And the Dead Shall Rise*, 188.

[158] "Watchman Tells of Finding Body," *Atlanta Georgian*, 28 July 1913, 2.

[159] Ibid.

[160] *Atlanta Constitution*, 29 July 1913.

[161] Ibid.

[162] Ibid.

[163] "Negro Watchman Swears Frank Acted Oddly Day of Crime," *Atlanta Georgian*, 28 July 1913 (night edition), 1–2. See also *Brief of the Evidence*, Part 1, 1–3.

[164] *Atlanta Georgian*, 29 July 1913.

[165] "Tragedy Ages Old, Lurks in Commonplace Court Setting," *Atlanta Georgian*, 29 July 1913 (night edition), 3

[166] Cross-examination of Newt Lee, *Brief of the Evidence*, Part 1, 4.

[167] "Frank and Wife Perfect in Poise; Mother Pitiful Figure," *Atlanta Georgian*, 30 July 1913 (home edition), 3.

[168] Testimony of Grace Hicks, *Brief of the Evidence*, Part 1, 16.

[169] Ibid., 17

[170] "Factory Girl Says Frank Seldom Spoke to Women Worker in Pencil Plant," *Atlanta Georgian*, 31 July 1913 (extra edition), 4.

[171] "Frank and Wife Perfect in Poise; Mother Pitiful Figure," *Atlanta Georgian*, 30 July 1913 (home edition), 3.

[172] Re-cross Examination: Mrs. J. W. Coleman, Re-called for the State, *Brief of the Evidence*, Part 1, 20.

[173] Re-cross Examination: J. M. Gantt, Sworn for the State, *Brief of the Evidence*, Part 1, 20.

[174] "Attorneys for Both Sides Riled by Scott's Testimony; Replies Cause Lively Tilts," *Atlanta Constitution*, 1 August 1913, 2.

[175] Ibid.

[176] "'I've Been Trapped by Witness' Cries Dorsey When Holloway Goes Back on His Affidavit," *Atlanta Constitution*, 1 August 1913, 4.

[177] "Frequent and Angry Clashes between Attorneys Mark the Hearing of Darley's Testimony," *Atlanta Constitution*, 2 August 1913, 2.

[178] Ibid.

[179] Testimony of Dr. J. W. Hurt, *Brief of the Evidence*, Part 1, 46–47.

[180] Testimony of Helen Ferguson, *Brief of the Evidence*, Part 1, 42.

[181] "Conley's Story in Detail; Women Barred by Judge," *Atlanta Georgian*, 4 August 1913 (final edition), 2.

[182] C. B. Dalton, a railroad carpenter, who would be called later to testify. See C. B. Dalton, Sworn for the State, *Brief of the Evidence*, Part 1, 50.

[183] "Conley Grilled Five Hours by Luther Rosser," *Atlanta Constitution*, 5 August 1913, 1–2.

[184] "Conley Continues to Withstand Fierce Attacks of Rosser," *Atlanta Georgian*, 5 August 1913 (1st edition), 1.

[185] "Negro Repeats Charge That Accused Man Asked Him 'Why Should I Hang?'" *Atlanta Georgian*, 5 August 1913 (Alabama edition), 2

[186] "Conley Swears He Heard Screams in Metal Room after Girl Entered Factory," *Atlanta Semi-Weekly Journal*, 5 August 1913, 1.

[187] "Conley Grilled Five Hours by Luther Rosser," *Atlanta Constitution*, 5 August 1913, 2.

[188] The following testimony appeared in the *Atlanta Georgian*, 5 August 1913 (Alabama extra), 4.

[189] The following testimony appeared in the *Atlanta Constitution*, 5 August 1913.

[190] Francis E. Price (photographer), "Women Are Playing Big Part in Trail of Frank," *Atlanta Constitution*, 6 August 1913, 1.

[191] "Mincey Affidavit Is Denied by Conley During Afternoon," *Atlanta Constitution*, 6 August 1913, 2.

[192] Ibid.

[193] "After 15½ Hours on Stand Conley Ends His Testimony," *Atlanta Georgian*, 6 August 1913 (final extra edition), 4.

[194] *Atlanta Constitution*, 7 August 1913.

[195] "Dalton Corroborates Statements Contained in Conley's Testimony," *Atlanta Constitution*, 8 August 1913, 2.

[196] "Defense Gives Up Futile Effort to Batter Down Sweeper's Main Charge," *Atlanta Georgian*, 7 August 1913 (Florida extra), 4.

[197] "Scott Called by Defense to Refute Conley's Story," *Atlanta Constitution*, 8 August 1913, 2.

[198] "Frank Takes Active Interest in Case and Assists His Lawyers," *Atlanta Georgian*, 8 August 1913 (evening edition), 1.

[199] Ibid., 2.

[200] Ibid.

[201] Ibid.

[202] "Street Car Crew Tell of Mary Phagan's Last Ride to Pencil Factory," *Atlanta Georgian*, 8 August 1913 (home edition), 2.

[203] "Architect Is Quizzed to Refute Testimony of Negro in Frank's Home," *Atlanta Georgian*, 8 August 1913 (home edition), 4.

[204] Ibid.

[205] "Holloway, Witness for Defense, Riddled by Cross-Examination," *Atlanta Constitution*, 9 August 1913, 2.

[206] "Women Never Came into Factory Office Witness Testifies," *Atlanta Georgian*, 9 August 1913 (home edition), 1–2.

[207] Ibid.

[208] Ibid.

[209] "Defense's Food Expert Is Grilled by Solicitor," *Atlanta Georgian*, 11 August 1913 (extra edition), 3.

[210] *Atlanta Georgian*, 12 August 1913.

[211] Ibid.

[212] "Testimony of Office Boy Causes Warm Clash between the Lawyers," *Atlanta Constitution*, 13 August 1913, 3.

[213] "Defense Threatens to Move for a Mistrial," *Atlanta Georgian*, 12 August 1913 (final edition), 4.

[214] "Cook Says She Signed Affidavit in Order to Get out of Jail," *Atlanta Constitution*, 13 August 1913, 3.

[215] "Mother-in-Law of Frank Denies Charges in Cook's Affidavit," *Atlanta Constitution*, 15 August 1913, 2.

[216] Re-direct of Mrs. Emil [Josephine] Selig, *Brief of the Evidence*, Part 1, 113.

[217] *Atlanta Constitution*, 14 August 1913. One New York newspaper reported her words as "No, nor you either—you Christian dog!" (see Dinnerstein, *The Leo Frank Case*, 51 and 190, and Oney, *And the Dead Shall Rise*, 286).

[218] "Frank's Neighbors Tell of Seeing Him on Fatal Day as He Left Home," *Atlanta Georgian*, 14 August 1913 (evening editing), 2.

[219] Ibid.

[220] Mrs. E. M. Carson, Sworn in for the Defendant, *Brief of the Evidence*, Part 1, 118–19.

[221] "Every Girl on Fourth Floor of Factory Will Go on Stand," *Atlanta Constitution*, 16 August 1913, 2.

[222] Defendant's Exhibit 42, *Brief of the Evidence*, Part 2, 294.

[223] Miss Irene Jackson, sworn for the Defendant, *Brief of the Evidence*, Part 2, 172.

[224] "Only One of Factory Women Fails to Aid Case of Their Chief," *Atlanta Georgian*, 16 August 1913, ed. 2, 1.

[225] "Profound Impression Made by Prisoner's Remarkable Story," *Atlanta Georgian*, 18 August 1913 (night edition), 1.

[226] Ibid.

[227] Testimony of Leo Frank, *Brief of the Evidence*, Part 2, 205.

[228] "Indirect Testimony Against Prisoner Is Forbidden by Judge," *Atlanta Georgian*, 19 August 1913 (home edition), 6.

[229] "Trial Nearing End and Leo M. Frank Should Know Fate by Next Saturday," *Atlanta Constitution*, 21 August 1913 (morning edition), 1.

[230] "Frank Case May Go to Jury Late This Afternoon," *Atlanta Constitution*, 22 August 1913, 1–2.

[231] "Arnold Ridicules Plot Alleged by Prosecution and Attacks the Methods Used by Detective," ibid., 2.

[232] "Arnold Opens Argument Charging Persecution," *Atlanta Georgian*, 21 August 1913, ed. 1, 3, 5.

[233] "Arnold Ridicules Plot Alleged by Prosecution and Attacks the Methods Used by Detective," *Atlanta Constitution*, 22 August 1913, 2.

[234] "Rosser Makes Great Speech for the Defense; Scores Detectives and Criticizes the Solicitor," *Atlanta Constitution*, 23 August 1913, 2.

[235] "Dorsey's Brilliant Address Attacking Leo Frank Is Stopped by Adjournment of Court Friday," *Atlanta Constitution*, 23 August 1913, 3.

[236] *Atlanta Georgian*, 23 August 1913; Matt 23:27; 2 Sam 11:15; Matt 26:15.

[237] Ibid.

[238] "Packed Courtroom Applauds as Dorsey Begins Closing Plea," *Atlanta Georgian*, 25 August 1913 (South Georgia afternoon edition), 1.

[239] "Solicitor in Final Plea Demands Leo Frank Be Sent to the Gallows," ibid., 2.

[240] Ibid.

[241] "Arnold's Motion for Mistrial Is Denied by Judge Roan," *Atlanta Journal*, 25 August 1913, 5.

[242] "Judge Thanks Jury," *Atlanta Constitution*, 26 August 1913, 1.

[243] "Wife Waits with Wife in Tower for News From Courtroom," *Atlanta Constitution*, 26 August 1913, 1.

[244] Ibid.

[245] "Friends Tell Frank of Jury's Verdict," ibid., 7.

[246] "Stepfather of Murdered Girl Thanks Members of the Jury," ibid.

[247] "Mary Phagan's Grandmother Dies after Dreaming Girl Was Living," *Atlanta Constitution*, 18 August 1913, 1.

[248] Ibid.

[249] "Shadow of Death on Mary Phagan's Home," *Atlanta Georgian*, 18 August 1913 (South Georgia afternoon edition), 2.

[250] "Mary Phagan's Grandmother Dies after Dreaming Girl Was Living," *Atlanta Constitution*, 18 August 1913, 1.

[251] "Cell of Leo Frank Now Like Living Room," *Atlanta Constitution*, 28 August 1913, 5.

[252] Oney, *And the Dead Shall Rise*, 346.

[253] "Many Errors Laid to Court; Charge Made of Jury Intimidation," *Atlanta Georgian*, fourth edition, 1 October 1913, 1.

[254] "Rosser Bitterly Attacks Dorsey," *Atlanta Georgian*, 22 October 1913 (evening edition), 1.

[255] Ibid.

[256] "Counsel for Doomed Man Begin Fight for Appeal Immediately," *Atlanta Georgian*, 31 October 1913 (evening edition), 1.

[257] Ibid.

[258] "Frank Still Stoic; Wife Breaks Down," ibid., 2.

[259] "Frank Case Will Go to High Court in Mystery," *Atlanta Georgian*, 2 November 1913 (*Sunday American*, Florida edition), 2A.

[260] "Leo M. Frank Has Not Lost All Hope," *Atlanta Constitution*, 18 February 1914, 1.

[261] Ibid.

[262] "Leo Frank Looks to Burns as Last Aid in Battle," *Atlanta Georgian*, 22 February 1914 (*Sunday American* extra edition), 1.

[263] "Statement of Harris Basis of Appeal," *Atlanta Georgian*, 20 February 1914 (night ed.), 1.

[264] "Sensational Admission by Chief Expert for State Made to Journal Friday," *Atlanta Journal*, 20 February 1914, 1.

[265] "State Hid Facts to Convict, He Says," *Atlanta Georgian*, 20 February 1914 (final edition), 1.

[266] Ibid.

[267] "Rosser Plans Renewed Fight for His Client," *Atlanta Georgian*, 22 February 1914 (*Sunday American* edition), 2.

[268] "Solicitor Asks Day of Death to Be Set," *Atlanta Georgian*, 4 March 1914 (home edition), 2.

[269] "Dorsey Asks Death Day Be Set; New Startling Charge Against Conley," ibid.

[270] "I'm on the Frank Case to the Finish—Burns," ibid., 1.

[271] "Execution Date His Thirtieth Birthday; Words Stir Hearers," *Atlanta Georgian*, 7 March 1914 (home edition), 1.

[272] Ibid.

[273] Ibid.

[274] Ibid.

[275] "Frank Convicted by Public Clamor; His Lawyer Makes Important Statement Here and Witness at Atlanta Accuses Negro; Says Conley Molested Her in the Very Spot Where a Week Later Mary Phagan Was Murdered," *New York Times*, 2 March 1914, 1, 2.

[276] "Finds Case Is Easier than He Thought," *Atlanta Georgian*, 19 March 1914 (evening edition), 1.

[277] *Jeffersonian*, 19 March 1914.

[278] *Jeffersonian*, 7 May 1914.

[279] Ibid.

[280] "Judge Hill Over Rules Plea without Hearing Dorsey's Argument," *Atlanta Georgian*, 6 May 1914 (final edition), 1.

[281] "William M. Smith Says He Has Faith Murder Mystery Will be Solved," *Atlanta Constitution*, 3 October 1914, 1.

[282] "Plea Made Too Late, Is Court Ruling," *Atlanta Georgian*, 14 November 1914 (home edition), 1.

[283] *Jeffersonian*, 3 December 1914.

[284] *Atlanta Georgian*, 28 December 1914.

[285] "Prominent Georgians Join Delegations to Save Doomed Man," *Atlanta Georgian*, 31 May 1915 (final edition), 1.

[286] Ibid.

[287] *Atlanta Constitution*, 1 May 1915.

[288] "Loyal Wife of Leo Frank, Condemned to Die, Begs Americans to Believe Him Innocent," *Atlanta Georgian*, 4 May 1915 (*Sunday American* edition).

[289] *Jeffersonian*, 27 May 1915.

[290] "Mrs. Frank Makes Plea in Clemency Hearing," *Atlanta Georgian*, 31 May 1915 (afternoon edition), 1.

[291] Archives, Breman Heritage Museum, Atlanta.

[292] *Atlanta Constitution*, 22 June 1915.

[293] *New York Times*, 22 June 1915.

[294] *Jeffersonian*, 24 June 1915.

[295] Lucille to Leo Frank, 29 June 1915, Archives, Atlanta History Center.

[296] Tim Alan Garrison, "*Worcester v Georgia* (1832)," *New Georgia Encyclopedia*, last modified 20 February 2018 (georgiaencyclopedia.org/articles/government-politics/worcester-v-georgia-1832/).

[297] Ben Brasch, "What is Cobb County named for? (It has nothing to do with salad)," *Atlanta Journal-Constitution*, 6 November 2017.

[298] "Marietta's Rich History," City of Marietta, Georgia (mariettaga.gov/1067/Mariettas-Rich-History).

[299] "Frank's Wedding Ring to Be Given to Widow," *Atlanta Georgian*, 19 August 1915 (night edition), 2.

[300] Ibid.

[301] *New York Times*, 20 August 1915.

[302] See Brandeis University Alumni Association, *The Leo Frank Case: On the Screen and in the Brandeis Archives*, presented by Thomas Doherty and Sarah Shoemaker, YouTube.com, at 47:10–33 (https://www.youtube.com/watch?v=iFCuitUsLRM).

[303] F. J. Turner to Lucille Frank, 17 August 1915, box 1, folder 106, Leo Frank Trial Collection, Brandeis University Archives (https://search.library.brandeis.edu/permalink/01BRAND_INST/8v7dkj/alma9924346873301921).

[304] *Augusta Chronicle*, 1 October 1915.

Index